NON-CIRCULATING

CISTERCIAN STUDIES SERIES: NUMBER NINE

Thomas Merton
on
Saint Bernard

CISTERCIAN STUDIES SERIES: NUMBER NINE

Thomas Merton
on
Saint Bernard

Cistercian Publications: Kalamazoo, Michigan
A. R. Mowbray & Co. Ltd.: London - Oxford
1980

Typeset by the Carmelites of Indianapolis.
Printed and bound by Edwards Brothers Inc., Ann Arbor, Michigan.
Published by Cistercian Publications Inc., Kalamazoo, Michigan
and A.R. Mowbray & Co. Ltd., Oxford-London.

ISBN   hardcover (Cistercian Publications)   0 87907 809 X
       paperback   0 87907 909 6
ISBN   hardcover (Mowbray)   0 264 66523 6
       paperback   0 264 66706 9

This volume is Number Nine in the Cistercian Studies Series.

'Action and Contemplation in St Bernard of Clairvaux' was originally published in *Collectanea O.C.R.*, 1953-1954. 'St Bernard on Interior Simplicity' formed a part of *The Spirit of Simplicity* (Gethsemani Abbey, 1948). 'Transforming Union in St Bernard of Clairvaux and St John of the Cross' appeared in successive issues of *Collectanea O.C.R.*, 1948-1950.

Library of Congress Cataloguing in Publication Data

Merton, Thomas, 1915-1968.
    Thomas Merton on St. Bernard.

    (Cistercian studies series ; no. 9)
    1. Bernard de Clairvaux, Saint, 1091?-1153--
Collected works.   I. Title.   II. Series.
BX4700.B5M43   1980   230'.2' 0924   79—27472
ISBN   0—87907—809—X
ISBN   0—87907—909—6 pbk.

Manufactured in the United States of America

TABLE OF CONTENTS

FOREWORD

This volume is made up of three studies on St Bernard of Clairvaux by Thomas Merton, two of which appeared serially in *Collectanea Cisterciensia*, and were written about the time of his ordination to the priesthood, and one later when he was Master of Students at the Abbey of Gethsemani. The first part, 'Action and Contemplation in St Bernard', developed from lectures on St Bernard which Father Merton was at that time giving to the students, and appeared in three installments in *Collectanea* (January and July of 1953, and April of 1954). A few years later it was published in French in expanded book form under the title *Marthe, Marie et Lazare*. Subsequently, it was brought out in Portuguese, but for some unknown reason it never made its appearance in English in book form.

We are indebted to Father Chrysogonus Waddell of Gethsemani for the second part of this volume. When he heard that we were considering the possibility of a collection of Thomas Merton's studies on St Bernard, he suggested that we include an important early study (written about 1948) on 'St Bernard and Interior Simplicity'. This was originally published as Part II of *The Spirit of Simplicity*, a commentary on various texts of St Bernard on the subject of interior simplicity. It sheds light on some of Merton's later writings on such themes as image and likeness, and affords the Merton student a good example of his translations of St Bernard from the Latin.

The third part of this volume is a comparative study on 'Transforming Union in St Bernard and St John of the Cross', which was first published in *Collectanea* in five parts (April and July of 1948, January and October of 1949, and January of 1950). This longer study reveals something of

Merton's preoccupations during those early years of his monastic life. The Spanish school of spirituality (especially St John of the Cross and St Teresa of Avila) Merton found very attractive, as this study bears witness, and was to have a distinct influence on his later writings.

During the summer of 1977 Father Hilary Costello, a cistercian monk of Mount Saint Bernard Abbey in England, made the suggestion that 'Transforming Union in St Bernard and St John of the Cross' be published by itself in book form. For quite some time the idea had been contemplated of publishing this study along with the later essay on 'Action and Contemplation in St Bernard' in its expanded form as it appeared in French and Portuguese. It was then suggested that both essays, together with the study on 'St Bernard and Interior Simplicity' might form a single volume, since all three studies are related, and the logical place of publication was Cistercian Publications, who were making great progress in getting the cistercian Fathers translated into English as well as publishing more serious studies on monastic tradition. At this point Father Jean Leclercq gave the manuscript a reading with a view to publication and his reactions were positive and encouraging, as his introduction indicates.

Anyone who has read Thomas Merton's writings over the years is aware of his lifelong concern with the question of action and contemplation in the monastic life, beginning with its biblical roots as found especially in the Fourth Gospel and in St Paul (See Daniel Adam's excellent work, *Thomas Merton's Shared Contemplation: A Protestant Perspective*, Cistercian Publications, 1979). Merton studied St Bernard and the other cistercian Fathers, as well as Cassian and the earlier Desert Father tradition, with a view to gaining insights into his own life. Similarly his comparative study of St Bernard and St John of the Cross on the subject of transforming union reveals something of this same desire for the mystical dimension of the christian life.

Someone may ask: why publish these studies now? I submit

that they are as relevant today as when they were written
— perhaps more so. We are witnessing in our day a renewed
interest in the contemplative aspects of the christian life. In
fact, the interest extends far beyond the monastic enclosure
to the university campus, the market place and even the
family household. Everywhere one hears the question: how
can I lead a deeply contemplative life in the midst of my present activities? How can I combine the activities of Martha,
the contemplative leisure of Mary, and the ascetical prac-
tices of Lazarus? Is union with God possible?

Thomas Merton struggled with these problems in his own
monastic life and finally came to the conclusion that there is
a Martha, a Mary and a Lazarus in each of us, and we must
learn to live together in peace, ever striving to arrive at a
balanced measure in our lives. Likewise, in each community
there will be some more closely resembling the contemplative Mary, while others will be more inclined to the
activities of Martha (or perhaps through the circumstances
of the community needs, find themselves assuming more active roles), and still others the penitent Lazarus. In the final
analysis, the most perfect way for each person is the total
response in faith and love to one's personal call, to one's
God-given vocation.

It is interesting to note that Thomas Merton in his study
'Transforming Union in St Bernard and St John of the
Cross', mentions Père Poulain's *The Graces of Interior
Prayer*, which had by that time been translated into many
languages including English, and was doubtless instrumen-
tal in reviving interest in mystical theology. Augustin
Poulain was a French Jesuit mathematician who surprised
everyone by publishing a volume on interior prayer and
mystical graces in 1901, although it may be questioned
whether he wrote from personal experience. In any case, it
was the beginning of what has turned out to be a renewed
universal interest in mysticism, both in the West and the
East. Merton, however, felt that Poulain did not appreciate

adequately St Bernard's contribution to the field of mysticism, although actually St Bernard was one of the greatest 'Christian doctors of mystical theology'.

Some clarification may be necessary where Merton speaks of the hermit versus life in the cenobium. The hermit was for Merton someone who ordinarily had been well-tried by many years in the monastic community and only then ventured out into the single combat of the desert, through a special call from God, verified by his superior. This was fully within the benedictine/cistercian tradition, and many examples could be noted of this movement throughout the course of monastic history. It was something Merton himself sought all his monastic life and only fully realized the last three years of his life, which were lived in a hermitage on the property of the Abbey of Gethsemani.

In regard to the translations of St Bernard and St John of the Cross, Merton's own translations are indicated as such throughout the text and footnotes. Whenever they are not supplied by the author, Dr Rozanne Elder has made translations, which are indicated by brackets.

Although in a sense Thomas Merton's tragic death was untimely, his work goes on as his own writings are being brought out in new editions and translations, while new collections of his works are being published. During the past decade nearly a hundred doctoral dissertations, magisterial theses, and serious studies have been written (or are in progress) on Merton and his life and thought. Merton seminars and courses are now given on many university and college campuses, which seems to indicate that the influence of Thomas Merton is increasing throughout the world. This volume, it is hoped, will contribute to a deeper understanding of both St Bernard and Thomas Merton, and their message for us today.

Abbey of Gethsemani   Brother Patrick Hart

INTRODUCTION

THE PRESENT VOLUME is composed of articles written some twenty-five years ago by Thomas Merton. The usefulness of reprinting them after a quarter of a century of bernardine studies reflecting considerable scholarly effort might at first seem open to question. The year 1953, commemorating the nine-hundredth anniversary of Bernard's death, especially witnessed great and decisive progress in this field, for a number of learned conferences were held then and their texts subsequently published. Have these early writings of a poet become monk, who had not been trained in historical and theological studies, retained their value? Or did they require, to be worthy of rebirth, a thoroughgoing revision which would have amounted to rewriting them? I feared it might be so, and in this frame of mind I began reading the essays—not re-reading, for I had scarcely paid attention to them in the past.

The result was a discovery quite different from what I had expected. Indeed these texts have lost nothing of their value or timeliness. One could even say that in this era of post-critical bernardine studies, it is useful to find an approach which is, so to speak, pre-critical: ingenuous, fresh, almost naïve. In each of these texts the reader will find an assemblage of sharp insights and justified admiration for Bernard. How it was accomplished for each text must now be outlined briefly.

I. At the outset, the first essay begins with an act of faith in Christ and in the possibility man has of contemplating God, like Christ and through Him. Christ is at once the

11

model and the source, the example and the principle for all contemplation, and consequently of all contemplative and monastic life. When he 'prays on the mount'—according to the formula inspired by Scripture and taken up by the Second Vatican Council—Christ manifests what he is at all times: a contemplator of the Father. Such an approach is conformable to what is most recent in the christology of our day. After an infatuation with the christologies 'from below'—and without sacrificing the positive element they brought—a number of theologians, and not the least informed of them, favor a christology 'from above'; it begins in an act of faith in Christ's divinity and everything else we can perceive is illuminated by that light. Thus it remains as legitimate today as it was when Merton wrote thirty years ago to put at the foundation of any reflection on contemplation an act of faith in Christ's contemplation and in the possibility given us of participating in it, and consequently of being united with the Father through the Spirit in Christ. From the promulgation of its first text, the Constitution on Liturgy, the Second Vatican Council was to insist that every effort of the Church was to be directed toward placing men in the presence of God. The Council was not afraid to use the vocabulary of contemplation. And it was to do so again in one of its last documents, the Dogmatic Constitution on Divine Revelation. Thus was reaffirmed, in conformity with tradition, the essential tie between contemplation on one hand and action, apostolate, on the other. It cannot be said that Merton anticipated the Council, but simply that he was witnessing to a tradition confirmed by the Council.

Today, no doubt, the theological formulation of these realities of faith could be stricter. But after everything one could read in the sixties on the liberation of theology, which often resulted in reducing it to another human science, the solid faith of a witness like Merton feels good. Nowadays it is no longer necessary, before using the vocabulary of contemplation, to apologize that 'the term contemplation suffers a little because of its pagan connotations'. After experiencing increasingly serious discredit in the sixties, the word contemplation is again being used without guilt; it is now in danger of becoming too much used, of becoming too fashionable and of losing its substance. The pages where Merton expresses himself with simplicity and clarity on the substantial content of contemplation according to St Paul and St John are a beneficial reminder of what is essential on that subject.

In regard to the basic principles of the New Testament as well as those found in the tradition up to the time of St Bernard, we see in Merton's pages how, through a direct reading of texts, all the positive and constructive elements were perceived by a non-scholar. He did not feel obligated to condemn or to criticize Origen and Cassian for having introduced greek philosophical influences into christian tradition. Weren't these great witnesses to the faith sufficiently penetrated by the Gospel to absorb cultural riches from another tradition without compromising the identity of the christian message? Merton's charisma, in fact, is that he was not a scholar who submitted ancient texts to a critical analysis, useful to be sure but always temporary, always open to new developments and destined to become more and more complex and less and less accessible to the average reader.

Thus the clear, simple and unsophisticated summary of Saint Bernard's thought given here is sound for non-specialists, not just for nuns and monks, but for all Christians interested in the life of prayer. Some elements are undoubtedly dated: the notion, for instance, that priests, because of their scholarship, enjoy a contemplation of some special quality which they are privileged to share with those who are not priests. Today the practice of 'shared prayer' has demonstrated that no single group of Christians possesses such a privilege. Also, when Merton has the courage to denounce activity which in the economic field might become excessive for a cistercian monastery, we ought to observe that such a danger is less serious today than when these pages were written.

But on the whole — and this denunciation proves it — these pages illustrate the importance a gift of balance and common sense must have for the reader of ancient texts which scholars tend to obscure and make difficult. Merton does not feel obligated to invent problems in order to have the satisfaction of solving them. What he says of cistercian life retains its value in other forms of monastic life — benedictine and other — and in christian life. He insists in particular on the freedom necessary for the development of each person. This is typically bernardine and Merton had the ability to find in St Bernard's works the appropriate citations and to present them with real 'practicability'. He had assimilated many historical facts, but he was more than an historian: he was a witness to the living tradition. Many references could be added as footnotes to his assertions. But what would be the point? Was he himself always conscious of depending on intermediaries between Christ and our time? He goes directly to the heart of the problem and the end result is a treatment contemplative in character, the fruit of his own meditated readings, offering the reader a possibility of prayer. This early Merton, already full of love and enthusiasm, still marked to some degree by ingenuousness, was building the solid foundation upon which would rise Merton the activist and social critic of the following decades.

The very term 'activist' as applied to him implies the conciliation achieved between the contemplative he wanted to remain and some share of action. We see here that long before he devoted himself to a certain degree of activity, Merton had praised Martha. He had reacted against the clear and absolute distinctions that recent canon law had introduced between the two lives, as if a person had to be either active or contemplative. Why not both? Merton — and all who were not purely canonists — knew the ancient meaning of the expression 'active life'; it applied, he reminds us, to the practice of asceticism. But he also knew that we must speak the language of our day; it is not necessary, not even possible, to go back to ancient greek terminology after fifteen centuries, during which the Church called *active* that life which was subsequently termed apostolic, and *contemplative* that life organized around prayer.

Yet Merton takes care not to proclaim one life superior to the other — Mary's over Martha's — even if he recognizes that for some it is 'preferable'. Similarly, when he develops the idea of 'consideration', he finds instinctively, probably unawares, the term and the idea which hold great importance at the beginning of one of Gregory the Great's works, paradoxically entitled *The Pastoral Rule*. Gregory was both a contemplative and a pastor, and he taught pastors to be contemplatives. But they cannot and must not lead a solely contemplative life. Merton succeeds in keeping an objective view of these two ways of life and above all he avoids the exaltation of Mary's. With the freedom that always characterized him, he shows the limits of monasticism and the dangers to which it is exposed. Because he does, his essay can be equally useful to those devoted to a contemplative life or to pastoral care.

Furthermore, and in this he reveals the breadth of his vision and understanding of the Church, what he says of contemplative life applies to all its forms. Thus he can suggest relationships with traditions nurtured on St Thomas Aquinas, St Teresa of Avila and St John of the Cross. His message encourages those who live according to those traditions. And this is not because of any vague thoughts forgetful of specificities, of different identities; his thinking is precise, vigorous, one might even say rigorous. His use of the category 'mixed life' could be challenged, for it is a concept missing in St Bernard and objected to by St Thomas in the last work in which he discusses the subject, the last Questions in the second part of the *Summa Theologica*. But we see clearly what Merton means. Let us not reproach him for ignoring what twenty years of thomist research subsequently brought to light. Besides, he is modest: 'Unless I am mistaken...' he cautiously writes before taking a position on delicate matters controverted even among Thomas specialists. Here, above all, Merton wishes to be practical, and he succeeds without giving in to over-simplifications, without establishing facile contrasts between Martha and Mary. Martha can also be a contemplative. The praise of an apostolate which leaves some room for contemplation is today more timely than ever.

II. After the text in which the bases for both ways of life have been laid, the brief essay on the Virgin Mary may justly be inserted because it is complementary. Its thesis is illustrated by means of admirable and extremely well-chosen texts from St Bernard. Again we are in the presence not of pious exhortations but of a real doctrine entirely centered on Christ. As the Constitution on the Church of Vatican II was later to do in its last chapter, Merton insists on the essential part of what we know of Mary: her faith. Later other theologians, Hans Urs von Balthasar among them, proposed better developed and more articulate considerations on what the experience of faith in the Mother of Christ Jesus might have been. Yet the condition for such an analysis is primarily belief in that faith. Schooled in St Bernard, Merton puts us face to face with this first requirement.

III. The essay on *The Spirit of Simplicity* offers an example of the way in which Merton, like Bernard long ago, could transform into a spiritual testimony what had at first been conceived and written as a practical text: it dealt with justifying observances which had become complicated while trying to show that they were not incompatible with an early cistercian spirit marked by a search for simplicity. Effortlessly, Merton goes from the letter to the spirit, from customs and observances to the inner attitude. In a three page letter sent to me in October of 1950, Merton referred in passing to this essay: 'A copy of *The Spirit of Simplicity* was mailed to you, but my own contribution to that work is confused and weak, I believe. I refer to the second part', the one reproduced here. He went on to raise questions or express ideas on subjects ranging from Antony the Great to Rancé and Daniélou.

To tell the truth, the text begins with a good summary of Saint Bernard's theology. Merton goes straight to the heart of the problem raised by the idea of simplicity and he expresses himself with precise vocabulary but also with such breadth that what he says is valid not only for the Cistercian Order but for all Christians. His carefully annotated *florilegium* establishes a good initiation to St Bernard, accented by balance of judgment and serenity of style. At the same time, Merton was working on Saint John of the Cross; hence the parallels drawn between John and Bernard. Without a scholarly apparatus, but with great control of his subject, he laid the foundation for a monastic culture. What historians toil to demonstrate, Merton grasps at once and explains with disarming clarity. He relies on key texts. He presents a positive view of Bernard and of his attitude toward religious knowledge while adverse slogans continue to circulate.

It is good for monks to return to these primary truths. This presentation, easy to read, in a conciliatory style, free of polemics, may seem too simple at a time when criticism is all important. Yet, is it not useful that some writers have had and yet have this 'simple eye', this child-like faith, ad-

miring yet nevertheless enlightened? Much of what Merton
wrote for his brothers applied to other forms of life in the
Church. He did not linger on details of observances, but the
spirit he defines was to be at the fountainhead of the renewal
to come, and it consists in simplifying existence.

IV. Finally, the comparative essay on Bernard and John
of the Cross is very revealing of Merton's tendency to recon-
cile rather than to oppose, to discern what is common to
both authors rather than to contrast them. Thus he succeeds
in throwing light on both subjects equally. He has and offers
a sound intuition concerning both. Of course we sense that
he is more familiar with Bernard than with John of the
Cross. He does not pretend to say anything new on the latter. But in his own way he illustrates, as his friend Maritain
had before him, the 'practical-ness' of the great carmelite
scholar whose sublimity and subtlety run the risk of being
discouraging. Such an introduction is therefore very useful.
It requires that the texts be read with realism and common
sense; then the solid teaching they contain becomes understandable and accessible. Merton does not write to satisfy a
scholar's curiosity but always in view of life, of a love which
implies knowledge but goes and sees beyond it, and is united
with its object.

Here again, Merton reveals his ability to grasp quickly
what is essential in a complex doctrine. He sees the whole.
He used Gilson's famous book on St Bernard,[1] yet he remained dissatisfied. In a letter to me, dated 9 October 1950,
he wrote:

> I am also very much interested in the question of Saint
> Bernard's attitude toward 'learning' and feel that a
> distinction has not yet been sufficiently clearly made
> between his explicit reproofs of *scientia* in the sense of
> *philosophia,* and his implicit support of *scientia* in the
> sense of *theologia,* in his tracts on Grace, Baptism, and

his attacks on Abelard, not to mention his attitude to
the Canticle which makes that commentary also *scientia* as well as *sapientia*.

He tried to overcome the difference he perceived in Bernard
between speculative knowledge and mystical experience and
he did the same for St John of the Cross. His education was
broad enough to let him place both in their proper perspective and to grasp the areas in which there are differences
that do not bear on the essential meaning. Let us
note in passing that he recognizes the importance of the
Song of Songs in the works of John of the Cross as well as in
those of Bernard. Since then this has been confirmed by a
voluminous and erudite thesis.[2] For Merton it was enough to
draw attention to this biblical poem as a privileged place for
the rhetoric of love. For Bernard and for John of the Cross
there is in it one source of inspiration, one means of expressing, by means of similar images yet with different personal
sensitivities, a common experience.

At Gethsemani I was privileged to see the edition of St
Bernard used by Merton, who had received permission to
make marginal notes. His careful reading is manifest in his
underlining of key passages, his marginal references to
parallel or complementary texts, his glosses and summaries.
He appears not to have used the indices. There the pages remain untouched. He worked with the text itself. He did not
annotate throughout but judiciously chose passages deserving careful study.

His patient association with St Bernard as well as his own
acuity explain Merton's special insights. Thanks to them
these works of his monastic youth on the Abbot of Clairvaux
preserve the true value of the texts. They are and remain
classics. Scholarly theses on the symbolism of Martha and
Mary, for example, have fallen by the wayside, but Merton's
essay on the same subject, because of his well-balanced

judgment, his understanding of human situations, remains true and useful.

A reviewer of mertonian essays written between 1950 and 1965 on the liturgy, an evolutionary topic profoundly renewed by Vatican II, made a comment which can be applied equally well to Merton's texts on Saint Bernard: 'Surprisingly little needs to be rewritten for 1977.'[3]

Jean Leclercq

Clervaux
Translated by Monique Coyne

Notes

1. *The Mystical Theology of Saint Bernard,* translated A.H.C. Downes (London-New York, 1940, 1958).

2. Fernande Pépin, *Noces de feu. Le symbolisme nuptial du 'Cantico espiritual' de S. Jean de la Croix à la lumière du 'Canticum canticorum'* (Paris-Montreal, 1972).

3. 'A propos de T. Merton, *Meditation on the Liturgy*' in *The Way* 17 (1977) 239.

Part I

Action and Contemplation
in St Bernard

1. Action and Contemplation in the
Mystery of Christ

BEFORE WE APPROACH the subject of this study, which is St Bernard's doctrine on the active and contemplative lives, let us first pause to consider the great mystery of action and contemplation in Our Lord Jesus Christ, as it is revealed to us in the New Testament. Here, of course, there is no mention of 'contemplation': the sacred book speaks rather of the infinite reality of the divine life which has been manifested and given to us in Christ and which far transcends our poor abstract notions of contemplation. A later generation could speak of the contemplation enjoyed by the soul of Christ, of his beatific, his infused and his acquired knowledge. The gospels tell us only of the ineffable mystery of the union of the Son with the Father, and teach us that the only true and perfect idea of contemplation is realized by the christian soul who, perfectly united to Christ in the charity of his deifying Spirit, enters with him into the Holy of Holies and becomes one with the Father in him, and one with all who are united in him to the Father.

'No one has at any time seen God,' says St John. 'The only begotten Son, who is in the bosom of the Father, He has revealed Him.'[1] The Word 'came forth' from the Father to assume a human nature. But all the while that he walked our earth, he remained in the bosom of the Father. The soul of Christ always enjoyed the most perfect and uninterrupted beatific intuition of the Father, of himself, the Word, and of their union in the Holy Spirit. He comprehended God in himself, and knew that he was God and knew that he and the Father were One. He saw all creation, past, present and to come, in his own divine Person, for he was the firstborn of every creature, and 'in him were created all things in the heavens and on the earth, whether visible or invisible...all things have been created through and unto him.'[2] All that was God's was his, for the Father had loved him and given all things into his hands.[3] Only during the passion was this glorious vision temporarily obscured in the human soul of the Redeemer. Yet even in the passion he was God of God, Light of Light, True God of True God. His experience was, then, still in a very particular way an experience of con-templation: the experience of the Light that shone in the darkness by which it was not comprehended. Jesus, in his passion, experienced in his soul that darkening of the divine light which every christian soul must in some way share before it can pass from its own darkness into his admirable light, drawn by the power of the Father who has hidden himself in darkness with his Son, our Christ. Even in the darkness of death before his resurrection Christ is a pillar of fire lighting our way through the Red Sea and the desert to the promised land, as the Church sings in the triumphant mystery of Easter.[4]

Jesus was united with his Father in the union of one divine nature, and in the union of perfect love and vision, being the splendor of the Father and the image of his glory. But besides this union of 'contemplation' and love, the Son of Man is united with the Father in action. 'I came forth from the Father and came into the world.'[5] 'I must do the works of Him that sent me.'[6] These are the words of Jesus, telling us that he came into the world with work to do for the Father. His very life, being and sustenance are involved in this work. 'My food is to do the will of him who sent me, to accomplish his work.'[7] The work that Jesus does is not his own, but the Father's and he has no reason for existing except to accomplish that for which he was sent.

It is in the works of the Son that the Father manifests himself to the world, because the works of the Son are at the same time the works of the Father. The doctrine of the Son is the doctrine of the Father. When the Son speaks, it is the Father who speaks in him. The works of the Son are inseparable from his ineffable union with the Father, and are simply an expression of that union, a witness to his oneness with the Father. 'If I do not perform the works of the Father, do not believe me. But if I do perform them, and if you are not willing to believe me, believe the works themselves, that you may know and believe that the Father is in me and I in the Father.'[8]

'Do you not believe that I am in the Father and the Father in me? The words that I speak to you, I speak not of my own authority. The Father dwelling in me, it is he who does the works.'[9]

But why does the Father seek to manifest himself in the Son? This action outside himself is not for himself alone. True, it gives him glory. But his glory is to bear fruit in his creation, in spiritual beings, in angels and men. His glory is to give them a share in his own divine life, his knowledge of himself, so that they become his sons and are one with his only Son, deified in him and caught up to the Father in the unity of the Holy Spirit. The action of Jesus in the world is then to draw all to his own vision of the Father and to unite them to the Father in himself. 'Everyone who has listened to the Father and has learned, comes to me.... As the living Father has sent me, and as I live because of the Father, so he that eats me he also shall live because of me.'[10] What is pro-

mised in these words is the most intimate possible union of
men with God, a union accomplished in the mystery of the
Eucharist which prefigures in time the everlasting contemplation of the Godhead in heaven.[11] If the Father is
working in the world, through his Incarnate Word, it is for
no other reason than to bring men to contemplation of him
in heaven, and to give them even on earth a foretaste of that
heavenly contemplation. Therefore, whether on earth or in
heaven, we are called to unite ourselves with the Son's contemplation of the Father. Yet this also involves our union
with the *action* of the Father in the Son. As the Father has
sent the Son into the world, so Jesus sends his apostles into
the world, and for the same reason. As the Father works and
manifests himself in his Son so the Son works and manifests
himself and the Father in his apostles. 'Even as you have
sent me into the world, so I also have sent them into the
world.'[12] 'Go therefore and make disciples of all nations,
baptizing them in the name of the Father and of the Son and
of the Holy Spirit.'[13] And what is baptism but an initiation
into the divine life, eternal life, the knowledge of the one
true God and Jesus Christ whom he has sent? The reason,
then, for the apostolate is that the whole world may be
brought to contemplation of the Father in the Son. An
apostolate that does not spring from contemplation and end
in contemplation is not the christian apostolate. It has
nothing to do with Christ. It cannot manifest him whom it
does not know, it cannot bring anyone to the knowledge of
him, since it is without power from on high, and no one can
come to the Son unless the Father draw him. An apostolate
that is not nourished in some degree by contemplation is a
work entirely human, not the work of the Father or of the
Son or of their divine Spirit. Since only the Holy Spirit is the
bond of union and the *vinculum perfectionis* [the link of
perfection] that holds everything together in the charity of
Christ, an apostolate that is not activated and driven on-

ward by the power of the Spirit cannot unite men in Christ. It will end only in division for the work of the human and earthly spirit is dissension and division.[14]

There is no contemplation for the person who is, by his own fault, divided from Christ, without whom no one comes to the Father. Therefore the contemplative life is first of all the realization of our union with God in Christ, and this invisible union is impossible without a visible union, in the Spirit of charity, with all our brethren in him. That is why St John says 'No one has ever seen God. If we love one another God abides in us and his love is perfected in us.... Everyone who loves is born of God and knows God.'[15] In saying this, the Apostle is saying that contemplation is a fruit of our union with all who are one in Christ. It is an expression of our incorporation in Christ, a consequence of our insertion into the unity of the Church. Mystical union with God is arrived at through union with the Church, considered not only as a juridical body but above all as a Mystical Person, the *pleroma* of the Incarnate Word, living by his divine Spirit.

Action and contemplation together are expressions of this life of the Church. They both flow from our life in Christ, completing and fulfilling one another. He is the Vine, we the branches. We can bear no fruit in action, taste no fruits of contemplation, unless we remain in his love. The discourse of Jesus at the Last Supper, as it is recorded in the fourth gospel, is at once the simplest and most profound exposition of his teaching on action and contemplation, contained in the mystery of our union with the Father in him. This discourse was given to the apostles as a divine legacy, together with the sacrament of love and union in which all its doctrine was to be concretized and fulfilled. The words of Jesus in the cenacle, and especially his high priestly prayer are the theological explanation of the ineffable mystery which he gave, that night, to his Church, in the Eucharist.

In this discourse Jesus tells us, as we have seen, that all

spiritual life consists in union with him. To love him is to be alive. To love him is to abide in him. Not to love him is to be dead, cut off from him, rejected like a withered branch. Love then is the ontological root of our new being in him. Love is the life which can manifest itself either in action or in contemplation. But we see at once that it must manifest itself in both these two. What is the active life? Keeping the commandments of Christ. 'If you love me, keep my commandments.'[16] Now the active life, in this sense, is of obligation for all who would abide in the mystical vine. 'He who does not love me, does not keep my words.'[17]

The active life, however, leads to 'contemplation'. For when we allow the life of love to develop in our hearts by carrying out the will of Love, we come eventually to know and realize the presence of the God of love dwelling and acting in our hearts: 'If anyone love me, he will keep my word, and the Father will love him, and we will come to him and make our abode with him... and the Father will give you the Spirit of Truth whom the world cannot receive because it neither sees nor knows him. *But you shall know him because he shall dwell with you and be in you.*'[18] And to make it quite clear that he indeed means the fulness of contemplation, Jesus adds: 'In that day you *will know that I am* in the Father and you in me and I in you.'[19] All our contemplation is a sharing in Christ's contemplation of his heavenly Father. All our action is valid only if it be a prolongation of the work done on earth by the Incarnate Word, and, through him, by the Father. In a word, the active and contemplative lives are simply two aspects of the divine life which Christ lives in his members, by the action of his Holy Spirit. The function of contemplation is to make us aware not only of God in himself but of God living in his Church, and the function of the active life is to diffuse the charity of Christ more widely throughout the world and make it penetrate into every field of human existence so that God may be all in all, and that all things may be restored in Christ.

All that the New Testament teaches us both of action and contemplation is therefore resumed and contained in the Mystery of Christ, or what St Paul calls, simply, 'the Mystery'. Mystery that is announced to men by the apostles, in order that all may contemplate Christ dwelling in them by faith and charity, and 'comprehend with all the saints what is the breadth and length and height and depth, and know Christ's love which surpasses all understanding and be filled unto all the fulness of God.'[20]

The beginning of contemplation is enlightenment as to the 'dispensation of the mystery which has been hidden from all eternity in God who created all things.'[21] And it is through the mystery, through the experience of Christ living in us and in our brethren, and in the whole Church, that we have access to the 'manifold wisdom of God'.[22] It is when, by the action of charity, we are fully inserted into this mystery, and find our providential place in it, that 'we receive the Spirit that is from God that we may know the things that have been given us from God'. It is then that, in the Spirit, 'we search all things, even the deep things of God'. And it is then that we can say: 'We have the mind of Christ.'[23] In these few phrases from the Epistles of St Paul, we find just as in St John, the same theology of action and contemplation as manifestations of our life in Christ.

But St Paul tells us more clearly than St John that action and contemplation do not take the same form or have the same importance in all the members of Christ. 'There are varieties of gifts... varieties of ministries... varieties of workings.... For the body is not one member but many.'[24] So though in all christian lives action and contemplation are to some extent mingled, and may even assume extraordinary and charismatic forms, the perfection of each individual member consists in finding his own providential place in the body of Christ, and carrying out the function which is peculiarly his own. Some therefore will lead active lives

devoted to bodily works of mercy, others will preach or ad-
minister the sacraments, others will exercise extraordinary
gifts, others still will bear witness to the union of Christ and
his Church by sanctity in the married state. There is a
special vocation for virgins, another for widows. The highest
perfection will be demanded of priests and bishops. Others
may not be required to go so far, but all must know and love
Christ, all must grow in him to the fulness of spiritual
maturity, within the limitations of their own calling, even if
they should remain only slaves in their social world.

In the sixth chapter of *Acts* we find the first intimated
division between what we shall later call the active and the
apostolic lives. The apostles decided to delegate some of
their duties to deacons, for (they said) 'it is not desirable that
we should forsake the work of God and serve at tables'.
Nevertheless even those who were to be selected for the
material care of the christian communities were to be chosen
on the basis of their interior lives. They would be 'of good
reputation and full of the Spirit and of wisdom'.[25]

That is to say, in the language of the New Testament,
they must be 'contemplatives'. The fact that it may seem a
little strange to us to suppose that the first deacons were
'contemplatives' only reflects the weakness and the limitations of our modern term. It is indeed far more expressive as
well as far more simple and less misleading simply to say a
person is 'full of the Holy Spirit' than to say he is a contemplative. The biblical expression conveys a much more integral and christian idea of contemplation, particularly of a
contemplation which is ready at any moment to divert itself
into action, without suffering any diminution of its own interior strength and vitality. We must frankly admit that the
term 'contemplation' suffers a little because of its pagan
connotations. Nevertheless it is the term we must continue to
use in this study. Meanwhile we need only illustrate our
point by alluding to the example of the first martyr, St

Stephen, 'full of grace and power', whose sanctity had reached such a height that 'he was working great wonders and signs among the people', and who was filled with such apostolic ardor that when he disputed with the Jews and laid open to them the hidden meaning of the Old Testament, 'they were not able to withstand the wisdom and the Spirit who spoke' in him.[26] Such is the spiritual perfection which the New Testament presupposes in what we would call a 'vocation to the active life'. Obviously, if one had to work miracles before being worthy of entering into christian action, there would be few vocations to the lay apostolate, and fewer still to the priesthood. The fact remains that in principle the active life is not possible without a deep interior union with Christ and a great docility to his divine Spirit.

St Paul does not speak much of what we would call a purely contemplative life. Yet there is one example of it in his chapter on the state of virginity. Here the Apostle admits that this state is in itself to be preferred to the married state, since it offers a chance to lead a deeper interior life. He counsels it, then, 'to make it possible for you to pray to the Lord without distraction'.[27] This suggests that there already existed a life of quasi-retirement and of prayer in the Church of God in apostolic times. St Paul nowhere implies that there is any contradiction between 'virginity' and an active apostolate.

St Paul himself tells us, in the epistle to the Galatians, that right after his conversion on the road to Damascus he retired into 'Arabia'. It is sometimes thought that he went into the desert for three years to pray, to prepare himself for his apostolic ministry. But it does not seem at all necessary to hold that he did not, instead, go south of Damascus and start at once to preach. Paul himself tells us no more than the fact that he went on this journey. He does not tell us what he did in those regions. In view of the tremendous importance of his miraculous vision on the road to Damascus, in which he saw, all at once, the whole 'Mystery of Christ' which was to be the substance of his gospel, there was really no necessity for Paul to spend a long time in contemplation and prayer. He had arrived, in one bound, at the very height of contemplation and was not only qualified to be an apostle by the depth of his interior life, but was actually sent by the risen Christ himself to the Gentiles. If we believe that Paul began at once to preach, this in no way weakens the traditional thesis in favor of the necessity of contemplation as a foundation for the apostolic life. On the contrary, the miraculous and perfect way in which Paul all at once became the greatest of contemplatives is a very strong argument in support of that necessity. What it tells us is that the christian contemplative is not one who has spent a very long time in retirement, or who has subjected himself to a series of techniques that have gradually raised him to a high spiritual state. The christian contemplative is one who, in the Spirit of Christ, full of wisdom and of charity, has a perfect knowledge and love of Jesus Crucified and is united to the Father in him. This union is always a gift of God, for which the best disposition is the simplicity of humble faith.

In the earliest years of the Church, the highest 'mystical graces' were in fact associated with the grace of martyrdom, which is the supreme expression of christian faith. As time went on, and as the charismatic fervor of the first centuries began to cool, and as the persecutions died away, the Holy Spirit began to lead Christians not to the arena of the pagan cities but to another, and more spiritual, arena: that of the desert where, like the Saviour, they were to suffer temptation.

The Desert Fathers, following Clement and Origen, began to make a clear separation between the active and contemplative lives. And it is here we see the first appearance of the doctrine which we shall study in detail in the pages of Bernard of Clairvaux.

A few words will suffice to sketch the broad outline of the

traditional teaching of the orient, as it is summarized by
Cassian: The monk leaves the world and all its cares in order
to seek the 'Kingdom of God'. What is this kingdom? Simply
the divinization of the monk's own soul by contemplation, in
this life, and the perfect vision of God in the next. The true
aim of all the monk's ascetic strivings is 'purity of heart'. To
this everything else in the monastic life is subordinated. Action and contemplation both tend towards this one end. The
active life predominates in the communities of the
cenobites, the contemplative life is purer and deeper, but
also more difficult of attainment, and is the privilege of the
solitary. In both the community and the hermitage, the
monk arrives at purity of heart. The sanctity of the cenobite
is less exalted but more evangelical and more sure. The
purity of the hermit is most perfect but far more rare. In any
case, contemplation is superior to action because it is meant,
ultimately, to fulfill the active life and supplant it altogether
according to Cassian. He says quite categorically: *Videtis
ergo principale bonum in theoria sola, id est in contempla-
tione, Dominum posuisse.*[28]

Cassian shows us that the monastic life by its very nature
tends to the constant and undisturbed union of the soul with
God. *Hic ergo nobis principalis debet esse conatus, haec im-
mobilis destinatio cordis jugiter affectanda, ut divinis rebus
ac Deo mens semper inhaereat.*[29] These are the first words of
a chapter in which he takes up the allegory of Martha and
Mary which had first been exposed by Origen. The sentence
we quoted before is Cassian's conclusion to the allegory. It
was in preferring Mary to Martha that Jesus, according to
the mind of the Desert Fathers, 'has placed the highest good
in contemplation alone'. Nevertheless, Cassian continues,
the praise of Mary implies no blame of Martha. The good
works of Martha are indeed less perfect than the contemplation of Mary, but both are necessary and both are pleasing
to the Lord. The implication is that in the monastic life,

even though the ideal may be that of Mary's contemplation, nevertheless in fact many will arrive at perfection by the labors of Martha. Martha and Mary belong together in the same household. They supplement one another, and neither one must expect to win the other over to her own function. If Mary has the 'best part', it does not mean that Martha must leave her work and become a Mary, because, in another place, Cassian tells us that Martha's active and cenobitic life has a peculiar excellence of its own which even the solitary life of contemplation cannot duplicate. 'The end of the cenobitic life is to mortify and crucify all the monk's own will and to bring him, by the salutary commandment of the Gospel, to live without any thought of the morrow. And it is *quite certain that this perfection can be achieved by no one, except the cenobite.*'[30]

Here, then, we have the foundations of St Bernard's teaching on the active and contemplative lives, which is nothing but a development of the tradition summarized by Cassian. We shall see that for St Bernard the monastic life includes elements both of action and contemplation. Contemplation is in itself the highest expression of the monastic and Christian lives, but it rests on action and tends to overflow in apostolic activity for souls. Not all need necessarily reach the heights of contemplation, but since the monastic life is the perfecting and maturing of our life in Christ, all must certainly live by his Spirit and be deeply united to him in whatever way he calls them to be so and in whatever function they may exercise, according to the injunctions of his will. However, St Bernard pays less attention than Cassian to the solitary vocation, nor does he, like Cassian, tend to make contemplation the privilege of the hermit. Although St Bernard himself permitted Blessed Conrad to leave Clairvaux and live as a hermit,[30b] he ordinarily envisaged the contemplative life within the ordinary framework of the cistercian community, and it was his characteristic task to show that a deep life of contemplation was possible side by side with its varied and numerous activities. We shall see that he assumes that the contemplative monk while retaining his place in the common life is not ordinarily immersed in these activities as much as the others.

So much for St Bernard and Cassian. But can we find, in the works of the Abbot of Clairvaux, anything to reproduce our summary of the New Testament teaching on action and contemplation? We shall find much that does so either explicitly or implicitly, later on in this study, in the eighth sermon *In Cantica,* where St Bernard describes union with God in mystical contemplation. This is one of the most important sermons in the series. It explains the mystical union in exactly the same terms as in the Gospel of St John.

The eighth sermon continues St Bernard's commentary on the opening lines of the Canticle: *Osculetur me osculo oris sui* [Let him kiss me with the kiss of his mouth]. Here he shows how the 'spouse', the contemplative soul, is expressing her desire for mystical union. What is mystical union? It is a participation in the love and knowledge that unite the Father and the Son. It is a sharing in the 'embrace' of these divine Persons. How? Through their Holy Spirit. To receive from God the kiss of his mouth is to receive the inpouring of the Divine Spirit — *non est aliud quam infundi Spiritu sancto* [it is nothing else than the inpouring of the Holy Spirit].[31] The Holy Spirit is the bond of union between the Father and the Son, their 'peace', their 'love', their 'unity'.[32]

In asking for the gift of the Holy Spirit, the spouse is asking the Father to reveal both himself and the Son. Note how St Bernard does not say that the spouse asks for 'contemplation' or the 'grace of infused prayer' or even 'mystical union', but for the Holy Spirit. She desires not an abstraction but a divine Person, not a transient subjective experience but the objective possession of God in his infinite reality and love. To receive the Holy Spirit is to receive the love of the Father

and the Son, to know the Father and the Son, and to know
also the Spirit whom they send into our hearts. It is furthermore an intimate contact with the freedom and liberality of
an infinitely loving God. In receiving his Spirit, we know
him in the mystery of his own divine freedom. He does not
yield up the secret of his inner life by necessity, compelled by
our virtue or by our discovery of some mystical technique
that compels him to make himself known. To those who seek
to force their way into the sanctuary of his Love, God remains unknown even though they may seem to have
discovered something about him. The spouse therefore does
not seek this kind of knowledge, but only that intimate
revelation of Himself which God grants out of love and mercy, to his little ones. It is this element of liberality, of free-
giving, which gives the experience of divine union its ineffable character and makes it, not a matter of knowledge in
the sense of science, but rather of wisdom. We know God,
not only in our love for him but far more in his gift of his
love for us. And in the mystery of his gift, we see that he
himself is his love and his gift. For here, in this union, God
gives not merely something he has created, or even all that
he has created. Far more than that, he gives himself. Outside this giving of himself, God cannot be intimately and
perfectly known.

> The Son reveals himself to whom he wills, and he reveals
> the Father. But he reveals him, without any doubt, by a
> kiss, that is to say by the Holy Spirit, according to the
> testimony of the Apostle, who says: 'God has revealed it to
> us by his Spirit.' In giving the Spirit, by Whom he reveals,
> he reveals also the Spirit. In giving him, he reveals him,
> and in revealing he gives him....
> A happy kiss indeed, through which God is not only
> known but loved as a Father: He who is not at all fully
> known except when he is perfectly loved.[33]

The effect of this reception of the Holy Spirit is that the contemplative is filled with charity, truth and wisdom. *In osculo isto nec error locum habet, nec tepor* [In this kiss there is no room for uncertainty or for lukewarmness].[34] St Bernard will explain later how this ardor of love overflows in apostolic zeal. Here he contents himself with giving us two great examples of this kind of contemplation: both of them are apostles of Christ—St John the Evangelist and St Paul, the Apostle of the Gentiles. There is also St John the Baptist, the model and patron not only of monks but also of missionaries and of all priests. Clearly, the source of their apostolate was a knowledge of God that had been received in the experience of divine union, and in the 'kiss of love and peace, of love which transcends all knowledge, and of peace which surpasses all understanding'.[35]

As for the diversity of souls and of their vocations, this is clearly explained in the preceding sermon, in which St Bernard identifies the 'spouse' as the *anima sitiens Deum*,[36] and suggests that her personal vocation is somewhat different from that of other souls who seek not God himself, nor the kiss of his mouth, but the reward of faithful service, or the inheritance of sons, or the doctrine of students. In distinguishing the spouse from the 'slave', the 'mercenary', the 'son', or the 'disciple' St Bernard is not only enumerating the different degrees of the spiritual life which he elsewhere elaborates in greater detail, but he is also suggesting the possibility of different vocations within the one monastic vocation, or the one christian vocation, as we shall later see. We might begin by considering the place of the active life within the monastery.

2. Action in the Monastic Life

In his ninth sermon on the Canticle of Canticles, St Bernard describes the apostolic fruitfulness of the contemplative. His doctrine is the traditional teaching of the Fathers. Echoing St Augustine and St Gregory the Great,[37] and sounding a note that will afterwards be taken up by St Thomas Aquinas[38] the first Abbot of Clairvaux declares that the zeal of apostolic souls, flowing from contemplative union with God, leads to an activity which is in a sense higher than and preferable to contemplation. For this activity contemplation must often be sacrificed, but the sacrifice, made under the inspiration of the Holy Spirit, will itself be more meritorious than the contemplation which is relinquished for the love of others. True, the sacrifice is a source of pain and anguish for the bride of the Word. But her companions assure her that nothing is lost. Indeed, they say, she must not insist too much upon the joys of contemplation, nor seek to retain these consolations against the will of God. Apostolic activity, they tell her, is better and more necessary than the joys of contemplation. *Ubera quibus parvulos alis, quos et paris,* meliora, hoc est necessariora, *sunt vino contemplationis.... Noli nimis insistere osculis contemplationis,* quia meliora sunt ubera praedicationis.[39]

Other statements, just as strong as this, can be drawn from other sermons of St Bernard. Putting them all together, we might feel justified in coming to the conclusion that St Bernard believes, simply and without qualification, that the 'mixed' or apostolic life is superior to the contemplative life, as well as to the merely active life.[40] If such a statement were to be made without qualification, it might lead to the practical conclusion that the apostolic life should always be *chosen* in preference to the contemplative life. And yet, such a conclusion would be far from the mind of St Bernard, as well as from the mind of St Thomas Aquinas, St Gregory or St Augustine.

As we know, there are other texts of the Abbot of Clairvaux in which he says, quite clearly and definitely, that contemplation is to be preferred to action. The apostolate interferes with that perfect unity of heart which makes the soul most pleasing to God.[41] Mary has indeed chosen the best part. It would be a disgrace for her to look with jealous eyes upon the activity of Martha and seek a part in the troubled life of her busy sister. Jesus has praised the choice of Mary, and therefore, insofar as we are able to make a choice, we should also aspire not to the labors of Martha but to the repose of Mary. *Pars ipsa (Mariae) quantum in nobis est est omnibus eligenda* [Her—Mary's—part should be chosen by us all insofar as it lies within us.].[42]

No one who understands the teaching of christian tradition on the respective merits of the active and contemplative lives will be surprised at this apparent contradiction. Nor will they find any real discrepancy between the strong assertion of Pius XI in *Umbratilem* on the superiority of the contemplative life and the complaint made by St Augustine that the contemplative life was relatively fruitless.[43] There is no contradiction on this point in St Bernard. His doctrine is clear and consistent, and his texts, when assembled and compared, reveal to us a coherent and practical structure of ideas. Needless to say, these ideas are of considerable importance in the study and appreciation of the cistercian vocation. It is from this point of view that they will be treated here.

However, before we go further, there are three cautions to be observed. First, St Bernard is not bringing into opposition the active, contemplative, and 'mixed' lives in the same way as St Thomas. Nowhere does he say that the cistercian monk is dedicated by his very vocation to a state of life with which activity would be incompatible. If we assert that the cistercian vocation is purely contemplative in the sense that it excludes any activity, in the sense that activity constitutes an infidelity to our vocation and to our state of life, we are immediately confronted by a contradiction. It would be dangerous to attract souls to our cloisters by leading them to expect a life devoted purely to the contemplation of God, without the risk of ever becoming implicated in material cares or even in the necessity of caring for other souls. True, our life ordinarily does not involve us in parish work or teaching, but the activity required to support a cistercian monastery, from a merely material point of view, can sometimes be very intense. And in any case, the priests of the monastery will generally be called to share with others the fruits of their contemplation in sermons, conferences and scriptural exegesis as well as in the confessional and in spiritual direction. As St Bernard clearly saw and taught, we are called to the monastery to seek God and indeed to find him. Just as there are many mansions in our Father's house, so too in the monastery there may be many different ways to heaven. The whole community is the generation of those that seek God. The life is preponderantly contemplative, but not all monks will be contemplatives in the strict sense of the word. Contemplation is indeed open to all, but it does not follow that all will attain it, or even that all should attain it. St Bernard is not worried by the fact that many of his monks will be leading effectively active lives. He only asks that they leave the contemplatives alone[44] and not trouble them with their activity. For as he shows, the cistercian life is not a mould into which all are poured alike, so that all emerge with the same identical form. On the contrary, the beauty of our life lies in its diversity, in the freedom of development which each person should be able to find, under the formative influence of grace, in the bosom of the monastic community.[45]

A second warning to be remembered is that St Bernard, here as elsewhere, approaches this problem not from a speculative but from a practical and indeed from an intimately personal point of view. Everything that St Bernard has to say about the interior life is colored by his own personal experience and by his contact with the souls whom God had given into his care. Therefore the strong contrast between the joys of contemplation and the fruitful sacrifice demanded by apostolic action derives its urgency from St Bernard's own feelings on the subject and from the problems he met with in his own monks. Nowhere is St Bernard's personal experience more telling than in this question, which was to remain a source of interior suffering throughout his whole life.[46] It was because he felt in himself the effects which could not help but be harmful even though the activity was imposed on him by obedience, that he *experienced* the opposition between contemplation and action in his own soul. But we must not exaggerate this into a speculative opposition which would make action and contemplation in themselves incompatible. On the contrary, in a more objective mood, he describes the way action and contemplation mutually assist one another in leading the soul to the perfection of charity.

The monastic life is simply the christian life in all its perfection, and so it is not strange that within our monastic vocation we should still find that various 'ways to God', various 'states', if I may employ the term loosely, remain open to us as vocations within our vocation. St Bernard treats these different levels of Christian life now in reference to the monastery, now in reference to the whole Church. Since the monastery is a little mystical body, a kind of microcosm within the organism of the Church, it reproduces something of the structure of the Church itself. So in the monastery we find the active life, the contemplative life and the 'apostolic' life being led side by side. I use the term apostolic life in preference to 'mixed' life, because it is more in harmony with the thought of St Bernard, even though he himself does not use it.

All these vocations, whether in the monastery or outside it, are ways to God. What is more, all these are ways of the *interior* life. It is because they all demand a deep interior life of intimate union with God, although in different degrees, that St Bernard does not scruple to admit them within the precincts of the monastery. God speaks to the heart of those who faithfully follow these three ways of life, and what he utters in their heart is his own peace. These three orders are symbolized by Noah, Daniel and Job. In the Church at large, these represent the married state, the monastic state, and the episcopate. In the monastery — where neither married life nor the episcopacy are found — the three Old Testament figures have a different meaning. Job represents the active life — officiales fratres *qui exterioribus et quasi popularibus negotiis occupantur* [the steward brothers who are taken up with outside and, as it were, secular business]; Daniel the man of desires, suitably represents the contemplatives — *claustrales quos nulla occupatio impedit, sed libere vacant ut videant quam suavis est Dominus* [the cloistered brothers whom no busy-ness impedes, but they are freely dutiless that they may see how sweet the Lord is]. Finally, there are the superiors — the *praelati* — who combine both lives because, like Jesus Christ whom they represent in the monastery, they are set as cornerstones upon which the two walls of action and contemplation must meet.[47]

This threefold division into *officiales fratres, claustrales,* and *praelati* is paralleled elsewhere by other triads familiar to all who know St Bernard's sermons. For instance, a slightly different division occurs in the third Sermon for the Assumption of Our Blessed Lady. Commenting on the Gospel of the Feast, St Bernard compared the monastery to the family which Jesus used to visit at Bethany. In the monastic community we find Lazarus, the penitent, Martha engaged in administration, and Mary the contemplative.[48]

All three are necessary to make the monastery what it ought to be, not only materially but above all spiritually. They are the effect of the good order of charity in the community. It would be a distortion and a caricature of moanstic life to demand that a community consist exclusively of one or the other of these 'orders'. It is a distortion of the cistercian ideal to insist that everyone confine himself exclusively to the vocation of Lazarus. It is a further distortion of the cistercian ideal when, in actual practice, the house becomes a collection of querulous and somewhat excitable Marthas. Mary has chosen the best part. And yet not even Mary has a monopoly on the cistercian ideal. The monastery is not expected to consist exculsively of Marys sitting at the feet of Jesus. If St Bernard makes this last qualification, it is certainly not because he regretfully accepts it as inescapable. We are not to think that the monastery *ought* to be peopled entirely by Marys but that, since human nature is what it is, we must be content to let two-thirds of the community live below the level of our true vocation. This is by no means the case. It is *better* that the community should live on these different levels, and all who live on their own level within the community are in fact *fulfilling* the cistercian ideal. *Tria haec distribuit ordinatio charitatis!*[49]

There is another interesting triad in the forty-seventh sermon *In Cantica*. Here St Bernard speaks of three vocations — to action, to virginity and to martyrdom.[50] Whatever St Bernard says about different ways of life within the monastery or within the Church will be clarified by his symbol of the three 'ointments' in the early sermons *In Cantica*. The anointing of compunction is what introduces us to the penitent vocation. Devotion makes us, in some sense, contemplatives. Piety *unguentum pietatis* is the overflow of the other two in an apostolic charity that brings souls to God.[51]

And here we find that, as a matter of fact, one may pass from one level to the other. One may start as a Lazarus and then become a Mary. What is more, one cannot fruitfully enter upon the apostolic life unless one is first of all both a penitent and a contemplative. The apostolate, without virtues and without a deep interior life, is of no value.[52]

3. The Contemplative Life

We have seen[53] that the monastic community, in all its integral perfection, is made up of men and women who seek
God and find him in different levels of the interior life.
Some find him in penance, others in charitable activity,
others still in contemplation, and finally others in sharing
the fruits of contemplation with their brothers or even with
the world outside. St Bernard emphasizes the fact that all
these vocations are good. Even though the monastic life may
be essentially contemplative, in the sense that it is centered
directly on God, the active life is not banned from the
monastic enclosure and when it is properly understood by no
means constitutes an infidelity to the monastic vocation.
Those who travel by these various ways are all travelling to
God. *Ad idem tendunt, licet non eadem via.*[54]

It is because our modern terminology is slightly different
from St Bernard's that these statements of the abbot of
Clairvaux may perhaps create a slight unrest in the minds of
a modern Cistercian. But we must remember that in saying
that some members of the monastic community lead 'active
lives' he is by no means saying, as we might imagine, that
they lead the kind of life one would expect to find in an active *order*. Activity has its place in the monastic life. To
begin with, according to the traditional meaning of the
term, the active life is first of all the life of virtue and of
penance which is the necessary preparation for contemplative prayer.[55]

The term 'active life' also embraces the necessary labors
and duties of the monastic community. St Bernard tells us
that those whom obedience obliges to live more active lives
lose none of the merit that is gained by the contemplatives.

Non minoris meriti apud Dominum humilis conversatio Marthae.[56] However, he adds that those who enter a monastery of our Order are normally seeking the contemplative life in its purity, and therefore they should not look for employments, charges or offices, but only accept them when they are commanded by superiors. A monk, if he can, should *choose* and *prefer* the contemplative life. Activity is not to be desired but *tolerated*. It should be *accepted* under obedience, not sought by our own volition. *Haec, si vero injungitur, patienter toleranda est.*[57]

Here, to be quite precise, we must make an important distinction. When the active life means merely the life of penance and laborious practice of virtue which we would call today the 'ascetic' life, it is not to be merely tolerated but also chosen. It is a necessary prelude to contemplation. In choosing contemplation we also, in fact, choose the active life in this particular sense. Indeed, it is all that we do choose: contemplation is a gift of God. All we can do for our own part is dispose ourselves to receive it by leading the kind of life that is most appropriate—a life of detachment, silence, recollection, humility, obedience, charity. This implies the 'activity' of many virtues. The active life that is to be *tolerated* rather than *elected* is the life of material or spiritual administration in the monastery or even outside it.

Hence, in a more precise statement of the relation between the three lives of contemplation, penance and the apostolate, St Bernard tells his monks to choose the lot of Mary or of Lazarus but not that of Martha. *Tibi vero cui necessitas haec (administrationis) non incumbit,* e duobus unum est necessarium: *aut non turbari penitus, sed delectari magis in Domino; aut si id necdum potes, turbari non erga plurima sed... ad teipsum.*[58]

Let us turn to a detailed study of that contemplative life which is to be preferred before all others: *omnino quod ad nos spectat, eligenda.*[59]

The contemplative life is in itself better than the active life and is always to be sought by us in preference to the active life. In other words, for St Bernard, the contemplative life is both speculatively and practically *preferable* to the active life in all the senses of that term. However, it is not necessarily *superior* to the apostolic life. However, the peculiar excellence of the apostolic life is derived from the element of contemplation that is in it even more than from the element of active charity. This is clear from the fortieth sermon *In Cantica*. This sermon deals with the perfect purity of heart by which the spouse captivates the Word of God. Contemplation, seeking God alone for his own sake, is the *amor castus*[60] which pleases him perfectly and brings us, at least momentarily, to intimate union with him.

Even though the apostolic life as St Bernard conceives it implies a heroic degree of selflessness, nevertheless it lacks this particular note of *castitas,* of spiritual purity, which contemplation alone can give.

> Porro intendere in aliud quam in Deum, tamen propter Deum, non otium illam Mariae sed Marthae negotium est. Absit autem ut qui hujusmodi est quidquam dixerim habere deforme. *Non tamen ad perfectam affirmaverim pervenisse decoris,* quippe quae adhuc sollicita est et turbatur erga plurima et non potest terrenorum actuum vel tenui pulvere non respergi.[61]

The apostolic life cannot help but be slightly stained with the dust of the world. It cannot avoid all solicitude, all misery, or all failure, and it therefore falls short of the perfection demanded for union. However, in practice, since St Bernard would deny the apostolate to any but true contemplatives, these souls recover their perfect purity when they return to that contemplation which gives meaning and value to their own life as well as to their apostolate. *Pulverem tamen cito facileque deterget vel* in hora sanctae dormitionis casta intentio *et bonae conscientiae interrogatio in Deum.*[62]

St Bernard can therefore say, succinctly, that the contemplative life is 'better'. 'Hoc enim melius, quiescere et cum Christo esse, *necessarium exire ad lucrum propter salvandos.*'[63]

The relation between the active and contemplative lives is seen from a slightly different angle in the *De consideratione.* Here, St Bernard shows considerable anxiety for the welfare of his spiritual son, Bl Eugene III. The urgency of St Bernard's counsels, and the solicitude which he displays seem to indicate that he thought the first cistercian pope was ascending the throne of Peter with an interior life barely sufficient to cope with his vocation as Supreme Pontiff. He urges upon him the practice of meditation (*consideratio*) and other exercises which are usually emphasized in the earlier stages of the spiritual life, or whenever the spiritual life must be lived under pressure of unfavorable circumstances. St Bernard's injunctions are clear and definite. 'Do not give yourself entirely to activity, and do not engage in active works all the time. Keep something of your heart and of your time, for meditation!'[64] But the holy abbot immediately adds that this is strictly an emergency measure. It would be far more desirable if Eugene could give himself much more time for prayer. The life of prayer is always and in all circumstances to be preferred to the life of action. It should always, if possible, prevail over activity. 'Nam si liceret quod deceret absolute per omnia et in omnibus praeferendam et vel solam vel maxime colendam eam quae ad omnia valet, id est pietatem, *irrefragabilis ratio monstrat. Quid sit pietas quaeris? Vacare considerationi.*'[65]

Pietas, and *vacare considerationi* are not strictly speaking the contemplative life,[66] at least not in St Bernard's terminology. They can of course enter into the contemplative life, but *consideratio* is not contemplative prayer. It is the meditation which spiritualizes the active life. It is the prayer of Lazarus, not of Mary.[67] Nevertheless even this should be chosen in preference to apostolic action or to exterior works if the choice is left up to us. And in the life of action itself, prayer, meditation, the consideration of divine things should always exercise the greatest attraction upon our heart, so that even in our activity we long to return to them.

However, if the apostolic life should not be chosen or desired, that is not because it is inferior to the contemplative life. On the contrary, the very *superiority* of the apostolic life demands that we avoid entering upon it without a special mission from God. That mission, as we shall see, is made known to us by obedience or by the interior inspirations of grace (which, in any case, must be controlled by obedience).

In an age when bishops were often chosen from communities of Cistercians, St Bernard advised his monks to revere the bishops but not to envy their apostolate or their dignity. *Fratres,* revereamur *episcopos sed vereamur labores eorum.*[68] And to those who might seem too eager to take contemplatives and put them to work in the Master's vineyard, St Bernard uttered a warning. Amplifying the Saviour's defence of Mary — *Quid molesti estis huic muliere* [Why do you pester this woman?] — the Abbot of Clairvaux defends contemplatives from the dangers of an activity of which they might well be incapable. Unlike St John of the Cross, St Bernard does not here argue that 'when the soul has reached (union) it befits it not to be occupied in other outward acts and exercises which might keep it back, however little, from that abiding in love with God, although they may greatly conduce to the service of God; for a very little of this pure love is more precious in the sight of God and the soul and of greater profit to the Church, even though the soul appear to be doing nothing, than are all these works together.'[69] St Bernard, believing that apostolic action is one of the fruits of mystical union, defends the contemplative who is perhaps far short of perfect union, against being engaged in activity before the time is ripe. St John of the Cross thinks that even though a contemplative may be capable of fruitful activity, it is still more profitable for him to remain hidden in the contemplative life. Speaking in the person of Jesus, St Bernard says: *Quid tentatis ei (Sponsae) imponere jugum* ad quod ego eam minus sufficientem intueor? ...stet in bono quandiu non convalescit in melius.[70]

The contemplative life is good, indeed. But the apostolic life is better. However, as one of the Desert Fathers remarked, it is better to be fervent in a less exalted vocation than to be found tepid in a higher profession.[71] The contemplative must seek rather to cling to the good which he has than lose it by reaching out for a higher good for which he is probably unprepared. Let him wait until God gives him the grace necessary for that special mission. Let him wait until God Himself calls, and let him be very hesitant to interpret every interior 'attraction' as an inspiration of the Holy Spirit.

The principal reason for this discretion is, of course, the dangers and difficulties inherent in the active life. The burdens of the apostolate should, ideally, be reserved for strong souls only. Such burdens are designed for 'men'. The cloistered religious, says St Bernard, in an expression well calculated to enable his followers to advance in humility, is more a woman than a man when it comes to shouldering the labors of the apostolate. *Non est vir, ut putatis, qui possit mittere manum ad fortia, sed mulier.... Adnoscamus impares vires nostras, nec delectet molles et femineos humeros virorum supponere sarcinis.*[72]

However, the saint instantly turns this same argument into a weapon against those of his cloistered monks who were prone to criticize the inevitable faults and failings of their brethren or superiors engaged in the active or apostolic lives—faults against which they themselves were protected by their enclosures and the advantages of their monastic retreat. For a contemplative religious to find fault with those engaged in a far more difficult and dangerous vocation is like a woman sewing in the window-seat criticizing the soldiers of a returning army.

> Temerarie objurgat virum de praelio revertentem mulier nens in domo. Dico enim si is qui de claustro est eum qui versatur in populo interdum minus districte minusve circumspecte sese agere deprehendit verbi gratia in verbo, in cibo, in somno, in risu, in ira, in judicio; non ad judicandum confestim prosiliat, sed meminerit scriptum: melior est iniquitas viri quam benefaciens mulier.[73]

The last words of this passage are a quotation from Scripture[74] and St Bernard makes the same curious application of them several times over, in connection with the same theme of action and contemplation. The contemplative life is, in a certain sense, easier. Not that the contemplative life lacks trials and difficulties of a very particular kind, but it affords us greater protection against spiritual dangers and more numerous helps to spiritual advancement.

> Non est ejusdem facilitatis devote quiescere et fructuose operari; humiliter subesse et utiliter praesse; regi sine querela et regere sine culpa; obedire sponte et imperare discrete; bonum denique esse inter bonos, et bonum inter malos; imo etiam esse pacatum inter filios pacis, et his qui oderunt pacem exhiberi pacificum.[75]

This humble and realistic view of the monastic vocation reminds us of all the advantages of the cloistered life and indeed recalls to our minds the debt of gratitude we owe God for having placed us in its shelter. But it should not make us think that our life is somehow less useful than any other. On the contrary, St Bernard strenuously defends the high value of the contemplative life. Indeed, the arguments we have been quoting are directed against those who complain, as did the disciples when Mary Magdalen poured out her precious ointment upon the feet of Jesus that this sacrifice is sheer waste: *ut quid perdito haec* [why should this be wasted]? No one knew better than St Bernard that the contemplative life was not a waste of time or talent. To direct such a criticism against the apparent idleness of the contemplative is to give evidence of a worldly and carnal spirit which is not able to appreciate the things of God. *Carnalis est et omnino non percipit quae sunt Spiritus Dei, si quis forte vacantem animam sua de vacatione redarguit.*[76]

In this text, St Bernard almost rejoins the thought quoted above from St John of the Cross. The 'idleness' he speaks of here is the apparent idleness of contemplative prayer, and he is defending true contemplatives not only against active persons in the world, but also against the Marthas of their own cloister who are often more uncomprehending and more bitingly critical than outsiders. Nevertheless he hastens to qualify his statement by saying that it is better for the contemplative to be able to unite action with contemplation, but that if God does not call us to this superior vocation our contemplation will remain most fruitful and meritorious by itself.[77]

Before we go on to treat of this apostolic life, we must pause to understand the full importance of the *quies contemplationis,* the fruitful and formative 'rest' of the soul in the secret embrace of the Word. This rest alone makes apostolic action fruitful. Woe to the carnal person who thinks such rest is a waste of time, or who condemns 'contemplative idleness' as a defection from duty or as a failure in generosity. What a mistake it would be to accuse a monk of self-love for desiring this hidden life, when St Bernard himself repeatedly reminds us that the holy sleep (*sancta dormitio*) of contemplation is to be preferred by us and sought out before every other vocation or activity.[78] Only the clear call of obedience or charity can dispense us from giving the primacy, in the matter of practical choice, to contemplation.

Monastic tradition teaches that the 'repose' of contemplation is not merely a rest from exterior labors and actions. The rest St Bernard speaks of is above all the fruit of liberation from slavery to our passions. The soul cannot be a spouse of the Word without this freedom to rest in his arms. She cannot rest peacefully in the embrace of his truth and his charity until contempt for all earthly things has given her the 'leisure' of the truly interior soul: *cui contemptus omnium otium dederit.*[79] This 'leisure' which enables the soul to rest in God is nothing else than pure love which is able to rise above the anxiety and concern of the *necessitas*[80] which continually nags the soul as long as it is in the body and exiled from the Lord. We can be most truly said to 'rest' when we are raised above our weak, deficient and human way of acting—above a way of knowledge and love still inhibited by human limitations. When pure love has perfectly liberated the will to allow it to rest in God, it is at least momentarily 'deified',[81] loving and acting as he loves and acts. In his earlier works, St Bernard lamented that this rest could never last long in this life, could never be perfect until the soul was entirely free from the flesh. We inevitably fall back to our own level. We are compelled to provide for the body and to go out of ourselves in a certain amount of social activity, no matter how contemplative we may be.[82] But during the brief rapture of perfect union the soul no longer engages in the activity of thinking about itself or about other people. It is lost in God—*ita ut nec ratio de se, nec voluntas de proximo cogitare sinatur.*[83] It could not 'work' even if it wanted to. This perfect union with God is described in a famous passage of the *Degrees of Humility*. The idea of 'rest' and quiescence is properly emphasized. It is the reward of a soul

that has previously shown much generosity in the active life
of acquiring virtue.

> Suffulta floribus ac stipata malis, bonis scilicet moribus et
> virtutibus sanctis, ad Regis denique cubiculum, cujus
> amore languet, admittitur. Ibi modicum, hora videlicet
> quasi dimidia, silentio facto in coelo, inter desideratos
> amplexus suaviter quiescens, ipsa quidem dormit, sed cor
> ejus vigilat, quo utique veritatis arcana rimatur: quorum
> postmodum memoria stati, ad se reditura pascatur.[84]

These terms clearly explain St Bernard's teaching that the
'repose' of contemplation is really a higher form of activity.
Indeed it is the highest activity and the most profitable
business the monk could possibly engage in. *Sapientiae otia
negotia sunt* [Wisdom's leisures are business]![85] Moved immediately and passively by the Holy Spirit, the soul penetrates
with Him into the deep things of God. He acquires a store of
experiential wisdom from which will later be drawn forth a
powerful and effective instruction, living and efficacious, if
and when there is a call to preach the word of God.[86]

Even when contemplation falls short of the perfection of
rapture, its ecstatic character generally brings 'rest' from the
exterior active life and from the interior activity of concern
with the accidents of a bodily and communal existence. It is
a life in which there is 'no disturbance' — *non turbari penitus.*[87]
Bodily activity is an impediment to contemplation.[88] It is
a life entirely of love, in which nothing is known or desired
but love.[89] Love is the one transcendent activity of the contemplative, which embraces all other activities and elevates
them to its own supreme level of liberty and rest.[90] To be
carried away by the Holy Spirit in this divine love means
therefore the renunciation of all other affections, all other
activities, even the comparatively mercenary interior activity
of hope, in the sense of a hope that hopes for something else
besides love. The repose of contemplation is achieved when
there remains no obstacle to our pure love for God.

The chief reason why this mystical and pure love for God is at once supreme activity and perfect rest is that it is produced in us not by our own energy or initiative, but by the direct activation of the Holy Spirit. Infused wisdom is, then, by its very nature, un-laborious because it is produced in us without efforts on our own part, passively and as a free gift of God. This tranquil passivity is one of the sources of the 'savor' or 'taste' (*sapor*) which makes wisdom (*sapientia*) the thing it is—*sapida scientia*'. *Ubi amor est, labor non est sed sapor.*[91] The sanctifying passivity of a love which recaptures the 'taste' for heavenly things through the secret interior action of the Holy Spirit repairs the disaster of original sin which doomed us to an Egyptian slavery in which we labor for the satisfaction of self and for the gratification of passion. But wisdom also raises us above the contrary labor, the *agere contra*, proper to the ascetic way, in which we struggle manfully against our passions in order to serve the Lord in fear.[92] Mystical contemplation completes and perfects the work of ascetic purification. It passively cures and heals the wounds of original sin and restores the health of the soul in a way that could not be achieved by our own action:

> Et nunc assidue sapientia vincit malitiam in mentibus ad quas intraverit, saporem mali, quam illa invexit sapore exterminans meliori. Intrans sapientia, dum sensum carnis infatuat, purificat intellectum, cordis palatum sanat et reparat. Sano palato sapit jam bonum, sapit jam sapientia, qua in bonis nullum melius.[93]

Elsewhere St Bernard explains that the sleep of contemplation is in reality an awakening to a higher life and a higher knowledge. In the embrace of mystical wisdom, the spouse is raised above the temptations and distractions that are the ordinary lot of men. In this sense also, therefore, contemplation brings rest from labor and surcease from interior activity. It delivers us, at least temporarily, from the necessity of struggling against temptation and distraction. It illuminates the intelligence without effort and carries the will away in a rapture of divine love.[94] Finally, contemplation is an 'angelic death' which delivers us even from the human mode of knowing through images and concepts. This too is a higher degree of 'rest' and quiescence — a sleep which closes our eyes to every human light but opens them to the divine.[95]

It is abundantly clear from all these texts that the contemplative life, as St Bernard conceives it, is by no means a life of study, still less of research scholarship. However, since mystical understanding is a penetration of the mysteries of our faith and since contemplative wisdom is nourished by the Word himself, it is clear that we prepare ourselves for it by our *lectio divina*. Contemplation is simply the possession, by experience, of what we have read in Scripture. Hence the soul spontaneously seeks God in Scripture, *sciens se ibi absque dubio inventuram quem sitit.*[96] This thirst is not to be satisfied by anything less than the 'kiss of his mouth' — by God himself, giving himself secretly to the soul in mystical experience, casting aside the sensible images and figures in which he came disguised.[97] St Bernard knew that these hidden meanings of Scripture were revealed more perfectly to the soul meditating in the woods than to the student in the scriptorium.[98]

There are two more aspects of the 'quiet' and 'rest' of contemplation. The repose of infused wisdom is proportionate to the secrecy and hiddenness of the truths we taste in their substance. And this secrecy in turn makes us rest in a purer and more intimate familiarity with the divine spouse, who only reveals himself perfectly in the inner sanctuary of the soul, to which no one but he alone can penetrate. St Bernard completes this teaching by adding that the quiescence of divine union flows essentially from an experience of God's infinite mercy. The 'place' in which we 'see' the divine mercy is the place of his peace where the 'tranquil God brings tranquillity upon all things'. *Tranquillus Deus tranquillat om-*

nia, et quietum aspicere quiescere est.[99] However, the context of this statement tells us that not all contemplation is perfectly 'quiet'. On the contrary, in a passage which recalls the 'Dark Night' of St John of the Cross, St Bernard describes another 'place' or another degree of infused contemplation in which God appears to us not mild and peaceful in his mercy but terrible in his judgements. And he also brings out the infused and experiential character of this contemplation.[100]

Finally there is a completely 'unquiet' contemplation, which is not infused at all. It is a kind of acquired contemplation which soars toward God in admiration but ends in anxiety and unrest, precisely because it is the work of our own powers which feel themselves frustrated by the divine light, which infinitely exceeds their grasp. We strive heavenwards and beat our wings vainly, but never leave the ground. There is no 'rest' in such contemplation as this, and yet it can have the merit of arousing in us the hunger and thirst for a true experience of God.[101]

The fact that this 'contemplation' is not restful means precisely that it is not contemplation. Since it is entirely laborious, it lacks the experiential element which goes to make up true wisdom. But the terror of God in darkness is passively infused, and though it is also without rest, it is the 'beginning of wisdom'.

St Bernard explains that contemplative wisdom is a sign of full spiritual maturity, and therefore of the perfection and sanctity of the soul. Maturity and beauty prepare the soul for marriage with the Word, and we shall see later on that one of the proofs that this marriage has taken place is the fruitfulness of a supernatural apostolate, nourished by mystical contemplation. St Bernard carefully distinguishes between the rapture of the soul resting in God and the other more fruitful *excessus* in which it goes out to souls. The apostolate is a great work and a great grace, but the labors it implies prevent perfect absorption in God until such time as we are again alone with him in contemplation. Then we may again achieve the liberty of a spirit lost in God and no longer able to think of itself.

> In hoc ultimo genere interdum exceditur et seceditur etiam a corporeis sensibus, ut sese non sentiat quae Verbum sentit. Hoc fit cum mens, ineffabilis Verbi illecta dulcedine, quodammodo se sibi furatur, imo rapitur et elabitur a seipsa, ut Verbo fruatur. Aliter sane afficitur mens fructificans Verbo, aliter fruens Verbo. Illic sollicitat necessitas proximi, hic invitat suavitas Verbi. Et quidem laeta in prole mater, sed in amplexibus Sponsi laetior... Bonum est salvare multos; excedere autem et cum Verbo esse multo jucundius.[102]

The divine Bridegroom himself, though sometimes sending forth his spouse to care for souls, more often seeks to guard and protect her contemplative peace with jealous care. Indeed, it is for this reason that he keeps his right arm around her and his left arm under her head, warning all others to allow her to rest on his bosom and not to disturb her contemplative sleep:

> vehementissime zelans pro quiete cujusdam dilectae suae, sollicitus servare inter brachia propria dormientem, ne qua forte molestia vel inquietudine a somno suavissimo deturbetur.[103]

Nevertheless, the repose of the Spouse in the arms of the divine Bridegroom cannot be considered on this earth as an end in itself. It must bring forth children of God, and apostolic fruitfulness is itself a proof that our contemplation is genuine. *Hinc te scilicet noveris osculum accepisse, quod te concepisse sentis.*[104] Although the soul finds the Word in deep solitude and secret intimacy, the contemplation of his mercy is not granted her for herself alone. Otherwise it would be, in a certain sense, sterile. *Sola introducta videor, sed soli non proderit. Vestrum omnium est meus omnis profectus.*[105] With these words of St Bernard, we can pass on to consider the meaning and value of the mixed or apostolic life.

4. The Apostolate

A curious error of the monk Joachim of Fiora, condemned by Alexander IV in 1255, bears on the relation of the active and contemplative lives. After stating, heretically, that Jesus and his apostles were not perfect in the contemplative life (!) the illustrious but misguided abbot went on to declare that the time had now come for cloistered monks to supplant the active ministry. The active life had hitherto been fruitful, in the hands of the *ordo clericorum*. But now, with the advent of Joachim, the contemplative life had at last come into its own, and the successors of the same Joachim would soon demonstrate that the contemplatives were to take the Church in hand. The active orders no longer mattered.[106]

A combination of loose thinking and badly documented zeal might perhaps remove certain passages of St Bernard from their context and interpret them as leading to some such conclusion as this. But that would be far from the mind of St Bernard. In the first place, Bernard is not interested in comparing active and contemplative *Orders*. His chief task is to clarify the functions of the active, contemplative and mixed lives *within the established framework* of the monastic order, or in any other established state, as the episcopate. We know that St Bernard attributes to the mixed life a certain superiority over the other two: but this superiority is never verified when the mixed life is not in fact the fruit of superabundant contemplation and intimate union with God. Thus even the superiority of the mixed life, since it depends in fact upon the element of contemplation which that life presupposes, is a most cogent argument for the primacy of contemplation. However, we must not interpret St Bernard's doctrine as if it instituted a comparison between the Cistercian Order and some other 'active' Orders, or with the secular clergy. No such comparison was intended by St Bernard in the texts with which we are concerned in the present study. The Abbot of Clairvaux has no chip on his shoulder and is not attempting to prove that we Cistercians, being 'contemplatives', are superior to other religious who are 'not contemplatives'. Still less does he suggest that we ought to leave the cloister and convert the world with the overflow of our contemplation.

He has shown us[107] that the contemplative life is to be sought and preferred to the active life, but that the 'mixed' life, composed of action and contemplation together, is in a certain sense more necessary to the Church than contemplation alone, and therefore it has a higher dignity than the life of pure or unmixed contemplation. Indeed the greater dignity and difficulty of the mixed life is the chief reason why humility and prudence will urge us to choose, for ourselves, the retirement and rest of contemplation.

A very high degree of christian perfection is necessary for the 'mixed' life, according to St Bernard. He says that the most perfect souls combine in themselves the vocations of Martha, Mary, and Lazarus. They excel at the same time in apostolic action, in contemplation and in works of penance.[108] He is speaking here of a perfection proper to the *monastic life,* for it is created 'in our house' by the *ordinatio caritatis.* It is the perfection proper to abbots and other superiors. But it is not necessary for a monk to be perfect in all these three if he is to become a saint and fulfil his vocation. It is more normal for the monk — and for the ordinary Christian — to attain sanctity by perfection in one or other of these 'ways' — active, contemplative, or apostolic.

In any case, perfection is not merely an individual matter. We are members of the Mystical Body of Christ, and the perfection of the member is nothing but a perfect integration in the life of the whole organism. In order to reach that integration, to find our place in Christ, we must indeed begin by emphasizing the work of our personal sanctification. What would it profit a man to save the whole world and suffer the loss of his own soul? But once our own perfection has been in some measure achieved (the result does not by any means have to be complete or total), our further development demands the unqualified gift of ourselves to the whole Christ. We must receive from Christ the grace which shows us our place in the Church, and we must *bear fruit* for him, grow in him, and radiate our own supernatural vitality to other members of his Mystical Body until we 'all meet into the unity of faith and of the knowledge of the Son of God unto a perfect man, unto the measure of the age of the fulness of Christ'.[109] It is thus that 'doing the truth in charity we grow up in him who is the Head, even Christ'.[110] Such is the doctrine of St Paul, and it is the doctrine of our Father St Bernard. A perfection that ends in ourselves, that does not contribute to the growth of the whole Christ, is not christian sanctity. Nevertheless, not all are called to preach.[111] Those who do not have to preach can still be perfect if they are 'zealous for the better gifts'.[112]

Unless I am much mistaken, it was St Teresa and the carmelite mystics of the sixteenth century who first brought into prominence the apostolic role and fruitfulness of the pure contemplative. The foundation of St Joseph, at Avila, which initiated the carmelite reform, was essentially apostolic. By their lives of prayer and penance, the contemplative nuns were to make reparation for the great heresies that were then dividing the Church, and they were to bring down grace upon the apostles whose mission it was to deal directly with souls.[113]

This implied no doctrinal innovation. It was the rediscovery of a truth which is clearly brought out in the Gospels: that there are certain 'great devils' which cannot be cast out except by prayer and penance.[114] The doctrine of the communion of saints vindicates the apostolic fruitfulness of every truly contemplative soul.

St Bernard, however, though he recognizes that the *otium sapientiae* (the repose of contemplation) is supremely profitable, considers the fruitfulness of contemplation in relation to the sanctity of the individual contemplative or apostle. He does not explicitly treat of the power of contemplation to bring down merits upon other souls and to win graces for the Church at large. On the contrary, St Bernard's contrast between the active and contemplative lives is incomprehensible if we forget that for him, as for the rest of the Fathers, contemplation is still the 'sterile Rachel'[115] whose embraces must be exchanged for those of blear-eyed but fruitful Liah before the contemplative can bring forth souls to Christ. St Bernard definitely believes that the contemplative life is 'for ourselves' and the mixed life is 'for others'. This is the precise reason why we must prefer the contemplative life, since charity begins at home. But it is also the reason why, if we are called by God to engage in activity, preaching, the care of souls, we must leave the quiet of the contemplative life in order to respond to his call; we must sacrifice the joy and security of our retirement in order to give light to others: *nec cuiquam sibi sed omnibus esse vivendum.*[116]

If St Bernard insists so strongly that the vocation of the monk is to weep and not to teach,[117] this is not because he considers that the monk's tears are in themselves more fruitful for the Church than apostolic preaching. It is because the urge to teach others must be regarded as a temptation when it interferes with the sanctification of our own souls, and we cannot safely presume, by an act of our own judgement, that we have reached a level of sanctity and union with God that would justify our taking upon ourselves the care of others,[118] especially when this does not enter into the field of our own vocation. Sermons 49, 50 and 51 *In Cantica* are important, for they give us the whole background of St Bernard's evaluation of the demands of action and contemplation upon one who is called to the care of souls. The standards he lays down are practical for anyone who is faced with apparently conflicting duties: on the one hand, the duty of carrying out God's will as it is manifested to us in the activities and responsibilities of our position, and on the other hand the duty to correspond to the clear call of God's grace inspiring us to seek a more perfect and more intimate union with him in contemplation.

St Bernard shows that perfection is not a matter of choosing between these obligations, of accepting one and rejecting the other. On the contrary, we must *harmonize the two*, achieve a perfect balance between them, give to each one its due. The soul that achieves this balance by dint of discretion and fidelity to grace finds itself perfectly ordered in charity. It is then able to retain the highest affective esteem for the thing which is greatest in itself: union with God in contemplation. It is able to *seek* and *prefer* contemplation before all else, while devoting itself (when necessary) to that which is less great in itself but which has a more intimate claim upon its time and energies: the care of souls and the other responsibilities of its office.[119]

This solution to the problem goes far to explain why St Bernard can say that contemplation is, in itself, superior and preferable to action, while on the other hand action is 'more necessary' and 'better' than contemplation. Contemplation takes precedence in the *ordo affectualis*. It is by its very nature better and higher than action, and we must always esteem it above action. Insofar as we are free to do so, we must seek contemplation rather than action. In practice, however, we are often bound to follow another order, the *ordo actualis*, which gives first place to that which has a more immediate claim upon our attention—the inevitable necessities of souls and bodies in the present life. To neglect the duties imposed on us by obedience, to fly from the activities which *must* be carried on for the salvation of souls, would be to disobey God. We cannot disobey him even in the name of contemplation. But at the same time, in turning to activity, we must never make the mistake of thinking that activity is by its nature higher than contemplation: we must remember that contemplation is worthy of our constant and unchanging desire.[120] We must remember that activity cannot legitimately claim *all* our time and all our energies. This will enable us to avoid the pitfalls of activism, and to seize all the opportunities for contemplation and solitude that God puts in our way.

One may legitimately refuse to accept a position which brings with it grave responsibilities, the duty to preach and to direct souls. But once the responsibility has been accepted, we are no longer free to abandon it in order to seek the repose of contemplation. Writing to Oger, a canon regular who had resigned his superiorship in order to return to the obscurity of the common life, St Bernard rebuked his 'false humility' as a defection from duty. *Placuit tibi magis quies tua quam utilitas aliena* [Your repose has pleased you more than outside usefulness] writes the Abbot of Clairvaux, and adds that Oger has resisted the *ordinatio caritatis* on which true sanctity depends.[121]

But before we go on, let us see what is the true nature of the 'mixed' or apostolic life in the mind of St Bernard. And first of all, let us consider what this life *is not*.

St Bernard has no patience for a febrile activism, nourished by no interior life, driven by no supernatural power but fomented by a natural restlessness which is really a subtle form of sloth. Such sloth, as Cassian and the Desert Fathers knew,[122] resorts to useless activities and contacts with the world because it cannot bear the effort demanded by a life of solitude and recollection. St Thomas Aquinas pointed out that although a certain sacrifice of contemplative quiet may be required of the apostle, for the good of souls, and that this sacrifice is an indication of greater love for God, it nevertheless happens in many cases that active men are drawn away from contemplation to activity merely because they find the interior life tedious.[123]

A truly supernatural apostolate cannot flow from mere *curiositas*. St Bernard will have none of that preaching which is nothing but an outburst of natural self-satisfaction, unable to contain its excitement at having discovered a 'new idea'. That would be merely the drunkenness produced by 'the wine of this world which inebriates us with curiosity and not charity, which fills us without nourishing us; which puffs up but does not edify, which stuffs the belly but gives no strength.'[124]

We must by all means resist the temptation to pour out our ideas upon others when we ourselves have not yet been filled with the Holy Spirit or called by him to the apostolate. It would be an utterly false charity to try to 'teach others what we have not learned ourselves and to try to govern others when we cannot even rule ourselves'.[125] Such inane presumption implies a desire to be greater and more perfect than God himself. For God pours out upon us light and love only from his own infinite plenitude. Are we then to try to pour out good upon others from our own emptiness?[126]

We cannot urge ourselves on to this false apostolate by arguing that 'charity seeketh not her own', and by asserting that we are obliged to place the good of others before our own advantage. We cannot give others what we do not have ourselves: and what would be the advantage of an apostolate that did not communicate to others the love of God?[127] Since contemplation is a gift of God and cannot be attained merely by human efforts[128] it is clear that the mixed life, which flows from the superabundance of contemplation, is also a special gift of God. We must be specially chosen for this life by God. The eighteenth Sermon on the Song of Songs is one of the most complete descriptions of the 'mixed' vocations according to St Bernard. Remember always that he is not speaking of the vocation of the 'mixed Orders', still less of the aptitudes that might be sufficient indication of a vocation to such an Order. He is speaking of the call to pass beyond contemplation to the care of souls. It is above all in the sphere of the monastic life that he considers this vocation. And he considers it insofar as it is an operation of the Holy Spirit.

Sermon 18 *In Cantica* begins with the declaration that the Holy Spirit works in the souls of monks in two different ways. In one way, he produces virtues within our souls, for our own salvation. In another he works through us for the salvation of others. It is the well-known scholastic distinction between *gratia gratum faciens* and *gratia gratis data*. Contemplation is of the first kind, the apostolate belongs to the second. Hence, from the very outset, St Bernard makes it quite clear that the 'mixed' life in its highest and strictest sense is a charismatic vocation. It bears fruit through the operation of special graces and gifts, in the spiritual order, given us not merely for ourselves but principally for their effect on others. St Bernard lists some of these. They are the charisms of St Paul and the early Church: 'Knowledge, the *word of wisdom,* the grace of healing, prophecy, etc.'.[129]

St Bernard then goes on to explain that it is the duty of the monk, if he has become aware of *both* these operations in himself, to take great care lest he give to others what is given him for himself, and even greater care lest he withhold from others what has been given him for their benefit. An example of the first error would be to pour out on others the fruits of an immature interior life that is not yet fully perfected, so that we lose the benefit of the grace that was given us for our own spiritual growth. The second error would be the 'false humility' which we have already seen St Bernard reprove in Canon Oger: the 'useless and damnable silence' in which we hold back the 'good word that could be of advantage to many'.[130]

This is immediately followed by the famous metaphor of the 'canals and reservoirs'. St Bernard seems to feel that the error of the prodigal 'canals' is more widespread than that of the avaricious 'reservoir'. And indeed who cannot see the facility with which human nature tends to presume without reason that it has arrived at the fulness of virtue and wisdom, and that the time has come to spread the good word and do good to many? This presumption is by no means charity. It does good neither to our neighbor nor to ourselves. The part of true charity is to wait until it has something to give, and then in abundance. *Benigna pruden-sque charitas affluere consuevit, non effluere.*[131]

The most important part of this sermon shows how the interior life gradually grows and builds itself up to the contemplation which most efficaciously produces a charity strong and pure enough to flow out and communicate itself to others without any but good results for our own souls. Let us quote the description of this infused love of God and of our neighbor, born of mystical contemplation.

> Such love burns with zeal; this is worthy of the friend of the Bridegroom; it is with such love as this that the faithful and prudent servant must be enkindled, when he is placed by the Lord over his household. This love fills, it grows warm and boils over, it is poured out without danger, overflowing and bursting its bounds and crying out 'Who is weak and I am not weak? Who is scandalized and I am not on fire?' Let this love preach and bear fruit, let it renew signs and change miracles: there is no place in it for vanity, for all is occupied by charity. For the fulness of the law and of the heart is charity, provided charity itself be full. *Plenitudo legis et cordis est caritas, si tamen plena.*[132]

St Bernard goes on to point out the great danger of promoting to the care of souls one who does not possess such charity as this. *Eam nondum adeptus periculossisime promovetur, quantislibet aliis videatur pollere virtutibus.*[133]

In order not to cause a universal wave of despair among Superiors and Novice Masters and Spiritual Directors, we may mention St Teresa's statement that even without the *prayer* of mystical union a soul can arrive, by the generous practice of virtues, at a degree of charity equal to that which is produced by union. This charity is, in effect, the same as mystical union, even though it may not taste the consolations of clearly recognizable mystical contemplation. 'The Lord asks only two things of us: love for his majesty and love for our neighbor. It is for these two virtues that we must strive, and if we attain them perfectly we are doing his will and so shall be united to him.'[134]

In comparing the purely contemplative life with the vocation to the care of souls, St Bernard tells us that the latter is more difficult, more dangerous, more meritorious, more necessary and more excellent. We have already seen some of the texts in which he makes these declarations. *Non est ejusdem facilitatis devote quiescere et fructuose operari; humiliter subesse et utiliter praeesse.*[135] Exposed to more numerous occasions of sin and imperfection, the Superior and guide of souls must be stronger than the monk called to the repose of Mary.[136] However, the very charity which impels the Superior to sacrifice the leisure and quiet of contemplation temporarily in order to help others to find Christ, will wipe out the stains of imperfection he has contracted in his apostolic labor. Charity covers up a multitude of sins.[137] Hence St Bernard concludes that the contemplative who, like Mary, enjoys purity of heart in a life of quiet and seclusion, indeed does well. But the one called by obedience or charity to the care of other souls has a vocation that is better and greater than that of Mary. 'Nam tu quidem in tui custodia vigilans, bene facis; sed qui juvat

multos *melius facit et virilius.*'[138] To be so carried out of
oneself by divine charity as no longer to live for oneself but
only for others is to possess the most precious ointment of
mercy and love by which to anoint not only the feet of Jesus
but his whole Mystical Body. This 'ointment' is more excellent by far, says St Bernard, than those other two which
symbolize the vocations to penance and to contemplation.

> O quaecumque es anima sic affecta, sic imbuta rore
> misericordiae, sic affluens pietatis visceribus, sic te
> omnibus omnia faciens, sic facta ipsa tibi tamquam vas
> perditum, ut caeteris praesto semper occurras atque suc-
> curres; *sic denique mortua tibi ut omnibus vives: tu plane
> tertium optimumque unguentum possides.*[139]

The call to Martha's life of self-sacrifice for souls in apostolic
labor is therefore superior to the penance of Lazarus and the
contemplation of Mary because it requires a superabundance of divine charity. This superabundance goes in a certain sense to the point of 'ecstasy' (*excessus*) carrying us completely out of ourselves. Hence St Bernard can declare that
the apostolic vocation is 'far superior to the two other'. *Am-
bobus longe antecellit.*[140] The most perfect souls in the
monastery are those who combine in themselves the abilities
of Mary, Lazarus, and Martha together. It is true, St Bernard admits, that the ordinary way to perfection lies along
one or another of these three roads. But nevertheless a
special sanctity is reserved for those who combine in
themselves the contemplation of Mary and the penance of
Lazarus with such copious fruits of charity that they are also
able to sacrifice themselves entirely for others in the
apostolic labors of Martha. *Habet haec simul quaecumque
perfecta est anima.*[141]

The charity of the 'mixed' life, nourished by a superabundant love of God found in contemplation, is something like
the intense charity of the martyr. Remember that St Bernard presupposes, all the time, that the apostle has an over-

whelming affective *preference for contemplation* and that
the call to aid souls, though appealing sweetly to his deep
fraternal love, usually means a costly sacrifice. Each time
the superior or director leaves the silence of contemplation
to attend to the needs of souls, he spiritually lays down his
life for his friends. And this is the mark of the highest
charity! *Quoties enim pro uno ex minimis ejus spiritale
studium intermittit, toties spiritualiter pro eo ponit animam
suam.*[142] To leave the embrace of the Word in order to bring
souls to him is to die at once for him and for them. This
charity unto death is the principal beauty of the Spouse. It is
this above all that makes her his 'love, his dove, his beautiful
one'.[143]

Clearly, if the charity of the apostle is superior to that of
the contemplative, there is only one reason: it is a *development* of contemplative charity, a *fruit* of contemplation. It
is one of the signs of a soul truly united to the Word in
mystical prayer, for it is an effect of mystical prayer. *Haec
siquidem vera et casta contemplatio habet, ut mentem
quam divino igne vehementer succenderit, tanto interdum
repleat zelo et desiderio acquirendi Deo qui eum similiter
diligant, ut otium contemplationis pro studio praedicationis
libentissime intermittat.*[144]

In the naive realism of his day, tempered none the less by
the euphemistic use of *osculum*, St Bernard says that the
proof that the soul has received the 'kiss' of the Spouse is that
she conceives and brings forth souls to his love. *Hinc te
scilicet noveris osculum accepisse, quod te concepisse
sentis.*[145] It is in this sense that St Bernard can say that the
work of preaching is better and more necessary than contemplation—*ubera quibus parvulos alis, quos et paris,
meliora, hoc est necessariora sunt vino contemplationis.*[146] It
is in this sense that, although he has strongly warned us that
we must always *prefer* and *choose* contemplation rather
than action, there nevertheless comes a time when we must

no longer cling too eagerly to the joys of contemplation, but renounce them for souls. *Noli nimis insistere osculis contemplationis, quia* meliora sunt ubera praedicationis.[146a]

There is another extremely important qualification of this doctrine. St Thomas, following St Augustine and using terms that St Bernard himself borrowed from the Bishop of Hippo,[147] shows that apostolic charity can never demand the complete *abandonment* of contemplation. How could it? If our charity for souls and our ability to help them depends entirely on our contemplative union with God, we must necessarily return to that union in order to recapture the ardor and strength which gradually grow cool as we spend ourselves in his service. Hence the apostolic vocation, as St Bernard and St Thomas conceive it, is not *substituted* for contemplation. It is *added* to contemplation, and becomes an integral part in the interior, contemplative life of the soul perfectly united to the Word.

And therefore, it is just as true to say that we must leave action for contemplation as to say that we must leave contemplation for action. Since the efficacy of our work for souls depends entirely on our union with God, we clearly have a twofold obligation: not only to work for others but to nourish our own souls in prayer and contemplation. Sanctity in the mixed life by no means consists merely in a generous sacrifice of our time and energy for other souls. It depends above all on the discretion which shows us the right balance between action and contemplation, in all the concrete situations and needs of our own lives. We must at all times respond to the inspirations of grace which do not always lead in the same direction. At one moment they call us forth from prayer to the help of souls, and at other moments they call us back again into the peace and silence of contemplation.

One of the most important and most characteristic features of St Bernard's teaching on action and contemplation is his insistence on the fact that Martha and Mary are not enemies but sisters. They live together in the same house. They love one another, help one another, complete one another. Neither one can do without the other. It is therefore folly to seek perfection by excluding one or the other either from our own souls or from our monasteries. *Quoniam sunt invicem contubernales hae duae, et cohabitant pariter; est quippe soror Mariae Martha.*[148]

We are by now convinced that contemplation helps action. The numerous texts we have so far quoted remove all doubt on this point. But are we equally convinced that action helps contemplation? Perhaps it may be a surprise to learn that even apostolic activity, with all its dangers, its difficulties and its distractions, supports and inspires the contemplative soul *even in his life of prayer and divine union.* We are perhaps too ready to oversimplify the relations between Martha and Mary and to declare that action is never anything more than a necessary evil. We assume that it always leads to distractions and faults. We feel that we must always lament the need which draws us from prayer to activity. Our only hope seems to be that the ill-effects of this sad necessity will be overlooked by Jesus, since we have incurred them under obedience, and out of love for souls beloved by him. But is this the true picture? No. Not according to St Bernard. For St Bernard did not think contemplative charity was only to be nourished by seeing no one, knowing no one, loving no one and remaining in a perpetual state of deep recollection. That is certainly not a practical formula for Cistercians, living the common life.

In the Fifty-seventh Sermon on the Canticle, we find St Bernard in one of his most characteristic moods, describing how the contemplative soul is one who is constantly on the alert for the 'visitations' of the divine Spouse. For, he says, if we are the sons of God we shall realize, through the action of the Holy Spirit, that we are also his heirs.[149]

What is our inheritance? God himself. To be sons and

heirs of God, co-heirs with Christ, means to receive the deep
interior assurance of the Divine Spirit that we are loved by
God. It means to be 'visited' in various ways by the divine
Spouse of our souls. It means to *know and recognize him* in
these visitations. *Visitabitur profecto frequenter, nec umquam
ignorabit tempus visitationis suae, quantumlibet is qui in
spiritu visitat clandestinus veniat et furtivus, utpote verecundus
amator.*[150] Furthermore it means to recognize him in *all* his
visitations, under all his disguises. Clearly, then, the truly contemplative soul who is also called to apostolic action will
recognize the coming of the divine Bridegroom not only in the
inspirations which call her to prayer, solitude and humility,
but in those which call her to the care of souls. Since it is he
who calls her, the soul most willingly sacrifices the repose of
prayer, in which she delights, in order to delight him by acting
as his instrument for the salvation of a soul dear to him. *Se-
quitur vox blande et leniter divinam insinuans voluntatem,
quae non est aliud quam ipse amor, qui otiosus esse non potest,
de his quae Dei sunt sollicitans et suadens. Denique audit sponsa ut surgat et properet, haud dubium quin ad animarum
lucra.*[151] After all, if her love for him is true, she will be
eager to see him loved by all other souls—*repleta zelo et
desiderio acquirendi Deo qui eum similiter diligant.*[152]

St Bernard then describes the fruitful alternation between
prayer and apostolic activity. The zeal for souls is a sign of
'true and chaste contemplation'. But at the same time, the
labor of preaching serves to make the fire of divine love burn
higher. It sharpens our taste for contemplation. It makes us
return to prayer with a greater hunger for God. And in our
prayer, the fire of love which hungers both for God and for
souls, rises to a consuming flame: *Et rursum potita votis, ali-
quantenus in hac parte tanto ardentius redeat in idipsum,
quanto se fructuosius interemisse meminerit; et item sumpto
contemplationis gustu, valentius ad conquirenda lucra solita
alacritate recurrat.*[153]

St Bernard does not deny that this *vicissitudo* — this alternation between prayer and action — cannot help but bring with it a certain anxiety. Desiring always to please her divine Lord, the soul realizes that her activity may be tainted with imperfection and false zeal. She remembers that it is dangerous for one to leave contemplation too soon. She is conscious of her weakness, her instability, her unworthiness. It is so easy to be deluded, to mistake the instigations of false zeal and presumption for the movements of divine grace. At the same time, her desire to remain in contemplative quiet may also be nothing more than a natural love of comfort and pleasure.

> Inter has vicissitudines plerumque mens fluctuat, metuens et vehementer exaestuans, ne forte alteri horum, dum suis affectionibus hinc inde distrahitur, plus justo inhaereat; et sic in utrolibet vel ad modicum a divina deviet voluntate.... Vides virum sanctum inter fructum operis et somnum contemplationis graviter aestuare: et in bonis licet semper versantem, semper tamen quasi de malis paenitentiam agere, et Dei cum gemitu momentis singulis inquirere voluntatem.[154]

What a beautiful text! It shows us the anxiety of a delicate love for God, a love that cleanses and purifies the heart, making it most pleasing to the divine Bridegroom. It drives us to him as our only refuge. It makes us men of constant and unwearied prayer, humble and poor of spirit, with our eyes fixed on him at every moment, in our action as well as in our contemplation. It establishes that perfect balance between effective and affective charity which is necessary for true sanctity.[155]

Filled with the discretion which can only be obtained by such love as this, the faithful Martha, who is also a Mary by virtue of her contemplation, is no longer one of those who are constantly moved by the impulsion of their own will. The secret of divine union is a pure and chaste love, a love that proceeds from God alone and terminates in him alone. Inspired and moved by this love, everything she does is pure and pleasing in his sight, whether it be action, penance or contemplation, prayer or preaching, labor or rest, superiorship or obscurity in the common life. Nothing inspired by self-love pleases him, not even the most brilliant of works, or apparently great gifts of interior prayer. The true contemplative will therefore be one who seeks something far better and greater than 'contemplation'. She seeks God, and him alone. She is the one who sings the *nuptiale carmen*. She is his 'love, his dove, his beautiful one'.[156] Curiously, in one of the many places where he quotes this text, St Bernard applies it to Martha rather than to Mary, in the third Assumption Sermon:

> An non amica est, quae Domini lucris intenta, fideliter ipsam quoque pro eo ponit animam suam? Quoties enim pro unus ex minimis ejus spiritale studium intermittit, toties pro eo ponit animam suam. An non formosa, quae revelata facie gloriam Domini speculando, in eamdem imaginem transformatur de claritate in claritatem, tamquam a Domini Spiritu? An non columba quae plangit et gemit in foraminibus petrae, in cavernis maceriae, tamquam sepulta sub lapide?[157]

But we notice that Martha, in this text, is the 'perfect' soul who combines in herself the qualities of Mary and Lazarus and adds to them a fruitful and apostolic zeal for souls.

This brings us to our conclusion, which has been evident for a long time. The vocation of Mary should be preferred to that of Martha, chosen rather than that of Martha. When Martha is only Martha, Mary has the best part. But when Martha is also a contemplative, then obviously she is better than Mary because she has Mary's best part along with something even better. Hence she has the *pars ipsa, quantum in nobis est, omnibus eligenda.*[157a] And she also possesses the *ubera praedicationis* which are better, more necessary and more fruitful than the wine of contemplation[158] not because they are opposed to it, but because they are nourished by it and are its perfection and its fruit.

She has the most difficult, the most perfect of all lives: but she has not chosen it for herself. It has been imposed upon her by her Lord and Spouse. It is in a certain sense a charismatic vocation to which not even St Bernard himself would dare to aspire, on the basis of a mere interior attraction.[159] The soul who is not called to the care of other souls must therefore not take that office upon herself. (He is speaking of those called to the monastic life and living in the monastery. His words in no way affect the vocation to life in teaching or preaching Orders which did not exist in his time.) On the other hand certain graces and lights are given us in prayer precisely in order that we may share them with others. We must know how to recognize such graces and to act upon them as the Lord wills.[160] We would certainly offend him if we kept for ourselves what was given us for others or, worse still, if we tried to appropriate his gifts for the satisfaction of human ambition, vainglory or pride.[161] *Rem profecto proximi retines tibi si verbi causa plenus virtutibus cum sis, forisque nihilominus donis scientiae et eloquentiae adornatus, metu forte aut segnitie, aut minus discreta humilitate verbum bonum, quod potest prodesse multis, inutili imo et damnabili ligas silentio; certe maledictus, quod frumenta abscondis in populis.*[162]

The generosity and self-sacrifice of the apostolic soul demands the greatest perfection because it is rooted and founded in a universal charity. St Bernard recognizes a perfect fulfilment of this ideal of charity in St Paul, a vessel of election, a vessel overflowing with sweet perfumes and spreading everywhere the good odor of Christ. The sweetness of his preaching sprang from his interior sacrifice — the characteristically apostolic sacrifice of his 'care for all the Churches': the sacrifice of his compassion for the weak.[163]

And in the eyes of St Bernard, the sacrifice of contemplation itself must enter into the compounding of this sweet ointment of mercy.[164]

But finally the secret of apostolic charity lies in the fact that it brings the soul closest to Jesus, and indeed it is the mark of the most intimate union and resemblance with him. In the final pages of the Sermons on the Canticle, St Bernard describes the soul united with the Word, penetrated within and without by the light of his Wisdom which shines forth in all her actions. In such a soul, there is no longer any contradiction between action and contemplation, for she is perfect in both. Perfect in both because she has risen above all things and possesses all in Christ. Jesus is her life, her career and her prayer. She has become so, not by her own efforts but by his gift of himself to her humility. And here is how St Bernard describes her perfection:

> Ergo quam videris animam relictis omnibus Verbo votis omnibus adhaerere, Verbo vivere, Verbo se regere, de Verbo concipere quod pariat Verbo, quae possit dicere Mihi vivere Christus est et mori lucrum: puta conjugem, Verboque maritatam. Confidit in ea cor viri sui, sciens fidelem, quae prae se omnia spreverit, omnia arbitretur ut stercora, ut sibi ipsum lucrifaciat.[165]

St Bernard has told us that the monk must not desire to preach. His office is to weep rather than to teach others. Yet there is no limit to our aspiration to love God, to renounce ourselves for him, to live by him and in him. If we give ourselves entirely to this 'one thing necessary', the speculative difference between action and contemplation will cease to seem important. If we give ourselves entirely to the love, the prayer, the humility which our vocation demands, we will be content to let Our Lord himself determine whether we are to lead active or contemplative lives within the monastic enclosure.

In principle, as St Bernard has told us all through the present study, it is the *contemplative life* which we have come to seek in the monastery. The monastery is for contemplatives. A certain amount of action is necessary to make the contemplative life easier and freer and more accessible. If there be an apostolate within the monastery, it must be a contemplative apostolate — it must form souls not to live lives of action but of humility and prayer. If Martha has the highest calling, it is only by reason of her contact with Mary and for the sake of Mary. St Bernard's teaching fully vindicates the primacy of contemplation.

5. Action and Contemplation in the
Blessed Virgin Mary

There is one exception to St Bernard's rule that every perfect soul combines in itself the vocations of Martha, Mary and Lazarus.[166] The highest perfection of all is that of the Virgin Mother of God, who had no reason for doing penance since she was free from all sin. St Bernard explains that the reason why the gospel of Martha and Mary was appropriately chosen for the Feast of the Assumption was because in the Virgin Mother of God the activity of Martha and the fruitful rest of Mary were united in their highest perfection.[167] At the same time, there was no mention of Lazarus in the gospel for the feast, because there was no place for penance in the house of the Virgin Mother. She had no need of Lazarus' broom where no sweeping was to be done.[168] Thus in the Virgin's bridal chamber only Mary and Martha were needed to receive the Word of God. As an example of Mary's active perfection, St Bernard refers in passing to the mystery of the Visitation. Her contemplation is hinted at in her silence, her keeping all the words of God in her heart.[169] Filled with grace by her divine son, Mary was the wisest of virgins, and the lamp of her sanctity by far outshines the holiness of all others, whether they be men or angels.[170]

The fifty-second Sermon *De diversis* sees the seven pillars of the house of wisdom as the fullness of Mary's virtues, and Mary herself is the 'house' built for himself by divine wisdom, that is to say by the Word of God. These virtues make Mary the model of the active life. St Bernard repeatedly calls her the 'mulier fortis' and applies to her the last chapter of the Book of Proverbs. And what greater 'work' was done by Mary than to crush the serpent's head and to destroy, by herself alone, all heresies. The last paragraph of this sermon suggests how the 'active' life of virtue prepared Mary to receive into her bosom the Word of God, that the very 'contemplation' of God himself might take flesh from her flesh. Her highest contemplative union with God was achieved in the Incarnation and was not lost thereafter. *Nam et ante mentem replevit [Verbum] quam ventrem; et cum processit ex utero, ab animo non recessit.*[171] Then the Incarnation itself is regarded by St Bernard as the fruit of Mary's contemplation and her communication to us of the fulness of her own interior life of union with God.[172] Therefore in the mystery of the Incarnation, Mary is the model of preachers and apostles, for he who preaches the Gospel to others brings forth Christ for those souls. *Qui aliis evangelizat, quasi Jesum in utero portat, ut eum aliis, vel potius alios ei pariat.*[173] This quotation is taken from a curious passage in which the Blessed Virgin Mary is compared to St Joseph and the old man Simeon in one of St Bernard's allegorical triads of the three lives. Joseph carries Jesus on his shoulder (going into Egypt), and is the symbol of the penitents. Simeon becomes the figure of the active life (*bonos operatores*) by holding Jesus in his arms. The Blessed Mother, carrying him in her womb, is the figure of preachers. One will ask where the contemplative life comes in these three: we seem to have nothing but works. Works of penance, corporal works of mercy (Simeon), and works of the apostolate (Mary). But the very nature of the symbol shows that in St Bernard's mind here, as everywhere else, the vocation to preach the Gospel implies the fulness of contemplation and the most intimate union with the Word. The preacher, with the Word in his bosom, is obviously a contemplative.

Needless to say, there is no lack of passages in St Bernard describing the perfect contemplation of Mary and her ineffable union with God. 'Rightly is Mary shown to us as

clothed with the sun, since beyond all belief she penetrated
into the deepest abyss of divine Wisdom: and thus she appeared to me immersed in inaccessible light as far as a
creature could be so, short of personal (hypostatic) union.'[174]

The divine fire which barely touched the lips of the
prophet in order to purge them and which enkindles the love
of the Seraphim not only touched Mary, says St Bernard,
but penetrated and enclosed her being from all sides so that
she was transformed in its flame. So perfect is her union with
the love of God that there is nothing found in her of
darkness, not the slightest shadow, not the faintest suspicion
that the flame of her own love could fall short of the most
burning ardor: *ut nihil in ea non dico tenebrosum sed ne
subobscurum saltem, vel minus lucidum, sed ne tepidum
quidem aliquid, aut non ferventissimum liceat suspicari.*[175]

Here again we see that Mary's contemplation leads up to
its perfect climax in Mary's union with the Word in his Incarnation. The 'Light' in whom she is clothed now clothes
himself in her, and we behold the mystery of a kind of cir-
cumincession in which Mary is in God and he in her. 'You
clothe the sun with a cloud, and are yourself clothed by the
sun with light.' *In te manet et tu in eo; et vestis eum, et
vestiris ab eo. Vestis eum substantia carnis, et vestit ille te
gloria suae majestatis. Vestis solem nube, et sole ipsa
vestiris.*[176]

Christian tradition has always seen a very close connection
between the contemplative life and the virginal consecration
to God. So too in Mary, and above all in Mary, do we see the
compenetration of these two mysteries. St Bernard
meditates on the fact that Mary knew, by some secret revelation, that virginity was pleasing to God, although con-
secrated virginity was unknown in Israel. *O Virgo prudens,
o virgo devota, quis te docuit Deo placere virginitatem?*[177]

And Bernard asks her where she had ever read that the
virgins would 'sing a new song, because they would follow
the Bridegroom wherever he went'? There was no precept
for this, no counsel, no example for her to follow. She was
taught by the grace of the Holy Spirit, who taught her all
things. The 'living and efficacious Word of God was thy
Master before he became thy Son, and instructed thy mind
before he assumed thy flesh'.[178]

Mary's virginity and her exalted contemplation are
therefore closely united in their common ordination to her
unique and supreme vocation to be the Mother of God. One of
the principal themes of the homilies on the *Missus Est*, which is
a kind of treatise on mariology and one of the first of its kind, is
to show how God prepared for himself, in Mary, a most perfect
mother for his divine Son, and then left the final decision, on
which the Incarnation was ultimately to depend, in her
hands. He made her capable of the most perfect act of love
for him, and then left the making of that act to her free will.
Mary's *fiat* which was her greatest work, and therefore the
culmination of all that we can call her 'active' life, is also the
crown of her contemplation. We shall see that it is, above
all, the very heart of her 'apostolate'. She is the Queen of
Apostles because without her there would have been no
Gospel, and no one to preach the Gospel.

But if the active preparation of virtue, which made Mary
perfect in the sight of God, led up to the Incarnation, and if
the 'apostolic' fruit of that mystery was the presence of the
Word in the world, and our redemption by his death on the
cross, it nevertheless remains true that the Incarnation itself
took place in the secrecy of Mary's contemplative solitude.
Truly, Our Lady of the Annunciation is Our Lady of
Solitude. St Bernard is convinced that the angel found her
'in the secrecy of her chamber, where having closed the door
she was praying to the Father in secret'.[179] He continued:
'The most prudent Virgin had enclosed herself in her room,

at that hour, shutting out men but not the angels.' And again: 'We cannot think that the angel found Mary's door open, for indeed her whole thought was to fly from the company of men and to avoid their conversation, lest the silence of her prayer should be disturbed, or her chastity be in danger.'[180]

For this reason, says St Bernard, the angel salutes her with the words 'Dominus tecum'. Truly, the Lord was already with her. She was indeed full of grace, for God was present in her and filled her immaculate and humble soul. For the perfume of her virtues and of her prayer, ascending like incense to the secret resting place of the Word in the bosom of the Father, roused him like a giant, ready to run his course, and coming forth from the height of heaven, he outstripped his own messenger and was himself present in the heart of the Virgin he had chosen before the angelic messenger could enter the silence of her room.[181]

In the sermon on the 'Aqueduct' St Bernard shows that it was precisely the spiritual desires and the prayer and the interior devotion of the Blessed Virgin that brought the Word into the world. So great was her thirst for grace that, although she was herself full of grace, she merited (in the broad sense) that the inexhaustible fulness of all grace should be poured out, through her, in Jesus Christ, upon the whole world.[182]

Once again St Bernard urges us to contemplate in Mary's contemplation, one of the great mysteries of Divine Providence. *Intuere, o homo, consilium Dei, agnosce consilium sapientiae, consilium pietatis. Coelesti rore aream rigaturus, totum vellus prius infundit: redempturus genus humanum, pretium universum contulit in Maria.*[183] What is most important of all is that we are nourished ourselves by the fruit of Mary's contemplation. Eve gave Adam to taste of the forbidden fruit, but we can say in all truth: 'The woman which thou gavest me has fed us with the fruit of blessedness.'[184]

The presence of God in the Blessed Virgin is something altogether unique in the history of mysticism. God is everywhere by his very nature. He is present in his rational creatures as an object of knowledge and in those who love him as the object of love. Indeed, such terms are too abstract and pale to convey the intimacy of the union of the soul with God, in Christ, by a charity which makes the two 'one spirit'. For the saints are so united to God that they will what he wills, and he wills what they will. More than a moral union, this identity of wills is a mystical embrace — *Parum dixi contractus, complexus est.*[185] But so perfect is the union of Mary with the Word 'that one Christ is made of her substance and his'.[186] Short of the hypostatic union itself, there has never been seen any union with God so close and so perfect as Mary's union with the Incarnate Word. For here we see the mystery of a human person who becomes 'one flesh' with God himself.

Through Mary's fulness of grace, and from her perfect union with God, we have all received the divine life. It is because of her union with him that we are able to be united to him and become 'one spirit' with the Word who was 'one flesh' with Mary.[187] When we talk of Mary's 'apostolate' we are using the term in a sense which exceeds its proper meaning. Mary was far more than an apostle, and in bringing God within our reach by her *fiat,* she is the Mediatrix of all grace. Her 'apostolic' work is not in the field of subjective redemption, like ours. With Jesus himself, and subordinated completely to him as his instrument, Mary has a part in the objective redemption of the whole human race. *Ipsa nempe Mediatrix nostra, ipsa est per quam suscepimus misericordiam tuam, Deus, ipsa est per quam et nos Dominum Jesu in domos nostras excipimus.*[188] *Omnibus misericordiae sinum aperit, ut de plenitudine ejus accipiant universi*[189] God's love for mankind is like an arrow which not only pierced the heart of Mary but passed straight through that heart, leaving no trace of herself in it, filling her with himself and reaching even to our own poor hearts. It is through her that Christ fills us with his love, and since we receive his grace only through her maternal heart, she is truly and in the strict sense the *mater caritatis* — the mother of that 'Charity' whose Father is God, and who is himself God.[190]

Speaking of Mary 'wounded with love' St Bernard touches upon a theme which will become very important in the writing of his followers — that of the mystical sufferings of the Mother of Sorrows.

The theme of the Mother of Sorrows is however less emphasized in St Bernard himself than the glory of Mary, the cause of our joy. Contemplating the glorious Assumption of the Mother of God and her reception into heaven where she is rightfully enthroned as the Queen of Angels, Bernard cannot help recalling that even on earth, when she was entirely unknown and hidden, Mary was able, by her salutation, to bring grace and joy to the soul of the unborn infant in the womb of her cousin Elizabeth. But, St Bernard asks, 'if the soul of an infant not yet born melted at the sound of Mary's voice, what think you was the exultation of the citizens of heaven when they merited to hear her voice and see her face and enjoy her blessed presence'?[191] Indeed, Mary not only has merited joy and salvation for men, but her presence adds something to the joy and the glory of the angels and saints in heaven. The brightness of heaven is intensified by the great light of her charity, and while she continues to pour out light and happiness upon the earth she especially increases the gratitude and consolation of those who have entered into their reward. *Mariae praesentia totus illustratur orbis: adeo ut et ipsa jam coelestis patria clarius rutilet virgineae lampadis irradiata fulgore... Maria tam copioso impetu laetificat hodie civitatem Dei ut sentiamus et ipsi stillicidia stillantia super terram.*[192]

Mary, therefore, becomes the center of all history because

she is the Mother of whom God descends from eternity into time in order to bring us from time into his eternity. Becoming incarnate in her blessed womb, God 'works out our salvation in the midst of the earth'. Bernard applies these words of the psalm to the Virgin Mother, and says that all generations and all ages, angels and men, saints and sinners, look to Mary as to the ark of God and the center of all things — *sicut ad arcam Dei, ad rerum causam, ad negotium saeculorum.*[193] 'All generations' cries St Bernard, 'shall call thee blessed for thou hast brought forth life and glory to all generations. In thee the angels find their joy, the just find grace, and sinners find pardon for ever.'[194]

Now if Mary enters into the midst of the greatest of God's works, and has an intimate part in it, St Bernard tells us that she does so by her faith more than by anything else. That is to say, in the terms of our present thesis, by her life of contemplation. This is clear from the second Christmas sermon of the Abbot of Clairvaux. Here he speaks of the union of the Word with the soul and the flesh of Christ in the Incarnation. In a characteristic allegory, Bernard compares these three to the three measures of flour in the parable, and Mary's faith becomes the leaven which is put in with them. Mary's womb is the oven in which is baked for us the bread of life, by the fire of the Holy Spirit. *Felix mulier quae in haec tria sata immisit fidei suae fermentum.*[195] and St Bernard adds at once: 'it is by faith that she conceived, by faith that she brought forth... blessed is she who has believed, for the things the Lord told her have been perfected in her.'[196]

If we understand this doctrine aright, it is clear that the most important factor in Mary's participation in the work of redemption is her contemplative union with God. But the separation of 'action' from 'contemplation' in Mary is, in fact, merely theoretical. So great was her perfection that there was, in fact, for her, no real separation. Her contemplation and her action were all one. They were perfectly united in the mystery of her divine motherhood, which so far transcends all other ways in which men have shared in Christ's work of redemption that there is but little profit in comparing with it. But insofar as the blessed Mother of God is the model of the active and contemplative and apostolic lives it is necessary for us to see how these lives exist in her. We have looked into that mystery. Now it remains for us to seek, by prayer and ardent desire, for a charity that will bring us to that spiritual maturity in Christ which will, to some extent, unite both action and contemplation in our own souls.

In the last sermons on the Canticle of Canticles, St Bernard, having himself achieved this great perfection, spoke of the 'victory of wisdom' which he experienced in the final unification of his own soul. Wisdom is the house which is built upon the foundation of active virtue.[197] It is the true maturity of the soul — *in sapientia postremo maturitas.*[198] The soul that has attained wisdom 'no longer finds anything in itself that makes it blush in the presence of truth, nothing that obliges it to turn away her face, as though confused and driven back by the light of God'.[199] But this interior radiance of the soul necessarily shines forth in its acts — *prodeat foris necesse est.* Above all, the soul that is thus united in all things to the Word is, in the truest possible sense, married to him, and the marriage is fruitful both in preaching and in contemplation at the same time: *cum sanctae matres aut praedicando animas, aut meditando intelligentias pariunt spirituales.*[200]

This, then is that supreme wisdom, that perfect maturity in Christ, in which contemplation does not rob a man of his senses and prevent him from carrying on an ordinary life, and in which action does not disturb the tranquillity of divine union, or produce any of that self-seeking that would make the soul avert its eyes from God even while it is serving him. The maturity of the perfect contemplative, who is always worthy to bring forth apostolic fruit for the Father, in the vine of Christ, is most like the blessed Mother of God. And it is due to Mary that such wisdom is possible in the world at all. Not only has she left us an example of such perfection, but her own perfection proved to exercise a causal action in restoring the defaced image of God, in man, to the divine likeness. It was by her wisdom, in union with the wisdom of the Father, the Son and the Holy Spirit, that malice has been overcome in the world, 'For see, once again wisdom has filled the heart and the body of a woman, in order that we, who were corrupted by a woman and made foolish should be restored and reformed in wisdom by a woman.'[201]

Notes

1. Jn 1:18.

2. Col 1:15-16.

3. Jn 3:35, 17:10.

4. Paschal Vigil, Blessing of the Paschal Candle: *Haec igitur nox est quae peccatorum tenebras columnae illuminatione purgavit* [This then is the night which has cleared away the darkness of sins by the light of the paschal candle].

5. Jn 16:28.

6. Jn 9:4.

7. Jn 4:34.

8. Jn 10:37-8.

9. Jn 14:10.

10. Jn 6:46.

11. Postcommunion, Mass for Corpus Christi: *Fac nos quaesumus, Domine, divinitatis tuae sempiterna fruitione repleri: quam pretiosi corporis et sanguinis tui temporalis perceptio praefigurat.* [We beseech you, O Lord, fill us with the eternal fullness of your divinity, which the receiving of your precious body and blood prefigures in time].

12. Jn 17:18.

13. Mt 28:19.

14. 1 Cor 3:3, Jm 3:14-18.

15. 1 Jn 4:12, 7.

16. Jn 14:15.

17. Jn 14:24.

18. Jn 14:23, 17.

19. Jn 14:20.

20. Eph 3:17-19.

21. Eph 3:9.

22. Eph 3:10.

23. 1 Cor 2:12, 10, 16.

24. 1 Cor 12:4-6, 14.

25. Ac 6:2-3.

26. Ac 6:8, 10.

27. 1 Cor 7:35.

28. Cassian, *Collatio* I.8; PL 49:492 [You see, therefore, that the Lord places the chief good in *theoria* alone, that is, in contemplation].

29. Ibid.; 490. [This therefore should be our chief endeavor, this the unswerving goal of our heart constantly to be sought: that our mind may cleave always to God and to godly things].

30. *Collatio* XIX.8; 1138: *Finis coenobitae est omnes suas mortificare et crucifigere voluntates, ac secundum Evangelicae perfectionis salutare mandatum nihil de crastino cogitare. Quam perfectionem prorsus a nemine nisi a cenobita impleri posse certissimum est.*

30b. [Conrad of Bavaria, a Guelf prince, entered the cistercian monastery of Morimond in 1123. Two years later, with the permission of the Pope and despite Bernard's best efforts to dissuade him, he went to Palestine to live as a hermit. Merton seems here to have been misled into accepting a long-standing but undocumented tradition that Bernard had approved of the venture. See 'Blessed Conrad the Hermit', *Cistercian Studies* 4 (1969) 159-62, by Conrad Greenia OCSO, who holds that 'it is now morally certain that St Bernard never granted any such permission'.]

31. SC 8.2; PL 183:811.

32. Ibid: *Patris Filiique imperturbalis pax, gluten firmum, individuus amor, indivisibilis unitas* [the imperturbable peace of the Father and the Son, their fast bond, their fast bond, their undivided love, their indivisible unity].

33. SC 8.5, 9; PL 183:812B and 814B.

34. SC 5.6; 813.

35. SC 5.7; 813: *Osculum plane dilectionis et pacis; sed dilectio illa supereminet omni scientiae; et pax illa omnem sensum exsuperat.*[It is clearly a kiss of love and peace, but a love which goes beyond all knowledge, and a peace which surpasses all our senses].

36. SC 7.2; PL 183: 807: [a soul athirst for God].

37. Cuthbert Butler, *Western Mysticism,* 2nd edition (London, 1951) 191.

38. *Summa Theologiae* II IIae. Q.188, a.6.

39. SC 9; PL 183:818. [The breasts with which you feed your children are preferable to, that is, more necessary than, the wine of contemplation.... Do not insist too much on the kiss of contemplation, for the breasts of preaching are better].

40. J.M. Déchanet OSB writing in the *Dictionnaire de Spiritualité* ('Contemplation au XIIᵉ siècle, Vol.2², col. 1958), interprets St Bernard's doctrine in this sense. He says: *S'il faut marquer entre eux (prière, action, contemplation) une hiérarchie, témoigner quelque préférence, on se gardera d'exalter la contemplation aux dépens de sa compagne: Rachel est plus belle mais Lia est plus féconde; c'est chose excellente de demande pour nous-mêmes la joie du coeur et l'enivrante possession divine, c'est chose plus excellente encore de travailler à l'édification des autres; ce que le Seigneur nous donne, quand il nous confie le ministère de la parole, vaut mieux que ce baiser de la contemplation que nous lui demandons.* [If we mark out a hierarchy between them (prayer, action, con-

templation), show some preference, we must beware of exalting contemplation at the expense of its partner: Rachel is more beautiful but
Leah is more fecund. It is a wonderful thing to ask for ourselves our
hearts' delight and the intoxicating divine possession; it is another, more
wonderful thing to work for the edification of others. What the Lord gave
us when he entrusted us with the ministry of the Word is better than the
kiss of contemplation which we entreat him for.]

41. SC 40.3; PL 183:989. Cf. St Thomas, *Summa Theol.* II IIae, Q. 182,
a. 2.

42. *Sermo III de assumptione;* PL 183: 422: *Mariae Martham aemulari
prorsus indignum, prorsus illicitum est. Absit, absit ut qui Deo vacat ad
tumltuosam aspiret fratrum officialium vitam* [For Mary to envy Martha
is utterly unworthy and unauthorized. Heaven forbid that anyone who
rests in God should hanker after the tumultuous life of looking out for the
brethren]. Cf. Div 9.4-5; PL 183:566.

43. *Contra Faustum,* c. 53; PL 42:434.

44. Div 9.4-5; PL 183:566. Asspt 3; 183:422-3.

45. SC 22.9; PL 183:882: *Nec currimus aequaliter omnes in odore omnium unguentorum: sed vides* alios vehementius studiis flagrare sapientiae, *alios* magis ad poenitentiam *spe indulgentiae animari, alios amplius*
ad virtutum exercitium *vitae et conversationis ejus (sc. Christi) provocari
exemplo, alios* ad pietatem *passionis memoria plus accendi.* [We do not
all run equally in the fragrance of all the ointments, but you see that *some
burn to study wisdom,* others are motivated *more to penance* by the hope
of pardon, still others are summoned *to practise virtues* by the example of
his (Christ's) life and behavior. Others are more enflamed *to fervor* by the
memory of the Passion.]

46. See, for instance, *Epistola* 48; PL 182: 154-7.

47. Div 9.3, 4, 5; PL 183: 566-7.

48. Asspt 3.4; PL 183:423: *Consideremus, fratres, quemadmodum in hac
domo nostra tria haec distribuerit ordinatio charitatis, Marthae ad-
ministrationem, Mariae contemplationem, Lazari poenitentiam... ut alii
vacent sanctae contemplationi, alii dedili sint fraternae administrationi,
alii in amaritudine animae suae recogitent annos suos tamquam vulnerati
dormientes in sepulchris. Sic plane, sic opus est ut Maria pie et sublimiter
sentiat de Deo suo, Martha benigne et misericorditer de proximo, Lazarus
misere et humiliter de seipso.* Here, too, St Bernard alludes to Noah,
Daniel and Job. Cf. Ezech 14:14-16. [Let us take thought, brothers, how
this threefold ordering of love is arranged in this house of ours: the administration of Martha, the contemplation of Mary, the penitence of
Lazarus... so that some may rest in holy contemplation, some may devote
themselves to brotherly administration, some may reflect upon their passing years in bitterness of soul, as if they were sleeping wounded in their
graves. It is plain in this that it is necessary for Mary to be sensitive lovingly and loftily of God, Martha kindly and mercifully of her neighbor,
Lazarus wretchedly and numbly of himself].

49. Ibid. [The ordering of charity apportions these three].

50. Speaking on Sg 2:1—*Ergo sum flos campi* [I am the flower of the

field]—St Bernard says that Jesus, the flower blooming in the 'open field' is the king of martyrs who died in the arena for his love. The vocation to be a *flos campi* is the vocation to martyrdom at least in the broad sense of a life of suffering. The *flos horti* [garden flower] is the virgin, growing in a garden enclosed. Then there is the *flos thalami* [the flower in a room] which might, at first sight, suggest the contemplative life. but the interpretation of this symbol goes back to Sermon 16 on the Canticle *(lectulus noster floridus)* where St Bernard says that the flowers scattered over the couch of the bride are her virtues and good works.

51. See Sermons 10-13 on the Canticle and also Sermon 90 *De diversis*.

52. SC 18.4; PL 183:861: *Disce et tu nonnisi de pleno effundere, nec Deo largior esse velis.... Implere prius et sic curato effundere. Benigna prudensque charitas affluere consuevit, non effluere.* [May you also learn to spill over only from fulness and not want to be more generous than God.... Be filled first and then spill over under supervision. Kind and prudent love usually floods, it does not run over.]

53. *Collectanea O.C.R.*, January 1953.

54. Div 9.4; PL 183:566. [They tend to the same end, although not by the same route]. He adds: *Est psalterium jucundum cum cithara, nec minus jucundus est sonus citharae quam psalterii, licet haec ab inferioribus reddat sonum, illud a superioribus.* [The psaltery should be enjoyed with the lute, nor is the sound of the lute less enjoyable than that of the psaltery, although it produces its sound from the bottom and the other does it from the top].

55. St Augustine, *Contra Faustum*, 22.52; PL 42:432 ff. St Thomas, II IIae, Q. 182, a. 4.

56. Div 9.4; PL 183:566. [The humble behavior of Martha is no less meritorious with God].

57. Ibid. [But if such a thing is enjoined, it shall be borne patiently]. Compare the same terms in St Augustine, *Contra Faustum*, 22.54: *Duae sunt uxores Jacob.... Una amatur et altera toleratur.* [Jacob had two wives.... One was loved and the other put up with].

58. Asspt 3.4; PL 183:423. [But for those of you on whom this duty (of administration) is not incumbent, one of these two is necessary: either not to be disturbed at all but to delight in the Lord, or—if you cannot yet do that—to be greatly disturbed not against but... for yourself].

59. Div 9; PL 183:566. [What pertains to us must surely be chosen].

60. SC 7.3; PL 183:807: *Amat profecto caste quae ipsum quem amat quaerit; non aliud quidquam ipsius.* [One loves chastely when one seeks him whom he loves, not something of his].

61. SC 40.3; PL 183:983. [But to give your attention to something other than God, even for God's sake, means to embark on Martha's busy-ness rather than on Mary's restfulness. I do not say that someone like this is deformed, but he has not attained to perfect beauty, for (the soul like this) worries and frets about many things and is bound to be stained to some extent with the grime of worldly affairs].

62. Ibid. [Chaste intention and the examination of a good conscience

before God quickly and easily cleans this grime *at the hour of a holy falling asleep*.] The *sancta dormitio* is not, of course, the kind of thing that takes place in the dormitory. It is a traditional cliché for contemplative prayer. St Bernard is not here referring to an evening examination of conscience.

63. SC 46; PL 183:104. [It is better to rest and be with Christ, yet necessary to go out and work at saving souls].

64. Csi I.7.8; PL 182:736: *Nunc autem quoniam dies mali sunt sufficit interim admonitum esse non totum te nec semper dare actioni; sed considerationi aliquid tui et cordis et temporis sequestrare.* [But since these are now evil days, it is enough to have warned you not to give yourself completely or continually to activity, but to set aside something of yourself—your heart and your time—to consideration.]

65. Ibid. [Yet if we were permitted to do what we ought, we would always, everywhere and utterly prefer that which is of value in every way and cherish it alone, or at least above everything else. And this is piety, as irrefutable logic shows. What is piety, you ask. To take leisure time for consideration]. The nature and practical character of *consideratio* is shown by the detailed description which follows, col. 737. *Et primum quidem ipsum fontem suum, id est mentem de qua oritur, purificat consideratio. Deinde regit affectus, dirigit actus, corrigit excessus, componit mores, vitam honestat et ordinat, postremo divinarum pariter et humanarum rerum scientiam confert. Haec est quae confusa disterminat, hiantia cogit, sparsa colligit, secreta rimatur, vera vestigat, verisimilia examinat, ficta et fucata explorat. Haec est quae agenda praeordinat, acta recogitet, ut nihil in mente resideat aut incorrectum, aut correctione agens. Haec est quae in prosperis adversa praesentit, in adversis quasi non sentit: quorum alterum fortitudinis, alterum prudentiae est.* [Now consideration purifies first of all its own source, that is, the mind from which it arises. Then it rules the affections, directs actions, corrects excesses, improves behavior, confers order and integrity on life, and even confers knowledge of divine and human realities. It puts an end to what is confusing, it closes gaps, gathers up what is scattered, roots out secrets, investigates truth, weighs out what appears to be true, and explores what is false and deceitful. It decides what is to be done and reviews what has been done in order to eliminate from the mind anything deficient or in need of correction. It anticipates adversities in time of prosperity and in adversity is, as it were, unaware of it; showing both prudence and fortitude].

66. For the difference between *consideratio* and *contemplatio* see *De consideratione* II, 2, 5; 745.

67. See SC 9, esp. 9.9.

68. SC 12.9; PL 183:832.

69. *Spiritual Canticle*, b, Stanza XXIX, annotation; Peers edition 2:346.

70. SC 12.8; PL 183:832 [Why are you trying to impose on her (the Bride) a yoke which I consider her incapable of bearing? ...Let her stay in a good (work) as long as she is incapable of a better].

71. Cassian, *Collatio*, 19; PL 49:1132. *Melius enim est devotum in minoribus quam indevotum in majoribus professionibus inveniri.* [It is

better to be faithful in little undertakings than unfaithful in great ones].
These are the words of Abbot John, the hermit who returned to the
cenobium after many years in the desert. Here, curiously enough, the
contrast is between the 'active' life of the cenobite and the 'contemplative'
life of the hermit. The 'active' life in this particular case is safer, less exalted, more obscure. Naturally there is no question of apostolate.

72. SC 12.8-9; PL 183:832. [It is not, as you think, a man who can handle
great enterprises, but a woman.... Let us admit that our powers are un-
equal to the task, that our delicate feminine shoulders cannot delight in
supporting men's burdens].

73. SC 12.9; PL 183:832. [A woman at home spinning rashly reprimands
her husband returning from battle. And I tell you: if someone in the
cloister happens to notice that a prelate working among the people
handles himself with less constraint that he himself does, and with less cir-
cumspection—for example, in speaking, eating, sleeping, laughing, getting angry, passing judgement—let him not leap to pass judgement
precipitately but remember scripture: better the wickedness of a man
than a woman doing good].

74. Si 42:14.

75. Div 90.3; PL 183:709. [It is not within one person's capability to be
quiet faithfully and to work faithfully, to submit humbly and to rule effectively, to be governed without complaint and to govern without fault,
to obey freely and to command discreetly, finally to be good among the
good and good among the wicked—even less to be peaceable among the
sons of peace and to show himself a peacemaker to those who hate peace].

76. Asspt 3.3; PL 183:423. [A person is carnal and does not in the
slightest perceive the things of the Spirit of God if he has somehow refused
his leisured soul its leisure].

77. Div 90.3; PL 708D. *Nec reputo perditionem unguenti hujus effu-*
sionem. [Nor do I think the pouring out of this ointment a waste]. SC 85.8;
PL 1191: *Ergo sapientiae otia negotia sunt, et quo otiosior sapientia eo exer-*
citatior in genere suo. [Therefore the idlenesses of wisdom are business, and
wisdom is idler when she is busier in her own kind of activity].

78. Div 9; PL 183:566. [Whatever pertains to us must surely be chosen].

79. SC 74.3; PL 1140. [To whom contempt of all things has given leisure].

80. Dil 28; PL 182:991: *Delectabit sane non tam nostra vel sopita*
necessitas, vel sortita felicitas, quam quod ejus in nobis et de nobis volun-
tas adimpleta videbitur. [Having our needs lulled to sleep or our happiness obtained will delight us less than seeing his will fulfilled in us and
for us]. A well-ordered self-love begins the laborious ascent to union with
God by begging him to provide for the ordinary needs of our material and
spiritual lives. This preoccupation governs the prayer of those in the first
and second degrees of love, and is called *necessitas.* It turns to *suavitas*
when we begin to love God, the bounteous Giver of all gifts, more than the
gifts themselves. See Dil 23-6; PL 987 f.

81. Dil 28; 991: *O amor sanctus et castus! O dulcis et suavis affectio! O*
pura et defaecata intention voluntatis! Eo certe defaecatior et purior, quo

in ea de proprio nihil jam admistum jam relinquitur: eo suavior et dulcior quo totum divinum est quod sentitur. Sic affici deificari est. [O holy and chaste love. O sweet and gentle affection. O pure and undefiled intention of the will! The more undefiled and purer in that nothing of its own remains still unalloyed; sweeter and gentler in that what is sensed in it is all divine. To be touched like this is to be deified].

82. Dil 29; PL 992.

83. Hum 21; PL 182:953. [so that the reason stops thinking about itself and the will about others].

84. Ibid. [Cushioned by flowers, surrounded by apples—that is, by good habits and holy virtues—she is led at last into the chamber of the King for whose love she languishes. There for a short time, perhaps half an hour, while there is silence in heaven, she rests gently in that desired embrace, she sleeps but her heart keeps watch. In that (experience) she is fed with the secrets of truth on which, recalled to memory later, when she comes to herself, she can graze].

85. SC 85.8; PL 1191. [Wisdom's leisures are business].

86. Cf. SC 41.5-6; PL 986-7.

87. Asspt 3.4; PL 183:423.

88. Ibid. 1.422: *Marthae corporis utitur instrumento, cum Mariae sit potius impedimento.* [Martha's body was an instrument; Mary's was more an impediment].

89. SC 83.3; PL 1182: *Quae amat, amat et aliud novit nihil....* [What she loves, she loves, and knows nothing else...].

90. Ibid. 3-6; 1182-4: *Amor... caeteros in se omnes traducit et captival affectus.... Amor praeter se non requirit causam, non fructum. Fructus ejus, usus ejus. Amo quia amo, amo ut amem.... Sponsae res et spes unus est amor.... Merito cunctis renuntians affectionibus aliis soli et tota incumbit amori....* [Love... absorbs into itself and conquers all other affections.... Love asks for no reason beyond itself, no fruit. It is its own fruit, its own purpose. I love because I love. I love that I may love.... The bride's being and her one hope is love Rightly renouncing all other affections, she lies down to be loved completely...].

91. SC 85.8; PL 1191. [Where there is love, there is no effort but there is savor].

92. This passage in St Bernard, SC 85.8-12, should be seen against the background of St Benedict's Rule, the end of chapter seven, where we are reminded that perfect love casts out fear. Cf. Etienne Gilson, *The Mystical Theology of St Bernard*, p 24.

93. SC 85.8; PL 1192. [Now wisdom continually vanquishes malice in the minds into which it has entered and drives out by a taste for better things the taste for evil which (malice) has instilled. Wisdom, when it enters, makes the fleshly sense taste flat, cleanses the understanding, heals and restores the palate of the heart. Once the palate is cleansed, it tastes what is good, it tastes wisdom, than which there is nothing better].

94. SC 52.3-4; PL 1031: *Istiusmodi vitalis vigilque sopor sensum in-*

*teriorem illuminat et morte propulsata vitam tribuit sempiternam.
Revere enim dormitio est quae tamen sensum non sopiat, sed abducat....
Et ego non absurde Sponsae extasim vocaverim mortem, quae tamen non
vita sed vitae eripiat laqueis.... Quid enim formidetur luxuria, ubi nec
vita sentiatur? Excedente anima etsi non vita, verte vitae sensu, necesse est
etiam ut nec vitae tentatio sentiatur.* [It is a slumber which is vital and
vigilant, which enlightens the heart, drives away death, and communicates eternal life. For it is a genuine sleep that still does not
stupify the mind but transports it.... And I do not foolishly call the
Bride's ecstasy death, which does not snatch her from life but from
life's snares.... Why dread wantonness where there is no sense of life?
Since the ecstatic soul is cut off from awareness of life, even if not
from life, it must certainly be insensitive to life's temptations].

95. SC 52.5; PL 1031: *Sed moriatur anima mea morte etiam, si dici
potest, angelorum, ut praesentium memoria excedens, rerum se in-
feriorum corporearumque non modo cupiditatibus, sed et similitudinibus
exuat, sitque ei pura cum illis conversatio cum quibus est puritatis
similitudo.* [But let my soul die the death even of angels, if one can say
such a thing, so that, transcending the memory of things present, it may
strip off not only the desire for things physical and inferior, but even their
likeness, and may have with those with whom it shares the likeness of purity, pure conversation]. Cf. SC 31.6; 945.

96. SC 23.3; 885. [Knowing without doubt that there she will find him for
whom she thirsts].

97. SC 74.2; 1139: *(Scriptura) nostris verbis sapientiam in mysterio
absconditam loquitur; nostris affectibus Deum, dum figurat, insinuat;
notis rerum sensibilius similitudinibus, tamquam quibusdam vili oris
materiae poculis, ea quae pretiosa sunt, ignota et invisibilia Dei mentibus
propinat humanis.* [(Scripture) tells in our words the wisdom hidden in
mystery. It insinuates God into our affections while it is uttering him, by the
written likenesses of sensible things, like precious draughts in cheap vessels,
it lets human minds drink the unknowable and invisible things of God].

98. Ep 106.1-2; PL 182:241-2: *Quid quaeris verbum in Verbo, quod jam
carnem factum praesto est oculis? ...Experto crede, aliquid amplius in-
venies in silvis quam in libris. Ligna et lapides docebunt te quod a
magistris audire non possis.* [Why seek the word in the Word, when he is
now before your very eyes made flesh? ...Believe someone experienced: this
is something you will discover better in the woods than in books. Branches
and boulders will teach you what you cannot hear from a professor].

99. SC 23.16; PL 893. [The tranquil God brings tranquillity on all things,
and to behold him quiet is to be quietened].

100. SC 23.13-14; PL 891-2: *Terribilis est locus iste, et totius expers
quietis.... Est tamen Dei locus et iste, plane non aliud quam domus Dei et
porta coeli.... Nec te moveat quod initium sapientiae huic demum loco
dederim... hic Sapientiam suscipimus... hic afficimur. Instructio doctos
reddit, affectio sapientes... tunc primum Deus animae sapit, cum eam af-
ficit ad timendum....* [That place is terrifying and utterly devoid of
repose.... But it too is God's place, plainly none other than the house of

God and the gate of heaven.... Nor should it disturb you that I have placed the beginning of wisdom precisely in this place... here we listen to wisdom... here we are attracted (by it). Instruction makes us learned, affection makes us wise.... God first savors the soul then, when he so affects it that it fears him].

101. SC 23.11; PL 890: *Est locus iste altus et secretus, sed minime quietus... contemplantem qui eo loco usque pervenerit, quiescere non permittit; sed mirabiliter, quamvis delectabiliter, rimantem et admirantem fatigat, redditque inquietum....* [This is a lofty and secret place, but not in the least a quiet one... the contemplative who penetrates even that far is not allowed to rest, but, miraculously, yet wonderfully, (God) exhausts the person who investigates and struggles to acquire; he renders him unquiet...].

102. SC 85.13; PL 1194. [In this last kind, (the soul) leaves and is even separated from its physical senses, so that (the soul) who is aware of the Word is unaware of herself. This happens when the mind, seduced by the unutterable sweetness of the Word, withdraws somehow from herself, or rather, she is snatched away and escapes from herself so that she may enjoy the Word. The mind made fruitful in the Word is affected one way; the one enjoying the Word in another. In the one the needs of a neighbor cause anxiety. Here the sweetness of the Word draws her on. A mother is happy with her offspring, but she is happier in the embrace of her Spouse.... To save many is a good thing, but to step out of oneself and to be with the Word is so much happier].

103. SC 52.2; PL 1030. [zealously concerned for the quiet of his beloved, eager to hold her in his arms as she sleeps lest perhaps she be disturbed in her utterly sweet rest by some annoyance or disquiet].

104. SC 9.7; PL 818. [You will know you have received this kiss if you are aware that you have conceived].

105. SC 23.2; 884. [I seem to have been led in alone, but it does not profit me alone. Every preferment of mine is also yours].

106. De Guibert, *Documenta Christianae perfectionis studium spectantia*, n. 185: *Activa vita usque ad tempus Joachim fructuosa fuit, sed modo non est fructuosa; contemplativa vero ab ipso Joachim fructificare coepit, et amodo in perfectis successoribus suis perfectius manebit. Et per hoc datur intelligi quod ordo clericorum, ad quos pertinet activa vita, amodo non fructificabit in aedificatione et conservatione Ecclesiae nec omnino in regimine, sed ordo monachorum amodo in his fructificabit.* [The active life was fruitful until the time of Joachim, but it is no longer fruitful. Instead the contemplative (life) began to become fruitful from that same Joachim, and from henceforth it will remain more perfect in his perfect followers. And by this one is given to understand that the order of priests, to whom the active life belongs, henceforth will not be fruitful in building up and maintaining the Church, not even in governance, but the order of monks will henceforth be fruitful in these things].

107. *Collectanea O.C.R.*, January-April, 1953.

108. Asspt 3.4; PL 183:423B: *Sed consideremus, fratres, quemadmodum in hac domo nostra tria haec distribuerit ordinatio caritatis, Marthae ad--ministrationem, Mariae contemplationem, Lazari paenitentiam. Habet*

haec simul quaecumque perfecta est anima. [But let us consider, brothers, how this triple ordering of love shall have organized in our house the administration of Martha, Mary's contemplation, Lazarus's penitence. Any soul having these at one and the same time is perfect].

109. Eph 4:13.

110. Eph 4:15.

111. 1 Cor 12:29.

112. 1 Cor 12:31.

113. See, for instance, *The Way of Perfection*, c.1; E. Allison Peers, *The Collected Words of St Teresa*, 2:3.

114. Mt 17:20. The change of tempo taken by Catholic life in the chaotic period following World War II should not lead us to forget or despise two classic expositions of this doctrine: *La vie contemplative et son rôle apostolique* by a Carthusian, and *The Soul of the Apostolate* by Dom Jean-Baptiste Chautard OCSO.

115. SC 9.8; PL 818C.

116. SC 41.6; PL 987B. [No one must live for himself but for all].

117. SC 64.3; PL 1085A: *Scimus monachi officium esse non docere sed lugere.* [We know that a monk's business is not to teach but to weep. A medieval commonplace, taken from St Jerome, *Contra Vigilianum* 15; PL 23:367A — ed.] This temptation is one of the 'little foxes' which destroy the 'vines' that are just beginning to flower in the contemplative soul. Cf. Ep. 89.2; PL 182:221A: *Docere itaque nec indocto est in promptu, nec monacho in ausu, nec poenitenti in affectu.* [An unlearned man is not competent to teach, a monk does not dare do so, and a penitent does not have the heart for it].

118. SC 18.3-4; PL 860-1.

119. SC 49.6; PL 1019B: *Utinam et in me Dominus Jesus ordinet et tantillum charitatis quod dedit; ut sic mihi curae sint universa quae sunt ipsius, ut tamen quod mei potissimum propositi seu officii esse constiterit, ante omnia curem: sed sane ita id prius, ut tamen ad multa, quae mihi specialiter non attinent, afficiar amplius.... Si vero me et ad id amplius, quod specialius incumbit, sollicitum; et nihilominus ad illud, quod majus est, magis affectum exhibeam: utrobique invenior charitatis ordinem assecutus.* [Would that the Lord Jesus would set in order in me the tiny bit of love he has given me, so that as I take care of everything that is his, I may above all care for what he has assigned as my special duty or responsibility; but that I may first be drawn more to the many things which do not particularly concern me.... Now if I should prove more solicitous for that which is especially incumbent and yet am more drawn by affection to what is greater, on both counts I am found to follow the order of love].

120. SC 50.2, 5; PL 1021-23: *Est charitas in actu, est et in affectu... illa mandatur ad meritum, ista in praemium datur.... Actualis (charitas) inferiora praefert, affectualis superiora.... Quoties pie ceditur negotiorum tumultibus pia quies?... Ordo praeposterus, sed necessitas non habet legem.* [There is love in action, and love as well in affection.... The first is commanded by merit, the second given in reward.... Active (love) prefers

lowly things, affective higher things.... How often does devout repose give way to the devout uproar of business?... A preposterous order, but necessity knows no law].

121. Ep 87.3, 5; PL 182:213, 214: *Congratulor quidem tibi, quod sis exoneratus: sed vereor ne Deus a te, quantum in te est, exhonoratus sit; cujus procul dubio ordinationi resistis, dum promotus ab illo tu te dejicis.... Nihil hoc quoque superbius. Dei quippe consilio tuum praetulisti, magis eligens tibi quiescere quam ejus operi deservire, ad quod te ipse assumpserat.* [I congratulate you that you have unburdened yourself, but I am afraid that you may have dishonored God, in so far as you can. You have doubtless resisted his ordering of things when you cast yourself down after being promoted by him.... There is nothing haughtier than this, for you have preferred your own counsel to God's, choosing to be at rest for your own sake rather than to do his work, to which he had taken you up].

122. See, for instance, *Collatio* 18; PL 49:1105.

123. *De perfectione vitae spiritualis,* c. 23: *Intendere saluti proximorum cum aliquo detrimento contemplationis propter amorem Dei et Proximi, ad majorem perfectionem caritatis videtur pertinere quam si aliquis in tantum dulcedini contemplationis inhaeret quod nullo modo eam deserere vellet etiam propter salutem aliorum.... Quae tamen perfectio caritatis in plerique proximorum utilitate vacantibus non invenitur, quos magis contemplativae vitae taedium ad exteriora deducit.* [For the love of God and neighbor to strive for the salvation of one's neighbors, with some detriment to contemplation, seems to belong to greater perfection of love than if someone were to cling to the sweetness of contemplation in such a way as to be quite unwilling to give it up even for another's salvation. This perfection of love in neighborly usefulness is not found in many at rest, whom boredom with the contemplative life leads into external works].

124. SC 9.7; PL 183:818C.

125. SC 18.3; PL 860B.

126. SC 18.4; 861B: *Disce et tu nonnisi de pleno effundere, nec Deo largior esse velis.* [Learn to overflow only from fulness. Don't try to be more generous than God].

127. SC 18.3; 860C: *Caritas non quaerit sua sunt...* plane quia non desunt. *Quisnam quaerat quod habet?* [Love does not seek its own... obviously, because it does not lack. Who in the world seeks for what he has?]

128. Div 87.2-3; PL 183:704.

129. SC 18.1; PL 183:859C.

130. SC 18.2; PL 860A: *Rem profecto proximi retines tibi si, verbi gratia, plenus virtutibus cum sis, forisque nihilominus donis scientiae et eloquentiae adornatus, metu forte aut segnitie, aut minus discreta humilitate, verbum bonum, quod posset prodesse multis, inutili immo et damnabili ligas silentio; certa maledictus quod frumenta abscondis in populis. Rursum quod tuum est spargis et perdis, si priusquam infunderis tu totus, semiplenus festines effundere, contra legem arans in primogenito bovis et ovis primogenitum tondens.* [Actually, you are keeping what belongs to your neighbor if, for example, you are filled with virtues and adorned as

well with the outward gifts of knowledge and eloquence, yet through fear perhaps, or laziness, or a false humility you muffle in useless and even damnable silence the good word that could be of advantage to many—cursed among the people indeed, because you hide the grain. On the other hand, you squander and lose what is yours if, before you are completely filled, you—half-full—hurry to spill out, ploughing contrary to the law with the firstborn ox and shearing the firstborn sheep]. Cf. Dt 15:19, Pr 11:26.

131. SC 18.4; PL 861C. [Generous and prudent charity spills over; it does not seep out].

132. SC 18.6; 862C.

133. SC 18.6; 862D. [Someone not yet attained to this (love) is advanced at the greatest risk, no matter how strong he may be in other virtues].

134. *Interior Castle*, V, 3 (Peers 2:261). The context explains that this union of wills is practically equivalent to mystical union.

135. Div 90.3; PL 183:709. [It does not take the same facility dutifully to be quiet and fruitfully to toil, humbly to be under, and usefully to be in, authority].

136. SC 12.8-9 (PL 832), Div 90.3-5 (709), SC 46.3 (1004).

137. SC 12.9; 832. Cf. I Pt 4:8.

138. SC 12.9. [Now in watching out for yourself, you do well, but anyone who helps many *does something better and manlier*]. Note the allusion to 1 Cor 7:38.

139. SC 12.1; PL 828. [O you who are a soul thus affected, thus imbued with the dew of mercy, thus abounding in the bowels of devotion, thus making yourself all things to all men, thus having made yourself like a lost vessel, so that you may always be present and helpful to all, *thus dead to yourself, you live to others; clearly you have the third, and best, ointment*].

140. SC 12.1; PL 828. [It far surpasses both].

141. Asspt 3.4; PL 183:423. [For as often as he interrupts his spiritual study for one of the least (of his brothers), he is laying down his soul for him spiritually]. Cf. St Thomas II, IIae, Q. 182, a. 1, ad 1.

142. Asspt 3.4; PL 424. Cf. SC 47.5; 1010.

143. Asspt 3.4. Cf. SC 2.10.

144. SC 57.9; 1054. [Real and selfless contemplation is marked by this: it kindles the mind so strongly with divine fire, it is filled with such zeal and such desire to gather to God those who love him similarly, that it very willingly interrupts the leisure of contemplation for the endeavor of preaching].

145. SC 9.7; 818. [You will know you have received this kiss because you will sense that you have conceived]. *Tantae nempe efficaciae osculum sanctum est ut ex ipso, mox cum acceperit illud, sponsa concipiat, tumescentibus nimirum uberibus, et lacte quasi pinguescentibus in testimonium.* [This holy kiss has such potency that by it, as soon as she receives it, the bride conceives, and her breasts swell and fill with milk in witness.

146. SC 9.8; 818. [The breasts at which you nurture the little ones, those you beget, are better, that is, more necessary than the wine of contemplation].

146a. Ibid. [Do not insist too hard on the kiss of contemplation, because *the breasts of preaching are better*].

147. St Thomas, II IIae, Q. 182, a. 1, ad 3. Cf. St Augustine, *The City of God*, XIX, 19. Bernard, SC 50.6; PL 1023.

148. SC 51.2; 1026. [These two are companions and they live together, for Martha is Mary's sister].

149. Rm 8:6, quoted by St Bernard in SC 57.4; PL 1051: *Spiritus Dei testimonium perhibet spiritui nostro quod filii Dei sumus.* [The Spirit of God bears witness to our spirit that we are sons of God].

150. SC 57.4; 1052. [He will be visited often. Never will he be unaware of the time of his visitation, even though he who visits in spirit comes furtively and secretly, like a shy lover].

151. SC 57.9; 1054. [There follows, gently and caressingly insinuating God's will, a voice which is none other than love, which cannot be idle, persuading and beckoning towards the things of God. Then the bride hears and arises and hastens, doubtlessly, to the welfare of souls].

152. Idem. See above, n. 144.

153. Idem. [And again, having been partially satisfied, she sometimes returns to that better part, more ardent because she remembers she has been so fruitfully interrupted. And again, having had a taste of contemplation, she hurries back to her search for (other's) welfare with her usual haste and even more vigorously].

154. Idem. [In the midst of these alternations, the mind vacillates, fearful and greatly agitated lest perhaps it cling more than it should to one of them while it is distracted by its affections and thus lest it may turn away even a little from God's will in either direction.... You are looking at a holy man grievously torn between the fruit of works and the slumber of contemplation. And although he is always directed towards good, he is a man always doing penance as if for some evil, and seeking the will of God with tears every moment].

155. See especially, SC 50.5-7; PL 1022, 1024.

156. Sg 2:10.

157. Asspt 3.3; PL 183:422. [Isn't she the friend who, directed toward the Lord's gain, faithfully lays down her soul for him? For as often as she interrupts spiritual study for one of the least of his brethren, she lays down her soul for him. Isn't she the beautiful one who, revealed in seeing the glory of the Lord face to face, is transformed into that same image from glory into glory, as by the Spirit of the Lord? Isn't she the dove who wails and weeps in the cleft of the rock, in the secret places in the wall, as buried beneath a rock?]

157a. Asspt 3.3; 422. [that portion which every one of us, as far as we can, should choose].

158. SC 9.8; 818. [the breasts of preaching].

159. SC 46.8-9; 1007-8. Cf. SC 19.1; 859.

160. SC 41.5, end; 987.

161. SC 41.6.

162. SC 18.2; 859. The last line is quoted from Proverbs 11:26. [You keep for yourself a thing of your neighbor's if, for example, you are filled with virtues and adorned as well with the outward gifts of knowledge and eloquence, yet through fear, or laziness, or a false humility, you muffle in useless and even damnable silence the good word that could be of advantage to many. He is cursed indeed, by the people, who hides the grain].

163. 2 Cor 11:29, quoted in SC 12.2; 828: *Quis infirmatur et ego non infirmor, quis scandalizatur et ego non uror?* [Who is weak and I am not weak? Who is offended and I do not burn?]

164. SC 41.5; 986. SC 47.5; 1010.

165. SC 85.12; 1194. [Therefore when you see a soul leaving everything to cleave to the Word with all her will, to live in the Word, to rule herself by the Word, to conceive by the Word what by the Word she will bring forth, a soul that can say 'for me to live is Christ and to die gain', think of her as a bride, married to the Word. The heart of her husband trusts in her, knowing that she is faithful who has spurned everything but him, who has considered everything else as dung that she might win him for herself].

166. Asspt 3.4; PL 183:423.

167. Asspt 2.9; 421: *In hac una et summa Maria et Marthae negotium, et Mariae non otiosum otium invenitur.* [In this one and greatest Mary are found both Martha's business and Mary's not idle rest].

168. Asspt 2.8; 420: *Absit enim ut proprii quidquam inquinnamenti domus haec aliquando habuisse dicatur, ut in ea proinde scopa Lazari quaereretur.* [God forbid that this house be said ever to have had anything of its own filth, that in it might be sought Lazarus' broom]. In this passage, St Bernard holds that Mary was not immaculately conceived but sanctified after her conception like Jeremiah.

169. Asspt 2.8; 421.

170. Asspt 2.9; 421. *Clarius enim ceteris rutilabat, quam repleverat oleo gratiae prae participibus suis Christus Jesus; ... Virgo... cujus lampas ardentissima ipsis quoque angelis lucis miraculo fuit.* [She casts her light more brightly on others; her Jesus Christ has filled with the oil of grace above her companions... the Virgin... whose lamp by that miracle was far brighter than even the lights of the angels].

171. Epi 1.2; PL 183:155. [Now (the Word) has filled the mind before the belly. And when he proceeded from her womb, he did not withdraw from her soul].

172. Div 52.4; PL 183:675. Asspt 1.1; 415. Asspt 2.2; 417, etc.

173. Div 51; 674. [He who preaches the Gospel to others carries Jesus, as it were, in his womb, so that he may bring Him forth to others, or better, others to Him].

174. O Asspt, 3; PL 183:431.

175. Ibid. [Fr Merton's translation given in text].

176. Ibid. 6; 432. [He dwells in you and you in him. And you clothe him and you are clothed by him. You clothe him in the substance of flesh, and he clothes you in the glory of his own majesty. You clothe the sun with a cloud and you are clothed with the sun itself].

177. Miss 3.7; PL 183:74. [O prudent virgin, o holy virgin. Who has taught you that virginity pleases God?]

178. Miss 3.7; 75.

179. Miss 3.1; 71.

180. Miss 3.1; 71.

181. Miss 3.2; 72: *Nam cum esset Rex in accubitu suo, nardus Virginis dedit odorem suum, et ascendit in conspectu gloriae ejus fumus aromaticus, et invenit gratiam coram oculis Domini.... Statimque Rex egrediens de loco sancto euo, exsultavit ut gigas ad currendam viam: et licet a summo coelo egressio ejus, nimio tamen praevolans desiderio praevenit suum nuntium ad Virginem quam amaverat.* [Now while the king was on his couch, the virgin's nard was giving out its odor and an aromatic smoke was rising up in the sight of his glory, and she found grace in the Lord's eyes.... The king, suddenly leaving his holy place, rejoiced as a giant to run his course. And although his starting point was the highest heaven, yet flying ahead in so great a desire he came ahead of his messenger to the Virgin whom he loved].

182. Nat BVM, 5; PL 183:440: *Sed quomodo noster hic aquaeductus fontem illum attigit tam sublimem? Quomodo putas, nisi vehementia desiderii, nisi fervore devotionis, nisi puritate orationis? Sicut scriptum est: oratio justi penetrat coelos. Et quis justus si non Maria justa? ...Quid? Plena est gratia, et gratiam adhuc invenit? Digna prorsus invenire quod quaerit, cui propria non sufficit plenitudo sed... petit supereffluentiam ad salutem universitatis.* [But how has our aqueduct here reached that fount so sublime? How do you think, if not by the strength of her desire, if not by the fervor of her devotion, if not by the purity of her prayer? As it is written: The prayer of the just pierces the heavens. And who is just if not Mary the Just? ...How? She is full of grace and finds grace like this. She is utterly worthy to find what she seeks. She is not satisfied with her own fulness but... asks that it flow over for the salvation of the whole world].

183. Nat BVM, 6; 440:1. [Regard, o man, the counsel of God. Recognize the counsel of wisdom, the counsel of godliness. He sets out to moisten the earth with heavenly dew, and first poured it wholly into the fleece; the human race which is to be redeemed has bestowed its universal value in Mary].

184. Nat BVM; 441.

185. SC 83.3; 1182. [I have said 'engaged' too slightingly; they are embraced].

186. Miss 3.4; 73: *Cum (Maria) utique tanta ei consensio fuit, ut illius non solum voluntatem, sed etiam sibi carnem conjungeret; ac de sua Virginisque substantia unum Christum efficeret, vel potius unus Christus fieret.* [She consented to him so fully that she joined not only her will but even her flesh to him, that from his own and the Virgin's substance he might make one Christ, or better, he might become one Christ].

187. Ann 3.8; Pl 183:396.

188. Asspt 2.2; 417. [She is our mediatrix surely. It is through her that we receive your mercy, O God. It is through her that we welcome the Lord Jesus into our homes].

189. O Asspt, 2; PL 183:430. [She opens the embrace of enveloping mercy, so that everyone might share in her fulness].

190. SC 29.8; 932: *Est etiam sagitta electa amor Christi, quae Mariae animam non modo confixit sed etiam pertransivit ut nullam in pectore virginali particulam vacuam amore relinqueret.... Aut certe pertransivit eam ut veniret usque ad nos, et de plenitudine illa nos omnes acciperemus, et fieret mater caritatis, cujus pater est caritas Deus....* [There is too a chosen arrow, the love of Christ which not only pierced the soul of Mary but passed through it until not even the tiniest part of her virgin breast was left untouched by love.... And it passed through her surely so that it might come as far as us, and we all might receive from her fulness, and she might become the mother of love, whose father is God (who is) love...].

191. Asspt 1.1; 415.

192. Asspt 1.1; 415. [The whole globe is enlightened by Mary's presence: so much so that the heavenly fatherland shines more brightly in the glow irradiated by the virgin's lamp.... Mary today makes glad the city of God with so bountiful an impulse that we sense its droplets falling, drop by drop, upon the earth].

193. Pent 2.4; PL 183:328. [as to the ark of God, to the cause of all things, to the hub of the world].

194. Ibid.

195. Nat 2.4; PL 183:121. [O happy woman who kneaded into these three measures the leaven of her own faith].

196. Ibid.

197. SC 85.9; 1192: *Virtus est quasi stabile fundamentum, super quod sapientia addificat sibi domum.* [Virtue is, as it were, a firm foundation on which wisdom builds her home].

198. SC 85.10; 1192.

199. SC 85.13; 1194.

200. SC 800.13; 1193. [When spiritual persons, holy mothers, give birth to souls by preaching, and to understanding by meditating].

201. SC 85.8; 1192.

Part II

*St Bernard on
Interior Simplicity*

St Bernard on Interior Simplicity

T HE WHOLE AIM of the cistercian life — and the Fathers of the Order are unanimous on this point — is to set men apart from the world that their souls may be purified and led step by step to perfect union with God by the recovery of our lost likeness to him.

The fall and redemption of man, especially in their psychological aspects and implications, consequently become in the writings of St Bernard matters of cardinal importance to which he frequently returns. It is in the finest sermons, the climax of his unfinished series on the Canticle of Canticles that St Bernard enters most deeply into this subject, as a preparation for the great discourses on the mystical marriage. And it is here that we find him introducing the topic of simplicity.

The soul was created in God's image and likeness. St Bernard's whole treatment of the fall can be summed up in this: that man lost his *likeness* to his Creator and Exemplar, but retained the *image,* ingrained in and inseparable from the very essence of his soul. To understand all that is implied by this is to possess the key to the whole mystical theology of St Bernard and to hold the solution of all the problems which some may find in the apparent harshness of some of his early

statements about humility. The whole tragedy of fallen
man, from the point of view of his own spiritual condition,
and the proximate cause of all unhappiness is the constant
self-contradiction generated within him by the confronting
of the essential *image* of God in his soul with the *lost likeness*
that has been unutterably disfigured by sin.

Worse still in the soul of unregenerate man, slavery to sin,
to pride and concupiscence only make this contradiction at
once more horrible and more inescapable. In hell, the process goes on without end and with consequences that are
unthinkable.

Now one of the ways in which St Bernard, departing from
the traditional augustinian treatment of the subject, describes
the divine image in the soul is to say that it consists in three
things: man's natural *simplicity,* his natural *immortality,* and
his inborn *freedom of will.* We shall see in a moment how the
simplicity of man's soul, for which being and life, *esse* and
vivere, are one and the same thing, stands half-way between
the greater complexity of animal and vegetable creation,
where matter lives by a principle other than itself, and the
perfect simplicity of the Word for whom not only being and
life are one, but life and happiness are also one and the same
thing. For him, *esse* is the same as *beatum esse.*

Now the true greatness of man consists not only in his own
essential simplicity, but in his ability *to rise to a participation* in the infinitely perfect simplicity of the Word.[1] We too
can share by grace, the unity of *esse* and *beatum esse* which
is his by nature. We too can be raised to such a state that to
live will be perfect and unutterable delight, and life and joy
will become in our souls the very same thing just as life and
being are now one in them.

This greatness, of course, was not lost in the fall. Without
the redemption, this capacity would have remained forever
unfulfilled, but it would have remained. What was lost was
not the soul's greatness but its *rectitude,* its uprightness, its

justice. To put it in other words, when Adam fell, he ceased to be *rectus,* he ceased to be *right,* that is, he ceased to be true to his own nature. He lost his *rectitudo,* and from then on it became impossible for him, without grace, to be true to himself or true to the obediential potency for union with God which is, according to St Bernard, the most glorious property of human nature.

God made us what we are, in his image. However, he did not make us *more* than this. The human soul is only made *ad imaginem,* in the image, a copy of the image. It is not *the image* itself (*Imago*), for only the Word, the second person of the Holy Trinity, is that. Satan, however, tempted Eve to desire what man was not made to desire: divinity not *by participation* but independently of God's free gift, by our own right, by our own nature. It is in this sense that *eritis sicut dii*[2] is to be taken. Eve was tempted to think human beings could become gods by natural right.

This pride was the birth of sin and the immediate ruin of our simplicity, involving as consequences our fall into servitude to sin and death. How was our simplicity lost? Not by being destroyed. St Bernard is always careful to insist that human nature was in no way harmed, in its essence, by the fall. We always remain what God has made us *in our essence,* but the tragedy is that God's good work is overlaid by the evil work of our own wills. Hence our simplicity was not taken from us but, and this was far worse, it was concealed under the disfigurement of a duplicity, a hypocrisy, a living lie that was not and could not be natural to us or part of our nature, and yet which would inevitably cling to us as a kind of hideous second-nature, but for the grace of God, who in his infinite mercy, sent his beloved Son to deliver us again by his death on the Cross.

The following quotations have been selected to amplify St Bernard's thoughts on our essential simplicity, and its corruption by the fall. But they must be seen against their own proper background, the background of the cistercian life. And the whole purpose of the Rule of St Benedict and the Cistercian Usages is, according to St Bernard, to keep man in an atmosphere where, by obedience, poverty, solitude, prayer, fasting, silence, manual labor and the common life, he will be constantly running into occasions where he will be brought face to face with the truth about himself, and forced to recognize his misery without God, with the result that he will turn to God in supplication, begging him for that grace and infused charity which will enable him to purify his soul of the hideous layer of duplicity and free the divine image within him from all the sordid appetites and evil habits that cling so obstinately even to souls that have devoted themselves for years, with the most ardent generosity, to the whole-hearted service of God in the cloister.

But this purification is only the beginning. As the Father looks down from heaven into the loving soul that seeks him in 'tears of compunction' and beholds there the likeness to his Son reappearing, as the simplicity of the concealed image begins to be freed from the dark crust of sin, he instantly pours more love into the soul and raises it up towards him ever more and more, until finally, by a faithful correspondence to grace, the perfect image is restored, and the soul is now utterly purged of all the 'fear' that is inseparable from 'unlikeness' to God. From then on, the way to heaven is nothing but confidence and love, and St Bernard does not hesitate to promise, as the *normal term* of the cistercian life of simplicity, a perfect union of wills with God, by love, which he calls the mystical marriage.

NOTES

1. See SC 80.
2. [You will be like gods: Gen 3:5.]

1. Man's Original Simplicity

TEXT 1: SERMON 81.2 ON THE SONG OF SONGS

LET THE SOUL *therefore realize that by virtue of her resemblance to God, there is present in her a natural simplicity in her very substance. This simplicity consists in the fact that for the soul it is the same thing to* be *as to* live, *but it is not, however, the same to* live *as to* live well, *or to* live happily. *For the soul is only like God, not equal to him. This is a degree of nearness to him, but it is only a degree.*

For it is not an equal excellence or distinction to have an existence that is identical with life, and to have an existence that is identical with happy life. *So, if the Word possesses this latter perfection, because of his sublime dignity, and the soul possesses the former by virtue of her likeness to him, without prejudice to his pre-eminence, it is easy to see the affinity of their natures; and it is equally easy to see the prerogative of the soul.*

To make all this somewhat clearer, let us say that only for God is it the same to be *as to* be happy: *and this is the highest and most pure simplicity. But the second is like unto this, namely that being and life should be identical. And this dignity belongs to the soul. And even though the soul belongs to this inferior degree, it can nevertheless ascend to the perfection of living well, or indeed of living in perfect happiness: not in the sense that being and happiness will ever become identical for her, even after she has completed the ascent.*

111

Thus the rational soul may ever glory in her resemblance to the Divinity, but still there will also ever remain between them a gulf of disparity whence all her bones may cry out, 'Lord, who is like unto Thee?'[1] Still, that perfection which the soul possesses is great indeed: from it, and from it alone[2] can the ascent to the blessed life be made.

SERMON 82. 2-3.

The fact that Scripture speaks of our present unlikeness *to God does not mean that Holy Writ maintains the likeness has been destroyed, but that something different has been drawn over it, concealing it. Obviously, the soul has not cast off her original form, but has put on a new one foreign to her. The latter has been added, but the former is not lost, and although that which has been superinduced has managed to obscure the natural form, it has not been able to destroy it. 'Their foolish heart was darkened,' said St Paul, and the Prophet cried: 'How is the gold become obscured and the finest color changed?' He laments that the gold has lost its brightness, and that the finest color has been*

---

[1] Statements like this one occur very frequently in all the works of St Bernard and they give us the very core of his doctrine of humility. The reason he insists so much on self-knowledge is not merely that we may be convinced of our 'vileness'. Humility is truth, and our vileness is only half of the truth. The other half is our greatness: our likeness to, our capacity for union with, God. *But he is, and will ever remain, infinitely above us, and in his sight we are always as nothing.*

[2] The brute animals, having no rational soul, do not have this perfection of simplicity, and they will never be able to ascend to the blessedness of participation in the divine life, God's own vision and love of his own infinitely simple reality.

obscured: but the gold is still gold, and the original base of color has not been wiped out. And so the simplicity of the soul remains truly unimpaired in its essence, but that is no longer able to be seen now that it is covered over by the duplicity of man's deceit, simulation and hypocrisy.[3]

What a contradiction it is, this combination of simplicity and duplicity! How unworthy of the foundation is the structure we have erected upon it![4] This was the kind of duplicity the serpent put on when he pretended to be counsellor and a friend in order to deceive. And his victims, the two dwellers in paradise, put on the same duplicity when they tried to conceal their now shameful nakedness in the shadows and foliage with garments of fig-leaves and words of excuse. From that day forth how terrible has been the spread of that infection

---

[3] The saint is not here accusing all men of conscious and deliberate hypocrisy. What he means will be clear from the example of Adam and Eve: fallen man seeks, by a perverse quasi-instinct, which he has acquired with the fall and which the saint calls duplicity, to conceal from himself, from other men and from God the truth about himself: his own insufficiency in himself, his utter dependence on God for everything. There is always in fallen man this persistent tendency to make himself like unto God, to put himself in the place of God, that is, to make his own ego the center of the universe.

[4] Once again, we are gravitating about the fundamental paradox on which is based St Bernard's whole theory of humility. We are at once great, and nothingness. The greatness in ourselves is God's work; the evil, the vileness, is the work we have done with our own will, in direct contradiction to our own nature as it was created by God. Cf. *Rule of St Benedict, ch. IV: Bonum aliquod in se cum viderit Deo applicet et non sibi, malum vero semper a se factum sciat et sibi reputet.* Let the monk attribute whatever good he finds in himself to God and not to himself, but let him know that the evil is always his own work, and let him attribute it to himself.

of hereditary hypocrisy throughout the whole race. Is it possible to find a single son of Adam who, I do not say is willing, but can even endure to be known for what he really is?

Yet nevertheless in every soul there still remains the natural simplicity of man together with the duplicity that came with original sin, in order that these two contradictories might persistently confront one another within us, to our own greater confusion. . . .

Add to this the fact that the desire for earthly things⁵ (all of which are destined to perish) increases the darkness of the soul, so that in the soul that lives in such desires nothing can be seen any more on any side, save the pallid face and the image, as it were, of death. Why does not this soul, since it is immortal, love the undying and eternal things which are like itself that thus she might appear as she truly is and live as she was made to live? But no, she takes her delight in knowing⁶ and seeking what is contrary to her nature and, by living in this manner that is so far beneath her, placing herself on the level of perishing things and becoming like them, she blackens the whiteness (candor) of her immortality with the pitch of this familiarity with death.⁷ For it is not to be won-

---

⁵For their own sake, as ends, not means. The saint is now discussing the corruption of our immortality by death, which is parallel to the contradiction generated within us between simplicity and duplicity. We are immortal, and yet we die. The ultimate contradiction is the eternal living death of hell. Our mortality is connected with the love of earthly things, *quae quidem omnia ad interitum sunt,* for they are all destined to perish.

⁶*Sapit*—literally, knows, as it were, by tasting. Hence *Sapientia,* wisdom, is the knowledge of God by the experience of (tasting) his infinite goodness.

⁷In other words: the being, the reality of material things is unstable and impermanent. Therefore the soul, loving these things, becomes itself unstable, vacillating, weak, confused, as the saint will show in the next paragraph.

dered at that the desire of material things makes an immortal soul like unto mortal beings, and unlike to the immortal. 'He that toucheth pitch,' says the Wise Man, 'shall be defiled with it.' The soul that seeks to rest and take its fill of delight in mortal things[8] puts on mortality like a garment, and yet the garment of immortality is not put off, but discolored by the arrival of this likeness of death.

Consider Eve, and how her immortal soul overlaid the glory of her own immortality with the shadow of death, by giving her love to perishing things. For since she was immortal why did she not despise mortal and transitory things and remain satisfied with the things on her own level, immortal and eternal? 'The woman saw that the tree was good to eat and fair to the eyes, and delightful to behold.' O woman! That sweetness, that beauty, that delight do not belong to thee! Or if they do pertain to thee, according to the portion of clay that is thine, they are not thine alone, but are common to thee and to all the animals on the earth.[9]

---

[8] *Fruendo mortalibus mortalitatem se induit...*
The verb *frui*, in the Fathers of the Church and the Scholastics, has a special meaning beyond the ordinary one: 'to enjoy.' It is the precise technical term used to describe the act of the will resting in the possession of something as in its last end. Hence, properly speaking, the only object of *frui* for the human soul is God himself. We may try to possess creatures in this way, but our attempt is necessarily doomed to failure. It is a metaphysical impossibility. Creatures are for our *use (uti)* as means to lead us to 'fruition' in God.

[9] The implications of this are very far-reaching. The goodness, beauty, usefulness, etc., of material creation have a definite purpose: to bring men to God, and in a wider sense to be used by all living beings for their own good. If, then, we desire to *possess* any part of this goodness and beauty for ourselves alone, we automatically enter into competition with all the other beings for whose use it was created. This, then, in addition to the natural instability of material things, is a second source of unrest, the

That which is thine, and really thine, is not to be found here: it is something totally different from these: for it is eternal, and of eternity. Why do you force your soul to take on the impress of an alien form, or rather an alien deformity? Yea, indeed, that which she loves to possess, she fears to lose. Now fear is a kind of color. It stains our liberty and, discoloring it, conceals it, and, at the same time, makes it unlike to itself.[10] How much more worthy of her origin would it have been if only this soul had desired nothing, feared nothing and thereby have defended its own liberty, remaining in her native strength and beauty![11]

Alas, she did not do so! The finest color is dimmed. Thou fliest away, Eve, and hearing the voice of the Lord thy God, thou hidest thyself! Why so, if not that him who thou once

---

second great source of *fear*. In connection with our topic, simplicity, it is also evident that these desires are in many ways causes of *multiplicity in the soul*. The very multiplicity of material objects multiplies our desires. The multiplicity of competitors, real and *imaginary*, multiplies our fears. The soul that loves material things finds simple recollection impossible: it is constantly tortured by a thousand images, spectres, phantasms, hopes, fears, loves, hatreds, etc.

[10] The saint here treats of the third of the three parallel disfigurements of the three elements of likeness to God in the soul. Simplicity was 'overlaid' by duplicity, immortality by death, now liberty is similarly obscured, though left essentially intact, by slavery to an inordinate desire of material things—i.e. to sin.

[11] This sentence is a perfect description of the state of *interior simplicity* as treated in the first section of the report. The soul is said to desire *nothing* because, in such a state, it is united to God and possesses him, although in another sense its love for him is always a mixture of satisfaction and desire, even in heaven. It is said to fear nothing, because its absolute confidence in God (*fiducia* is extremely important in the mysticism of St Bernard, and therefore an essential ingredient in cistercian simplicity) precludes all servile fear.

*didst love thou now fearest and the form of a slave has
superseded that of a free-born child.*

*. . . Therefore, because man neglected to defend the nobili-
ty of his nature by leading an upright life, it has come about
that by the just judgment of his Maker he has not been stripped of his liberty but has been 'clothed over with his confusion as with a double cloak'.*[12] *And the expression 'as with a
double cloak', is very apt, for now in the soul of man there
are found both the liberty which remains because it is essential to his will, and his servile manner of life which is proof of
his servitude. The same thing is to be observed in the case of
the soul's simplicity and immortality. In fact, if you consider
our present state well, you will see that* there is nothing in
the soul that is not in the same way reduplicated — likeness to
God being covered over with unlikeness. *Is it not indeed
'doubled', this cloak in which guile, which is no part of our
original nature, has been sewed on to our simplicity, death
stitched upon our immortality, necessity upon our liberty,
and all by the needle of sin? For duplicity of heart does not
exclude simplicity of essence, nor is our natural immortality
destroyed by death, whether the voluntary death of sin or
the involuntary death of the body. And the freedom of the
will, likewise is still there, underneath the servitude to sin.*

*And thus accidental evils superadded to the good that is
in our nature, do not suppress that good, but are impressed
upon it, defile it without destroying it, and lead to its
upheaval, not its total removal. This is the reason why the
soul is unlike to God, and why it is even unlike itself. This is
the reason why it 'is compared to senseless beasts and is
become like to them'.*[13]

---

[12] Psalm 108:29, [*Hebr 109:29*]. This psalm is traditionally interpreted as referring to Judas, in whom duplicity went to its
greatest limit — the attempt to betray God into the hands of death!
St Bernard is not concerned with Judas in this passage.

[13] It is interesting to compare this passage with a fundamental

PRACTICAL APPLICATION OF THIS
DOCTRINE OF ST BERNARD

Even a cursory reading of these notions, which are the very cornerstone of cistercian asceticism, will show that St Bernard has really vindicated the fundamental goodness of human nature in terms as strong as have ever been used by any philosopher or theologian. And if the first step in the cistercian ascent to God is for the monk to *know himself*[14] we may reasonably say that, in some sense, the whole life of such a one will consist in *being himself*, or rather trying to return to the original simplicity, immortality and freedom which constitute his real self, in the image of God.

---

text of St John of the Cross, who often greatly resembles St Bernard. The great Carmelite says:

'The reason why it is necessary for the soul in order to attain Divine union with God, to pass through this dark night of mortification of the desires and denial of pleasures in all things, is because all the affections which it has for creatures are pure darkness in the eyes of God, *and when the soul is clothed in these affections, it has no capacity for being enlightened and possessed by the pure and simple light of God* if it cast them not first from it; for the light cannot agree with darkness... It must be known that the affection and attachment which the soul has for creatures renders it like to these creatures; and the greater is its affection, the closer is the equality and likeness between them, for love creates a likeness between that which loves and that which is loved... And thus he that loves a creature becomes as low as is that creature, and in some ways lower: for love not only makes the lover equal to the object of his love but also subjects him to it. Wherefore in the same way it comes to pass that the soul that loves anything else becomes incapable of pure union with God and transformation in Him.' *Ascent of Mount Carmel. I. 4. (Peers translation.)*

[14] See Gilson, *Mystical Theology of St. Bernard*, pp 67 ff.

We will never completely succeed in being ourselves until we get to heaven. Meanwhile on earth our chief, in fact our only task, is to get rid of the 'double' garment, the overlying layer of duplicity that is *not* ourselves. Hence the cistercian stress on simplicity. Hence the fact that the whole of cistercian asceticism may be summed up in that one word.

And this is true even when the word is taken in several different senses.

1. The first step in the monk's ascent to God will be to recognize the truth about himself — and face the fact of his own duplicity. That means: *simplicity in the sense of sincerity*, a frank awareness of one's own shortcomings.

2. He will also have to overcome the temptation to excuse himself and argue that he is not, in fact, what he is (whether he argues with other men, with himself or with God, it does not matter). Hence: *simplicity in the sense of meekness* — self-effacement, humility.

3. He must strive to rid himself of everything that is useless, unnecessary to his one big end: the recovery of the divine image, and union with God. Now, simplicity takes on the sense of total and uncompromising *mortification*.

(a) *Of the lower appetites:* hence the simplicity in food, clothing, dwellings, labor, manner of life as laid down in the *Little Exordium, Consuetudines, Statutes of the General Chapters.*

(b) *Of the interior senses and the intellect:* This means simplicity in devotions, studies, methods of prayer, etc., and calls for the complete simplification in liturgical matters and the decoration of churches for which the early cistercians were so famous.

(c) *Of the will:* This is the most important task of all. In the works of St Bernard, the amount of space devoted to other forms of mortification is practically insignificant in comparison to the scores of pages which are given up to the attack on self-will and its utter destruction. Hence the stress on the great benedictine means of penance, which resumes all others for the monk: obedience. This will produce that simplicity which is synonymous with docility, the trustful obedience of a child towards his father; the supernatural, joyous obedience of the monk who seeks to prove his love for Christ by seeing him in his representative, the abbot. (See Text III.)

2. Intellectual Simplicity

TEXT II: SERMONS 35 and 36 ON
THE SONG OF SONGS

1. Culpable ignorance: There are two kinds of knowledge which all men are bound to have, and the lack of which will result in their damnation: knowledge of themselves and knowledge of God.

SERMON 35.6

MAN WHEN HE WAS in honor, did not understand.[1] What did he not understand? The psalmist does not tell us, but we shall say what it was. Man, being placed in a position of honor (in paradise) failed to understand that he was slime, and that he had been elevated to this culminating dignity. And therefore he soon found out, in himself, that whch many years later a man, a son of his captivity, also discovered and acknowledged in all truth saying: He who thinks he is something, when he is nothing, deceiveth himself.[2] And thus a creature that was above the run of other animals has been reduced to the same level as the rest of the herd[3]; thus it is that the likeness of God has been changed into the likeness of a beast[4] and thus it is, too, that man has exchanged the company of the angels for the com-

---

[1] Ps 48:13 [Hebr 49:12].
[2] Gal 6:3.
[3] Hinc egregia creatura gregi admixta est....
[4] Cf. the internal contradiction in man since the fall as expressed in Text I.

121

pany of the beasts of the field. You see, then, how much we ought to avoid this ignorance which was the cause of so many thousands of evils to our human-kind.[5] *For the prophet says that the very reason why man was made like to the beasts of the field was that* he did not understand.

But there is a second ignorance, even worse than the first. The first made us equal to the beasts, this second places us below them. It is the ignorance of God.

SERMON 35.7

He [the Wise Man] now shows us that there is a second ignorance which is far more to be feared, far more shameful than the first, for while the former made man equal to the beasts, this places him below them. For men deserve, by their ignorance, to be ignored, that is damned, by God, and to stand before his terrible judgment seat and to be cast into everlasting fire. None of these things will happen to the brute beasts.

Thus, the first reason why men are placed lower than beasts by their own ignorance, is the fact that they must go to hell. But even in this life they are lower in another way.

---

[5] The result of the fall was a quasi-natural duplicity, superimposed on the simple nature of man. But one of the chief causes of the fall was, according to the saint in this passage, the failure of man to consider the truth of his essential contingency upon God — a dependence which is his greatest glory, and the source of all his freedom. Consequently, culpable ignorance of the source of all the goods proper to his nature was the cause of all man's sorrows, and, likewise, the cause of the duplicity which keeps him a prisoner of weakness, darkness, mortality, suffering and sin. *But the first step in the recovery of our simplicity is the acknowledgment of the truth:* this truth has two aspects. The first, as we have just seen, is the truth about ourselves.

*Do you not think that a man, born with reason, yet not
living according to his reason, is in a certain way more of a
beast than the beasts themselves? For the beast, who does
not rule himself by reason, has an excuse in his very nature:
since this gift is denied him by nature. But man has no excuse, since reason has been given him by a special
prerogative.... Thus he is doomed to follow after the flocks
of the other animals in this life because he has depraved his
own nature, and in the next by reason of his extremely great
punishment.*

Why must we have this knowledge of God and of ourselves?
For the sake of knowing? No, but in order to love God. We
cannot love God unless we know him, and our love for him
cannot be properly ordered unless it befits our state and condition in his sight: i.e., unless it is rooted in a deep sense of
our misery and of our need for his mercy. (Sermon 37.1)

*Self-knowledge is the mother of salvation, and of this
mother is born humility, and the fear of the Lord which,
just as it is the beginning of wisdom, is the beginning of
salvation.... And what if you should fail to know God? How
can there be any hope of salvation[6], where there is ignorance
of God? It is impossible. For you can neither love one whom
you do know, nor possess one whom you have not loved.
Know yourself, then, that you may fear God; know God,
that you may also love him. Knowledge of yourself will be
the beginning of wisdom, knowledge of God will be the com-*

---

[6] 'Hope of salvation' is not here used as a more or less general expression (equivalent to 'You cannot be saved'.) The knowledge of
God, of his goodness and his mercy effectually begets hope in our
souls, to counterbalance the fear generated by knowledge of our
own helplessness. As the argument develops, it becomes apparent
that knowledge of ourselves without knowledge of God only begets
despair.

*pletion, the perfection of wisdom; because the fear of the
Lord is the beginning of wisdom and the fulfillment of the
Law is charity.*[7] *Beware, then, both of ignorance of
yourself and ignorance of God since there is no salvation
without the fear and the love of God. All other knowledge is
indifferent, since the possession of it does not give us salvation, and the lack of it will never cause us to be damned.*

SERMON 37.6

*But, just as the beginning of wisdom is fear of the Lord, so
the beginning of all sin is pride: and just as the love of God is
the perfection of wisdom, so despair is the ultimate consummation of all malice. And just as knowledge of ourselves
begets fear of God, and knowledge of God begets love of
God, so on the other hand, from ignorance of ourselves
comes pride and from ignorance of God, despair.... And
pride, the beginning of all sin, consists in this: that you
become greater in your own eyes than you are before God,
than you are in truth....*[8]

SERMON 38.1

*But in what manner does ignorance of God beget despair?
Let us suppose that someone enters into himself, and is filled
with sorrow for all the evil he has done, thinking to amend*

---

[7] Rm 13:10. Plenitudo legis est charitas.

[8] The text which space obliges us to omit, comprising most of
the last two sections of Sermon 37, contains some excellent rules
for the practice of humility, in which the saint explains why it is
always safer to place ourselves lower than we really are, although
the ideal would be to think of ourselves exactly as we are, neither
better nor worse, if we only knew how we and others stand in the
eyes of God.

his life and to turn back from his evil road, and from his carnal ways: if he does not know how good God is, how gentle and how kind, how quick to pardon: surely his carnal thoughts will rebuke him saying:... Your sins are too great... you will never be able to make satisfaction for them. Your health is weak, you have led an easy life, you will find it terribly hard to break your old habits. These thoughts, and others like them, drive back into despair the unfortunate man who does not realize with what great ease the omnipotent Goodness who is God would do away with all these obstacles.

2. SERMON 36.2: KNOWLEDGE: UNNECESSARY AND NECESSARY

Perhaps I seem to disparage speculative sciences and, as it were, to criticize learned men.[9] *Far from it. I am well aware how much good has been and is done in the Church by learned men, both in refuting the errors of her enemies, and in instructing the unlearned.*[10] *Indeed, I have read in Holy Scripture: 'Because thou hast refused knowledge, I will*

---

[9] St Bernard, like many others attracted to the cistercian cloister in his time (St Aelred, William of St Thierry, Alan of Lille, Guerric, etc.), belonged to the intellectual aristocracy of the twelfth century.

[10] It is intertesting to note that the Latin word here is *simplex*, simple. The simplicity of those who are merely ignorant is never proposed as an ideal by the early Cistercians and, in this place, St Bernard takes it for granted that they should be instructed by the learned, and that there should be learned men to instruct them. But it is not everybody's vocation to be a learned man, just as it would be better if no one passed his whole life in that form of 'simplicity' which is mere ignorance.

also refuse thee, and thou shalt not serve before Me as priest.'[11] And also: 'Whosoever shall be learned shall shine like the splendor of the firmament; and those who have instructed many in justice shall shine like stars for everlasting eternity.'[12] But I also know where I may read that 'Science puffeth up'.[13] And again, 'Bring in knowledge, and you bring in sorrow'.[14] So you see that there are different kinds of science, when one puffeth up, and the other makes sorrowful. Now I would have you tell me: which of these kinds of knowledge seems to you more useful, more necessary for salvation: that which puffeth up or that which causes pain? I do not doubt for a moment that you will prefer the science that fills you with sorrow to that which fills you with wind. The inflation of pride may make you feel healthy: but the sorrow of compunction will make you beg for real health instead of the illusory health of pride. But whoever begs for salvation is getting close to it already, because everyone who asks shall receive.

REMARKS

1. St Bernard applies the fundamental principle of simplicity to our intellectual life. The principle is: to eliminate all that is superfluous, unnecessary, indirect, and

---

[11] Hosea 4:6. Quia tu repulisti scientiam, repellam et ego te, ut non fungaris mihi sacerdotio.

[12] Dan 12:3. Qui docti fuerint, fulgebunt quasi splendor firmamenti; et qui ad justitiam erudiunt multos, quasi stellae in perpetuas aeternitates.

[13] 1 Cor 8:1. Scientia inflat.

[14] Persius, *Satires, 1.* This is not the only time when the saint paradoxically quotes a pagan poet in the midst of a passage where he is showing the vanity of secular culture.

to put in the place of these an exclusive concern with the one thing necessary—the knowledge and love of God, union with him, in the closest possible way. To simplify our understanding we abandon the knowledge of all that does not lead us more or less directly to God. In St Bernard's terms, since we cannot have any immediate knowledge of God in this life, we must at least seek that knowledge which fills us with love of God: for our love can attain immediately to him even on earth. Hence, simplicity in the intellectual order means subordinating all our knowledge to the *love of God*. We study in order to love. But it is by loving that we really begin to know God as he is in himself, not that love gives us new intellectual concepts of his essence or his perfections but nevertheless it endows us with an intimate experimental knowledge of God as he is in himself, by virtue of the immediate contact which it establishes with him.[1]

This is clear from a typical passage in St Bernard. In the fifth book of the *De consideratione,* having asked repeatedly 'Who is God?' 'Quis est Deus?' and attempted to answer the question by the most lofty intellectual speculations on the divine essence, the saint concludes:[2]

We know these things. But because we know them, do we imagine we have comprehended (comprehendisse) them? Philosophic argumentation can never comprehend them, that is a thing which sanctity alone can do if indeed, they can be grasped at all. (Non ea disputatio comprehendit sed sanctitas.) And yet unless it were possible, the Apostle would never have said 'in order that you may be able to comprehend with all the saints.... [3]

---

[1] Cf. St Bonaventure, II Sent. D xxiii, aii q. 3, ed. 4. 'Amor multo plus se extendit quam visio...ubi deficit intellectus ibi proficit affectus.' The Seraphic Doctor was inspired by St Bernard in this passage; cf. St Bernard, Csi V, 14; Div 4.3.

[2] Csi V, 14, 30.

[3] Eph 3:18.

Therefore the saints comprehend them. You ask how? If you are a saint, you comprehend, and you know; and if you are not a saint, then become one, and you will find out by experience. But it is a holy affection that will make you a saint[4] and that affection is twofold: the holy fear of God and his holy love. The soul that is altogether possessed of these two affections has, as it were, two arms with which it lays hold upon God and embraces him and hugs him to herself and holds him saying: I held him and I will not let him go.[5]

These words of the saint recall what he has just been saying about the one kind of knowledge that is necessary. That knowledge also was twofold: on the one hand it was necessary for us to know ourselves, in order to fear God, and on the other, to know God in order to love him. Therefore, that knowledge endows us with the means of arriving at an experimental knowledge of God by a direct contact with him. The knowledge itself does not enlighten our minds concerning him, but it leads to love and love gives us a concrete experience of God that tells us more about him than all the most sublime speculations of the theologians could ever do.

2.   Therefore, it would be far from the truth to say that St Bernard would have the monk renounce all knowledge and enclose himself in a kind of holy blindness and stupidity, making himself impervious to all truths and renouncing all books and all thought whatever. There is a certain holy ignorance which is incumbent on the saint: but this *docta ignorantia* is the ignorance of the things that are *useless* to him. And therefore, it is really a higher perfection of the mind, it is *docta*, 'learned'. It is more enlightened than the wisdom and prudence of this world, because it has renounced all the vain learning which only blinds the soul to higher truths and makes it incapable of the love of God.

---

[4] Sanctum facit affectio sancta.
[5] Sg 3:4.

St Bernard, therefore, teaches that there is a twofold obligation for the contemplative monk: he is obliged to know the things necessary for his state, and he is obliged to renounce all useless learning that would only stand in the way of his vocation.

Therefore when Pope Pius XI was drawing up a letter to the heads of all the religious orders in the Church, to remind them of the necessity of a thorough philosophical and theological training for all religious priests, he most aptly quoted the very text from St Bernard on which we are commenting. At the same time, the Holy Father recommended St Bernard, together with St Bonaventure and St Alphonsus Liguori as the most valuable masters of the spiritual life to whom religious ought to turn for guidance from the very first days of their vocation.[6]

In the sixty-ninth sermon on the Canticle of Canticles, St Bernard again speaks of this harmony between knowledge and love, and stresses the obligation of both: the need of a knowledge that is enlightened but humble, and the need of a love that is aware of the great love of God for us and free to respond to it — not impeded, that is, by self-love and pride. *Non decet Sponsam Verbi esse stultam porro elatam Pater non sustinet.* 'The Spouse of the Word,' he says, 'must not be stupid: but if she be proud, the Father will not be able to stand her.'[7] Let us consider more closely the two members of this statement.

Non decet Sponsam Verbi esse stultam

The soul of the contemplative monk — the souls of all rational beings, too, for that matter — is called to be the spouse of the divine Word. But the Word is the uncreated wisdom

---

[6] Unigenitus Dei Filius. (March 19, 1924.)
[7] SC 69.2.

of God, infinite wisdom communicated to the soul. He himself comes to teach her, to communicate to her his own substantial, uncreated truth. Is the soul that is destined to become the bride of uncreated truth to live in union with him as a fool? The thought is blasphemy.

But St Paul teaches us that 'The Wisdom of the world is foolishness with God'[8], and he also says that the learned men of the world 'professing themselves to be wise, have become fools'[9].

Therefore when St Bernard says that the spouse of the Word must not be a fool, he clearly means that she must not be guilty of the egregious folly of presenting herself for union with the uncreated wisdom of God, clothed in the darkness and ignorance which earthly wisdom is in the sight of God.[10]

When we come to ask what is the wisdom of this world, we find that it consists not in a certain *type of subject matter* so much as a certain manner of knowing. The knowledge of created things is not reprehensible: far from it; we know that God made them precisely in order that we might use them to arrive at the knowledge and love of him.[11].

---

[8] I Cor 3:19.

[9] Rm 1:22.

[10] St John of the Cross, *Ascent of Mount Carmel*, I, 4 (Peers 1:26). 'Any soul that makes account of all its knowledge and ability in order to come to union with God is supremely ignorant in the eyes of God and will remain far removed from that vision.'

[11] St Bernard says that the evidence of God in his creation, so visible even to natural reason alone without grace, is sufficient to oblige men to a complete and uncompromising *natural* love of God above all else. Dil 2.6. For the ascent of the mind to God through creatures, see especially St Bonaventure, *Itinerarium mentis in Deum*, I, 15: 'Aperi igitur oculos tuos, aures spirituales admove, labia tua solve et cor tuum appone ut in omnibus creaturis Deum tuum videas, audias, laudes, diliges et coles, magnificas et

And yet there is a certain manner of knowing not only creatures, but even God himself, a vain, self-centered, empty form of speculation which is true as far as it goes, but is useless to us because it does not end in the love of God. And hence its truth is imcomplete. Because if we really knew God, we could not help but love him. But God himself is Truth. Therefore, any knowledge of any 'truth' that does not directly or indirectly lead to the love of God is incomplete. If we possessed his truth, our possession would be manifested by our *love.*

In the eighth sermon on the Canticle of Canticles St Bernard develops at some length the distinction between false knowledge, the 'science that puffeth up,' the 'wisdom of this world' and knowledge of God by love. It is a distinction that had been long before set forth by St Paul. The Apostle said of the pagan philosophers that: 'When they knew God, they have not glorified him as God, or given thanks: but became vain in their thoughts, and their foolish heart was darkened.'[12]

St Bernard comments:[13] *these pagan thinkers, ... being satisfied with the knowledge that puffeth up, never arrived at the possession of that knowledge by charity that edifieth...and it is evident that they did not really know God if they did not love him. For if they had known him completely, they would have known that goodness of his which willed to be born in human flesh, and die for their Redemption.*[14]

---

honores, ne forte totus contra te orbis terrarum consurgat.' To ignore the voice of creatures crying out to us the glory of their Creator draws down upon us a terrible fate!

[12] Rm 1:21.

[13] SC 8,5.

[14] He does not mean that they ought to have known of the Incarnation of Christ before it happened, and by natural reason alone:

Then the saint continues: *Behold, these men pried into all there is of sublimity and majesty of God, prompted not by the Spirit of God but by the presumption of their own spirit: but they never understood that he was meek and humble of heart.*

The great contemplative, who knew the immense goodness of God by mystical experience, could not help but be overwhelmed at this spectacle of a selfish and self-complacent knowledge that used its gifts to adorn itself with grand and empty conceptions, at the expense of God himself: exploiting, as it were, the perfections of their own Creator, *not in order to admire him, but in order to admire their own wisdom.* Hence it was inevitable that they should be blinded, and that their pride should place an insurmountable obstacle between them and the Truth who is God and who is, at the same time, infinitely pure Love.

That brings us to the second half of St Bernard's sentence:

Animam elatam Pater non sustinet

We possess the Truth by a union of likeness with him. But what likeness is there between light and darkness, between infinite unselfishness and the narrowness of an almost infinitely petty pride? *Quid conventio luci ad tenebras?* [What contact has light with darkness?]

This kind of knowledge that instead of giving us the possession of truth, bars us forever from that possession goes, in St Bernard, by the technical name of *curiositas* — a term which the English 'curiosity' does not quite express. But the concept has already been adequately described. *Curiositas* is that vain and illusory knowledge which is really ignorance,

---

both would be impossible. But they should have recognized in God the *goodness* that would eventually show itself in Christ's birth and his death for us on the Cross.

because it is the exercise of our intellect not in search of truth but merely to flatter our own self-satisfaction and pride. The man who is 'curious' is the one who exercies his mind not in order to glorify God, but merely for the pleasure of exercising his own mind. How can such a one know the truth? He will deliberately avoid considering the facts that are displeasing to him; and the first of these facts will be his own limitations, his own failings, his own dependence upon God, his obligations towards God, and everything that reminds him of what christian ascetical tradition, since the Gospels and St Paul, calls his own *nothingness* — that is, his nothingness of himself, apart from God.[15]

This *curiositas* is the first degree of pride[16] and it was the cause of the fall of our first parents in Eden — the cause of the separation of the whole human race from God, and of the defilement of our own innate natural perfection of simplicity and liberty and immortality.

The serpent, in tempting Eve, told her two things: he promised her a knowledge beyond that which God had given her, and he promised her that she and Adam would be like unto gods. (*Eritis sicut dii.*[17])

But God had already given Adam and Eve all the knowlege that was worth having, all that really perfected their souls, all that was really true. Hence, the only addition the devil could contribute was the knowlege of evil, of falsity. In tempting them to know for the sake of their own glory and their own satisfaction, he was only offering them the useless knowledge of an untruth: he was making them a present of error, and in so doing he was acting in his true colors as the father of lies.

---

[15] Jn 5:30: Non possum ego a meipso facere quidquam. Gal 6:3: For if any man thinks himself to be something, whereas he is nothing, he deceiveth himself.

[16] Hum 10.

[17] Gen 3:5.

Non plus sapere quam oportet sapere:[18] St Bernard applies this text to the situation in Eden — and St Paul's words are the most eloquent of commentaries on the temptation of Eve. What is the wisdom that is fitting for us to have? The knowledge and love of truth. What is the wisdom that we should not seek? The knowledge and love of falsity. But all knowledge that would make us 'gods' is of the latter kind. And it is in that direction that we are led by *curiositas,* the love of knowledge for its own sake.

The application of this to the monastic life is too evident to need much development. Any monk who occupies himself with things that are outside his own vocation, without a justifiable and necessary cause, is on the path of *curiositas.* And one who studies even the highest and most perfect and most useful truths, theology itself, merely in order to please himself and to win honors and outshine everybody else and become famous and admired, is on the same wrong track.

But, to avoid the opposite extreme, St Bernard would have us realize that there is another ignorance which is just as dangerous as the ignorance of our nothingness. It is paradoxically the ignorance of *our own greatness.* This, too, we must study. It goes hand in hand with the first, and both come under the heading of that self-knowledge which grounds us in the fear of God and that knowledge of God which makes us trust in him. In the second chapter of the De diligendo Deo St Bernard tells us explicitly that it is the ignorance of our own greatness that has reduced us to a level below the beasts of the field. If we do not know our own greatness, we will never be able to have sufficient trust in God.[19] If we do not realize that

---

[18] Rm 12:3: Not to be more wise than it behooveth to be wise.

[19] Dil 2:4: Utrumque ergo scias necesse est, et quid sis et quid a teipso non sis: ne aut omnino non glorieris, aut inaniter glorieris.... SC 82: Homo factus in honore, cum honorem ipsum non intelligit, talis suae ignorantiae merito comparatur pecoribus.

our greatness is from him, and we are nothing of ourselves, then we will not even bother to trust in God, but will rely entirely on ourselves. That brings us back face to face with the same dilemma: presumption or despair, which we have been considering in the text from the thirty-seventh sermon on the Canticle.

3. The length of this discussion may seem only to complicate matters. To simplify them, let us consider one practical point. For St Bernard, the first step in acquiring intellectual simplicity is the *knowledge and imitation of Christ.* Among the many places in his works where the saint develops this theme, none is more explicit than the first chapters of the *Degrees of Humility.* He begins his tract by proposing the ascent of 'three degrees of truth,' and each degree is appropriated to one of the divine persons. The first degree, humility, self-knowledge, is the one in which the work of our enlightenment is appropriated to the incarnate Word, who sets himself before us in the Gospels as the 'way, the truth and the life'.[20] If anyone wants a brief and practical formula that sums up St Bernard's teaching on simplicity in the intellectual order, it is this: 'Allowing ourselves to be taught by Christ's love.'[21]

4. This intellectual simplicity, which begins with self-knowledge and the knowledge of the goodness of God as expressed by his love for us in our creation and in our redemption by Jesus Christ, paves the way for the higher simplicity of contemplation. That simplicity is even more a matter of love than of knowledge and therefore it demands a deep and searching simplification of the will that will be treated in the next selection of texts.

---

[20] Jn 14:6.
[21] For the details of the action by which the Word teaches the soul self-knowledge and draws it on to interior simplicity, see Hum 7.

But we may close the present topic with a view of contemplation as it affects the intellect, operating in the extreme simplicity of an intuition that is beyond all concepts and images and pictures and phantasms and discursive acts of the mind. Here we have the visit of the Word to the soul coming in person, without the medium of thought or image or anything that we can grasp by our ordinary understanding.[22]

But here is how St Bernard describes the visit of the Word to the soul in the simplicity of mystical contemplation:[23]

Take care lest you suppose that in this union of the Word and the soul we apprehend anything that has a body or can be imagined.... This union is in the spirit, because God is a spirit, and he desires the beauty of the soul of one whom he sees to be walking according to the spirit.... (The saint explains that such a one will never be content with ordinary or imaginary or rational apprehensions of God, or even with visions of him), but that soul will only be content when he receives God with secret love as He descends into the soul from heaven. For then he will possess the One he desires, not in a figure, but actually infused *(non figuratum sed infusum),* not under any appearance but in the direct contact of love *(non apparentem sed afficientem)....* For the divine Word is apprehended not by sound, but by his actual penetration into the soul *(Verbum non sonans sed penetrans).* He makes himself heard not by speech, but by direct action on the soul *(non loquax, sed efficax),* not calling out to the ears but delighting our inward love. His Face is perceived, not by an outward form, but by the form he imposes upon our very soul *(facies non formata sed formans).*

---

[22] St Bernard would agree with St Bonaventure that God is nevertheless present to the soul through some effect created in the soul by himself, not in the absence of all media whatever. That effect is love. Div 4.2. Cf. St Bonaventure, II Sent., D. xxiii, a ii, q. 3.

[23] SC 31.6.

3. The Simplification of the Will

TEXT III: OBEDIENCE—THE 'COMMON WILL'

We have now seen the great danger of ignorance in the spiritual life. And yet dangerous as it may be, it can be rendered completely harmless by a submissive and charitable will.

If only the soul will not cling to its own lights, to its own opinion, to its own way of doing things: if only the will can bring itself to consent to hand over its judgment to a superior or competent spiritual director, and to abandon its own way for the sake of peace and the common good, the battle for simplicity and sanctity is already won.[1]

The discretion and counsel of the greatest saints is a mystical grace of a high order: and yet the weakest of us can possess a virtue of almost equal power and value: the virtue of simple *obedience,* which does exactly what is commanded by the superior: *Nihil plus:* it adds nothing to his command by way of improvement upon it, or in order to make it a 'more perfect' sacrifice. (Self-will only makes the sacrifice less perfect, and in such a case even addition is rapine in the holocaust!)[2] It adds nothing to the austerities of the Rule

---

[1] Cf. Sermon III on the Circumcision. After describing the virtue of discretion as it is found in the highest degree of sanctity, and which sees through all the artifices of the demon and of our own pride, St Bernard concludes that this virtue is a 'rare bird' on earth, but assures his monks that its place is amply filled by simple obedience, which he describes thus: ut nihil plus, nihil minus, nihil aliter quam imperatum sit faciatis.

[2] Cf. 1 Sm 15 and Bernard, SC 33.10, on those who indulge in self-chosen mortifications. Cf. St John of the Cross, *Ascent* I. viii, 4-5.

without permission. It fears self-chosen penances. *Nihil minus:* It is hard to say which is worse—to follow self-will in doing more than is commanded or in doing less. Both are forms of self-love. But simple obedience is always generous enough to do what is required of it, and with a good heart. *Nihil aliter:* The perfection of simplicity in obedience is to do things in the precise way that the superior wants them to be done. We can be sure of pleasing God only when we abandon all internal arguments or attempts to find an opportunity to insinuate own own will on the grounds of *in dubiis libertas.* Let us simply try our best to do exactly what our superior seems to want, what the Rule seems to require, what the other monks, especially the seniors are doing or have done.[3]

If we were to enter into the question of obedience as it is treated by St Bernard, we would soon pass far beyond the limits of this little book. Suffice it to make two general statements on the simplification of the will before passing to the text of St Bernard himself.

1. Ignorance may be the ruin of simplicity and of sanctity: but only in so far as it springs from and is inseparable from pride. Obedience conquers ignorance, and even a man with the most erroneous ideas about the spiritual life can rapidly become a great saint if he places his judgment in the hands of a capable director. On the other hand, however, the greatest curse of the monastic life is the monk who not only has wrong ideas about the spiritual life, but clings to them with belligerent stubbornness and even tries to force them upon others.

2. The chief means for destroying self-will is not merely obedience. It is obedience regarded as subordinate to charity,

---

[3] Cf. RB 7, eighth degree of humility. Also Dom Godefroid Bélorgey *L'Humilité Bénédictine,* pp. 243-250.

and as integrated in the common life. The Cistercians were notable, among other things, for the emphasis they placed on fraternal charity and on unity in the spirit of divine Love. When St Bernard treats of the destruction of self-will, and the substitution of God's will for it, he speaks, very often, not of *voluntas Dei* but *voluntas communis:* and this common will is indeed the will of God but with an important added note: that the will of others, the will of the community with respect to the common good of the community, the Order, etc., is God's will, and to submit to our superiors and our brethren is to submit to God and become united to him.

This, it must be noted, is irrespective of whether our ideas may or may not be better than those of others. In all matters that do not clearly involve a fault, even when the community is wrong and the individual is right, he can best keep united with God by following the *voluntas communis,*[4] for the sake of peace and charity.

The chief characteristic of *voluntas propria* [self-will] is, as we have seen in Text I, a spirit of separation, of self-exaltation in a private heaven which belongs to us alone, by our own right, where we are our own gods, and where neither God nor man can interfere with our self-complacent desires. The type of this pride is the Pharisee of the parable.[5] To avoid falling into his sin, we must use the knowledge we

---

[4][common will]. This strong cistercian emphasis on fraternal union in the spirit of Love (*Deus Caritas est!*) is nowhere more strikingly evident than in the document which is the very legal foundation of the Order, the *Carta Caritatis.* The very title tells us so, and meditation of the first two pages will make it clear in no uncertain terms. This, indeed, is the whole basis for cistercian simplicity, i.e. for the unity of charity and mutual forbearance in following one rule, one set of usages.

[5] Lk 17:11.

have acquired of ourselves (Text II) to learn that we are no better than others, and that we suffer as they do, and they suffer as we do, and that we all need the grace of God. This substitution of compassion for suspicion, intolerance or contempt is a necessary degree in the ascent of the soul to mystical union with God which, to St Bernard, is unthinkable unless the soul is first prepared and purified by a true and deep and universal and supernatural love for other men.[6]

These truths are all reflected or included in the great third sermon for Paschal Time, one of St Bernard's most important expositions of his doctrine on the active purification of the will.

The subject is the purification of the leper Naaman.[7]

TEXT

SERMO III IN TEMPORE RESURRECTIONE, 3.

There is, in the heart, a twofold leprosy: our own will, and our own judgment. Our own will (voluntatem propriam), I call that which is not common to us and God and other men but is ours alone.[8] That is, when we carry out our will, not for the honor of God, nor for the benefit of our neighbor but simply for ourselves alone. Self-will means to will things that are intended not to give pleasure to God or to be of use to our brethren, but only to satisfy the selfish

---

[6] Cf. Hum 5, etc.

[7] 2 Kg 5:10.

[8] It would certainly be a grave error to say that all our desires were evil. The saint makes it perfectly clear that self-will is only to be applied to desires in rebellion against, in conflict with the will of God: and when our neighbor is in open rebellion against God, it is also God's will for us to resist him. Cf. Pre 4.

promptings of our own minds. Diametrically opposed to this evil is charity: and charity is God.

Self-will, then, is ever in a state of implacable hostility to God and constantly wages the most cruel warfare against him. What is there that God hates or punishes except self-will?

If self-will were to cease to exist, there would be no more hell. For what fuel would there be to feed those flames if there were no self-will?[9] Even now in this life, when we feel the cold or hunger or other such things, what is it that feels the suffering if not self-will? For if we willingly bear with these trials, our will becomes the common *will. What may be called our own will is really a kind of sickness and corruption of the true will: and it is this corrupt element that will continue to be the subject of every kind of suffering until it is totally consumed.[10]*

But now let those who are slaves to self-will hear and fear with how great fury self-will attacks the Lord of majesty. To begin with, it subtracts and withdraws itself from his domination and becomes its own master when by right, it should serve the God who made it. But will it be content to stop at this offence? By no means: its next step is to do all in its power to tear away from God and to destroy everything that is his. What limit does human greed avow? Is it not true

---

[9] This is to be taken in the sense that self-will itself is the object on which the flames of hell feed, not merely that it is the efficient cause of the flames of hell feeding on some other matter, viz., our bodies.

[10] We remind the reader of the contents of the first text quoted, in order to obviate the misinterpretation of these lines. Self-will belongs to the layer of corruption superinduced upon our true nature, upon our true freedom of will. It must be consumed before we can really become *ourselves.* Until then, it and it alone is the reason for our sufferings.

that the man who by usury has acquired a moderate sum of money would go on to gain the whole world if it were possible, and if his will could only find the way to do it?... Not only that, but self-will does all that it can to destroy God himself. For there is nothing it would like better than to have God either unable or unwilling to punish its sins, or else to have him ignorant of them. But when self-will would have God to be powerless, or unjust, or ignorant, that is the same as willing him not to be God. And that is the closest the will can come to destroying God... This, then, is that most filthy leprosy of the soul on account of which we have to bathe in the Jordan and imitate Him who came not to do his own will, whence in his very passion he cried out: Not my will but thine be done!

REMARKS: We interrupt this crucial text at the end of its first convenient division to make a few comments necessary to tie it in more closely with the theme of this book.

1. Self-will is in the *intention* to please ourselves: *(non intendentes placere Deo...sed satisfacere propriis motibus animorum)*. First, it must be made clear that self-will and the common will are not two separate faculties of the soul. There is only one will, but it can act in two diametrically opposed ways. Self-will and the common will are two mutually contradictory modes of action. And what must be stressed above all is the fact that it is the *common will that is natural to us* and self-will is simply a perversion.

By *intention*, St Bernard is speaking of the actual movement of the will towards what is, in real fact, its chosen object. He is not speaking of the intention which may exist in our imagination or on our lips, and which may be a self-delusion produced in a conscience completely warped and blinded by our own pride, as when the Jews crucified Christ 'that the people might not perish'.

What is meant by an *intention to please ourselves?* St Bernard says it is an act of the will moving primarily towards the satisfaction of our own desires. The will acts simply because we want this, we like that, we think this is right, we feel like doing such and such a thing. It is not always easy to say when such motives are the ones behind our acts until these desires come in conflict with (a) God's signified will, laws, rules, orders of superiors, duties and obligations, (b) the will or desires or interests of others, (c) providential circumstances. *If such obstacles destroy our peace of mind, cause us to rebel, to get excited, to lose our tempers, or to become depressed, despondent or, finally, to override the will of God and man alike to get our own way,* then we have clear evidence that our intention was more or less selfish (in proportion to the disturbance) no matter what fine reasons we may have given for our act beforehand.[11]

2. *Charitas...quae Deus est.* [Love...which is God.] This is an extremely strong sentence. But it is true. The common will is a participation in the life of God for it is charity. It is God's will, God's *love*, the *vinculum pacis*, the bond of peace uniting men to one another and to God himself. By this shall all men know we are Christ's disciples, if we love one another. And again, if we love him, we will keep his commandments. The case is perfectly clear from Our Lord's address to his disciples at the Last Supper.[12] Consequently, if we want union with God, let us obey our superiors and give in to one another, honoring one another, and seeking to do

---

[11] See Pre 10: 'It is a sign of an imperfect soul and of a very infirm will to argue insistently against the decisions of superiors...to demand a reason for every little thing, and to look with suspicion on every order the reason for which is not immediately apparent, and never to obey willingly except when you are told to do something you like to do, etc.'

[12] Jn 14-17.

what is profitable to others, not what happens to suit our own pleasure or convenience.[13] This is true simplicity, because it destroys diversity of wills and unites a multiplicity of characters and dispositions and interests in the harmony of one love, the bond of peace.

3. There is a well-regulated self-love, namely that which seeks the perfection of our own nature in the manner destined for it by God.[14] This alone should be enough to turn us away from the intolerable burden of unhappiness imposed by the unnatural tyranny of self-will. Self-will is the cause of all unhappiness, the subject of all unhappiness. This is a favorite theme with the Cistercian Fathers.[15] Why? Because, for our Fathers, unhappiness resided essentially in the conflict of our will with the will of God, with our brothers, with Providence, etc. Hence, lack of peace is identified with a certain lack of simplicity, a lack of union, of harmony with circumstances and events. Simplicity thus takes on the sense of abandonment. But even so-called passive abandonment in our Fathers was always so markedly positive in its act that it was never a merely passive acceptance of God's will, but an active desire that God's will be done.[16] This in itself is a more perfect union with God, a more perfect simplicity. There was no quietistic apathy at Clairvaux.

4. Finally, it is necessary to stress the fact that self will is a corruption of our natural freedom, our natural simplicity. In the last analysis, true simplicity for us can only mean the struggle to eliminate self-will and its concomitant, our own judgment (*proprium consilium*), the subject of the next division of the third sermon in Paschal Time.

---

[13] RB 71-72.

[14] Dil 2.

[15] To cite two other texts: St Bernard, Pre 10; St Aelred, *The Mirror of Charity*, II, 3-4.

[16] St Bernard, Miss 4: 'Fiat est desiderii indicium....'

OUR OWN JUDGMENT
TEXT III (Continued)

Now the leprosy of our own judgment is all the more dangerous, for it is the more hidden: and the more we have of it, the more we appear, to ourselves, to be healthy. This is the disease of those who have the zeal of God, but not according to knowledge, for they cling obstinately to their own errors to such an extent that they cannot bear to take advice from anybody else.

These are the kind who break up the unity of the Church or of the monastery, and are the enemies of peace, men without charity, puffed up with vanity, and thoroughly pleased with themselves, great in their own eyes, ignoring the justice of God, and desiring to set up their own standard of justice in its place.

And what greater pride is there than that one man should try to impose his own opinion upon the whole community, as if he alone had the spirit of God? Refusal to obey is the crime of idolatry and to resist is like unto witchcraft.[16] Woe, then, to those who make themselves out to be holier than everybody else, who are not like unto other men....

An excerpt from a beautiful passage on the same topic, Sermon 46.6, *In Cantica*, comes in appropriately at this point:[17]

Indeed I am amazed at the impudence of some monks among us, who, after they have upset the entire community

---

[16] 1 Sam 15:23: 'Idololatriae scelus est non acquiescere, et quasi peccatum ariolandi repugnare.' The reference is to Saul's self-chosen sacrifice, against the express command of God.

[17] The whole sermon should be studied carefully. It is a good exposition of the purgative way, according to cistercian asceticism: the stress being on *obedience* and *fraternal charity* as the two most essential prerequisites for the reception of graces of infused prayer.

with their singularities, have irritated us with their impatience, contemned us with their rebelliousness and their bad tempers, nevertheless dare to aspire, with the most fervent prayers, to mystical union with the Lord of all purity.... The centurion begged the Lord not to enter under his roof, because of his own unworthiness: and yet the fame of his faith went out through all Israel: and these men would compel him to enter in to their dwelling, vile with the filth of such great vices?

What would you have me do, such a one will ask. I would have you first of all cleanse your conscience of every stain of anger and quarrelsomeness, of murmuring and of bad temper and hasten to drive out of your heart whatever goes against peace with your brethren or obedience to your superiors. Then to adorn and prepare yourself with good-works, with priase-worthy thoughts, with the sweet-odor of virtues....[18]

Returning to the third sermon in Paschal Time, we find the saint even more explicit in his prescription of a remedy for *proprium-consilium*. He silences all objections, at least on the part of those who call themselves Christians, by the example of the obedience of Christ, who submitted his own infinite wisdom to the judgments and wills of two of his creatures, Our Lady and St Joseph.

But where can this leprosy be cleansed except in the Jordan (that is, in the humility of Christ)? Whosoever thou art that art thus afflicted, bathe therein, and observe what was done by the Angel of great counsel and how he subjected his counsel to the counsel, or rather to the will of one woman: the Blessed Virgin, and to the will of a poor carpenter, Joseph.[19]

---

[18] He sums up the dispositions required for intimate union with God in the following list: piety, peace, meekness, justice, obedience, joyfulness (hilaritas) and humility.

[19] Cf. Lk 2:46-51.

Who then would not be ashamed to cling obstinately to his own judgment when Wisdom himself gave up his judgment?

But perhaps we ought to inquire of him how it is that he gave up his will and abandoned his counsel.

The saint here passes to the agony in the garden and the problem of the divergence between the will of Christ as man, and his Father's will. Was there, then, self-will in Our Lord? Not in the sense of the corrupt mode of willing of which the saint has spoken above. That would be impossible. However, he did have his own human will.

Lord, concerning thy will, which thou didst say should not be done: if it was not good, how could it have been thy will? But if it was good, then why did it have to be given up? In the same way, concerning thy judgment: if it was not right, how could it have been thy judgment—and if it was right, why should it be given up? Both the will and the judgment were good, and they were both his: but it was none the less right that they be given up, in order that something better still might be accomplished. Therefore, when Christ said: 'If it be possible, let this chalice pass from me',[20] that was his will, and it was good. But the will with which he said Thy will be done was better because it was common to the Father, to Christ himself (since he was offered up because he himself willed it), and to us. For unless the grain of wheat, falling into the ground had died, itself would have remained alone: but dying, it bore much fruit.

And this was the will of the Father: that he should have many whom he could adopt as his sons. It was Christ's will to be the first-born of many brethren, and it was our will, because it was on our behalf that he did this thing, that we might be redeemed. The same may be said regarding his

---

[20] Mt 26:59.

judgment. When Christ said: 'I must be about my Father's business', that was his judgment, and it was good. But because Mary and Joseph did not understand, he changed his mind, in order to cleanse us of the leprosy of attachment to our own judgment.

REMARKS

1. In the first place, the distinction between corrupt self-will and well-regulated self-will now becomes apparent. The natural desire to avoid pain, to preserve life, etc., is in itself simply a movement of the sense appetite, and therefore in itself indifferent. We must not confuse the sense appetite with the will, still less must we regard it as a sort of an 'evil will'. This was the mistake of the Albigensian heretics, against whom St Bernard preached so vehemently. When Christ as man felt a desire to avoid the sufferings of Calvary which were not even strictly necessary to redeem us and which he was under no obligation to undergo, to have given the consent of his will to such repugnance would not have been an evil, but a good act in the natural order. It would have been perfectly reasonable, perfectly prudent, to avoid an unjust and cruel death, if God had not willed otherwise.

2. This brings us to the most important topic, of that 'social simplicity' which we call charity or the *common will*.

No matter from what angle we approach cistercian simplicity, the core and essence of it always turns out to be one thing: love. The will, for St Bernard as for all the augustinians, is man's highest faculty. Therefore the highest and most perfect simplicity attainable by intelligent beings is a union of wills. The all-embracing union of charity, which is effected by the Holy Ghost himself, unites men to God and men to men in God in the most perfect and simple union of one loving will, which is God's own will, the *voluntas communis*. This union is what Christ died to purchase for us. It is the work of his Spirit in us, and to realize it perfectly is to be in heaven: indeed the whole work of achieving this final magnificent and universal simplicity of all men made one in Christ will be his eventual triumph at the last day.

3. Hence we see that the very essence of cistercian simplicity is the practice of charity and loving obedience and mutual patience and forbearance in the community life which should be, on earth, an image of the simplicity of heaven. We now begin to see something of the depth of this beautiful cistercian ideal!

On the other hand, the devil is always working to break up this simplicity, to break the Order down into separate groups, the groups into conflicting houses, the houses into cliques and the cliques into warring individuals. St Stephen's Charter of Charity was explicitly directed against this work of hell.[21]

The chief weapon used by the devil in this conflict is our own corrupt self-will, our self-judgment, and the two together are commonly called pride, which makes us idolaters, self-worshippers and consequently *unitatis divisores*, disrupters of union, destroyers of simplicity.

Cistercian simplicity, then, begins in humility and self-distrust, and climbs through obedience to the perfection of fraternal charity to produce that unity and peace by which the Holy and Undivided Trinity is reflected not only in the individual soul but in the community, in the Order, in the Church of God. Once a certain degreee of perfection in this social simplicity is arrived at on earth, God is pleased to bend down and raise up the individuals who most further

---

[21] *Carta* (ed. Guignard, p. 79): '...Mutuae pacis futurum praecaventes naufragium....' [...guarding in advance against the future shipwreck of mutual peace....].

this unity by their humility and love to a closer and far more intimate union with him by mystical prayer, mystical union.

The culmination of cistercian simplicity is the mystical marriage of the soul with God, which is nothing else but the perfect union of our will with God's will, made possible by the complete purification of all the duplicity of error and sin. This purification is the work of love and particularly of the love of God in our neighbor. Hence it is inseparable from that social simplicity which consists in living out the *voluntas communis* in actual practice. This is the reason for the cistercian insistence on the common life: the Cistercian is almost never physically alone. He has opportunities to give up his will to others twenty-four hours a day. It is precisely this which, according to the mind of St Bernard, St Aelred and our other Fathers, should prepare him most rapidly for the mystical marriage.[22]

All this may be made plain in one final quotation, before passing on to the consideration of that ultimate perfection of simplicty which is the mystical marriage.

In his first sermon on the feast of St Michael and All Angels, St Bernard depicts the solicitude of the heavenly spirits for the perfection of this work of simplification which makes the Church on earth like that in heaven, a perfect union of souls in loving and praising God.

SERMON I.5 ON THE FEAST OF ST MICHAEL AND ALL ANGELS

There are many things which please the angels, and which it delights them to see in us, like sobriety, chastity, voluntary poverty, repeated sighs of desire for heaven, prayers accompanied with tears and with the heart truly directed to God. But above all these things, the angels of peace look to find

---

[22] This is especially stressed in St Bernard's Hum 5,7.

among us unity and peace. Is it surprising that they should take the greatest delight of all in these two things which show forth, as it were, the form of their own heavenly city among us, and allow them to behold their new Jerusalem on earth? And so I say, that just as that heavenly city 'participates in the selfsame'²³ so let us also think the same, say the same things, and let there not be divisions among us: but rather let us all together form one body in Christ, being all members one of another.²⁴

On the other hand, there is nothing so offensive to these heavenly spirits, and nothing which so moves them to indignation as dissensions and scandals, when such things are found among us. For let us hear the words of Paul to the Corinthians: 'When there is jealousy and contention among you, are you not carnal, and do you not walk according to man?'²⁵ And in the Epistle of Jude the Apostle we read: 'These are they who segregate themselves, brute beasts, not having the Spirit of God.'²⁶ Consider the soul of man, how it gives life to all the members of the body in their union one with another. But separate any one member from its union with the rest, and see how long it will continue to receive life from the

---

²³ Ps 121 [122]:3: Jerusalem quae aedificatur ut civitas, cujus participatio ejus in idipsum [Jerusalem which is built as a city, whose sharing is self-same] is one of the most perplexing lines in the Psalms. What is the meaning of this 'self-same?' For St Bernard, it is simply the *voluntas communis* or charity: the identical love of one object, *God's will* — and this love unites all the blessed among themselves as well as to Him.

²⁴ By the words *idipsum sentiamus* (let us think the same) St Bernard does not prescribe a stereotyped uniformity of thought, but a charitable agreement between differences of opinion springing from all the inevitable variety in temperament, background, education, etc., which it would be folly to try and destroy.

²⁵ I Cor 3:3.

²⁶ Jude 1:9.

soul!... That is what happens to every man who is cut off from unity with other men: there can be no doubt that the Spirit of Life withdraws from such a one. It is very just, then, that the apostles should call contentious men, and those who separate themselves[27] from others, carnal men and brute beasts, who have not the Spirit of God. And the saints and the blessed spirits in heaven say, when they come upon scandals and dissensions: 'What have we to do with this generation that hath not the Spirit?' For if the Spirit were there, charity would be everywhere diffused by him, and unity would not be broken.

The last sentence makes it once more perfectly clear that the operation of the *voluntas communis* (common will) and the operation of the Holy Ghost are one and the same thing, and the man who wishes to become united to the Holy Ghost only has to enter into participation in this unity of charity by humbly giving up whatever is disordered in his own will to that of the Church, the Order, his superiors, his individual brethren and through all these to God. Sanctified by this participation in the common will which is God himself working in men and in the Church, the individual monk is prepared for the graces of infused contemplation.

---

[27] It must not be forgotten that the precise meaning of the word *separate,* here is: to set one's self apart from others, in one's own estimation, by pride, self-esteem, self-congratulation, attachment to one's own opinion or one's own will. It means to say with the Pharisee: 'Non sum sicut caeteri homines.' [I am not like other men.] Pride is the root of all schisms and heresies.

4. Perfect Simplicity:
Unity of Spirit with God

We remember how, as we began this ascent of the holy soul to God, St Bernard told us that the fundamental thing was the recognition of God's image in ourselves: the end was to be the perfect rehabilitation of that image, in all its simplicity, in the purity of its original likeness to God. Now that this likeness is finally to be recovered by perfect love and confidence[1], it is fitting that we consider just how much it means.

This likeness produces more than a similarity between two separate objects. It takes the soul and makes it one with God: so close is this unity of the soul with God, that it is said *to become God*. The divine essence can never belong to us by nature and we shall always remain distinct, substantially, from God. But in the union of love which God has prepared for those that love him and seek him, everything that is his will become ours, not by nature *but by grace*.

We cannot, then, become one substance with God. But the union that we can achieve with him is only one degree less perfect than this. The union of *wills*, making us one

---

[1] On the importance of *fiducia*, confidence, see especially Sermon 83 *In Cantica*. This virtue is absolutely essential if the soul is to pass through the gruelling purification by the truth, that is, by an ever clearer and clearer knowledge of the hideous deformity that has been wrought on God's image, within her, by sin. Only perfect confidence in God's merciful love can draw the soul on towards him in spite of what she has realized about herself.

Spirit with God, is the highest and purest and most intimate union that can possibly be achieved by two individuals remaining essentially distinct.

This is the culminating ideal of cistercian simplicity!

The paradox is that the soul itself is more perfectly simple when absorbed in this union than it could ever be outside of it. The soul is never so truly itself as when it is lost in God and it is never so unlike itself as when it is completely separated from God and left entirely to itself. The reason for this paradox is in the fact that it is of the very essence of the soul to be like God and therefore it is most truly itself when it becomes, as nearly as is possible to a creature, *identified with him*.

In this perfect identification of the soul with God the soul is rightly said to lose itself in God: not in the sense of losing its substance, but in the sense of losing its *own will* in a perfect union of love with God's will that makes them truly one will, one spirit.

In such a state, the soul has completely forgotten itself and its own interests and desires for the simple reason that it no longer has any interests or desires other than those of God. It no longer has anything whatever of its own. It retains its own substance, but now it loves that substance with God's love rather than its own. The soul in this supereminent perfection of simplicity *now loves itself exactly as God loves it*, in the same degree, in the same manner—indeed, with the very same love. Even self-love is at last vindicated in this ultimate beatification of the soul! That is of course because the illusory personality, the false self superimposed upon the divine image by sin, has now been utterly destroyed in the successive purifications by the humiliating truth and by union with the *voluntas communis* (common will) in obedience and charity. St Bernard describes this union in the tenth chapter of the *De diligendo Deo*.

ON LOVING GOD, 10, 27.

*But when shall flesh and blood, this vessel of clay, this
earthly dwelling, attain at last to this fourth degree of love?[2]
When shall the soul experience this desire (affec-
tum) to the extent of becoming inebriated with divine love
and, forgetting itself, becoming to itself like a lost vessel[3] so
that it may pass over entirely into God and, adhering to
God, become one spirit with Him and say: My flesh and my
heart hath fainted away; Thou are the God of my heart, and
the God that is my portion forever.[4]*

*I should call that man holy and blessed to whom it may be
granted to experience such love, even were it only rarely, or
but once, and that in a brief flash (raptim) which might pass
and be all over in an instant. For to lose yourself, in a manner of speaking, and to become as though you did not exist,
and to lose absolutely all consciousness of yourself, and to go
forth from yourself, and to be practically annihilated, all
that belongs to heaven and is utterly above natural human
love (coelestis est conversationis, non humanae affectionis).*

The saint laments the fact that one must come back to

---

[2] There are four degrees of love for the monk in this tract on the
love of God. The first is that well-regulated self-love by which we
love ourselves enough to avoid the pains of hell and seek heaven.
The second is when a man begins to love God because of the gifts
and consolations God offers him. The third, the highest degree
reached in this life by many of the most spiritual men, is to love
God for himself alone. The fourth, and most perfect degree,
reached in this life only by a few great saints (the fewness is not
God's fault, but men's) is to love ourselves for the sake of God. All
souls attain to this if and when they reach heaven.

[3] Ps 30:13 [Hebr 31:12]. Tanquam vas perditum.

[4] Ps 72 [73]:26: Defecit caro mea et cor meum, Deus cordis mei,
et pars mea Deus in aeternum.

earth, to the necessities of one's own body, and to the duties
of the active life, after such an experience, then continues:

> *However, since Holy Scripture says that God made all
> things for himself,[5] the creature must surely at some time
> conform itself to its Creator.[6] Some day, then, we must at-
> tain to the same love that God has for us. We must reach the
> point where, just as God willed all things to exist only for
> himself, so we too may will to have existed and to exist, and
> will everything else to have been or to be solely for the sake
> of God and on account of his will alone, not for our own
> pleasure. We shall then delight, not in the fact that all our
> needs have been satisfied, and all our happiness carried to
> the ultimate consummation but in the fact that his will in us
> and for us will then be seen to be completely accomplished
> and carried out.[7] And this is what we daily ask for in our
> prayers when we say: Thy will be done on earth as it is in
> Heaven. Oh holy and chaste love! Oh sweet and delightful*

----

[5] Prov 16:4.

[6] Man is made for this perfect union with God. Capacity for it is
in his nature itself. That is, this union is within the scope of our
obediential potency, to be educed by the direct action of God on
the basis of our cooperation with grace. God does not create
beings with a potency for ends which they can never attain.
Hence, according to St Bernard, the fact that by our very essence
we are capable of this perfect union with God in love, means that
all men can attain it, if they will freely cooperate with God's love
drawing them to him. See Sermon 83.2, *In Cantica.* Also the article *'Transforming Union in St Bernard and St John of the Cross'*
below, Part III.

[7] Since God's will is the perfect beatification of the soul, the two
are, materially speaking, the same thing. But the formal reason of
the soul's happiness is to be found in the fact that this happiness is
God's will, not that it is the soul's own happiness.

affection! Oh pure, utterly clean intention of the will, all the clearer and more pure because no admixture of self remains therein; all the sweeter and more delightful in that what we feel is entirely divine. To love like this is to become a god. (Sic affici deificari est.)

This, then, is the ultimate limit of cistercian simplicity: the simplicity of God himself, belonging to the soul, purified of all admixture of self-love, admitted to a participation in the divine nature, and becoming one spirit with the God of infinite love.

Part III

Transforming Union in St Bernard and St John of the Cross

The Transforming Union in St Bernard and St John of the Cross[1]

ONE WOULD EXPECT that St Bernard, regarded for centuries as one of the greatest christian doctors of mystical theology, would have furnished modern writers like Fr Poulain[2] with a rich fund of evidence and examples in their discussion of the highest mystical states. Yet as a matter of fact although these writers respect St Bernard's authority and make use of it when they can, they do not seem to be able to use him as fully as one would expect. Dom Anselme le Bail in his article on the holy abbot of Clairvaux in the *Dictionnaire de Spiritualité,* has guessed the reason. St Bernard, concerned above all with the perfection of pure love and with degrees of charity, does not approach mystical theology from the same direction as modern writers and therefore does not directly help them to settle their most burning questions. And yet there are frequent passages on prayer in the Sermons *in Cantica* which recall St John of the Cross.[3]

And the truth is that while St Bernard and St John of the Cross tend to emphasize slightly different aspects of the spiritual life and above all to use terminologies that sometimes offer striking contrasts (as we shall see) nevertheless the same goal lies at the end of both their journeys.

161

In fact, in spite of the vague notion that exists in some minds that these two mystics differ to the point of being irreconcilable, they are in fact so close to one another that they support and fulfil one another's doctrine all along the line. However, since St John of the Cross was so profoundly influenced by the Pseudo-Dionysius—whose doctrine had little effect on St Bernard,— and since the Carmelite is so absorbed in the treatment of interior prayer before all else, the two mystics seem to ascend the mountain by different ways. The paths, however, are only parallel, and when they get to the top of the mountain it is definitely the same high peak on which they both stand together. That is the reason for this study: to draw attention to the close similarity between the teaching of the two saints concerning the final perfection of the spiritual life on earth, transforming union. This comparison will show us, without any doubt, the otherwise obscure interrelation between their directions and counsels for ascending to that height. Without going into too many details, we hope at least to sketch out enough of the principles to enable the reader to work out the conclusions for himself, in his own personal reading of the two theologians.

This study should lead those who have not already done so to seek in the *Spiritual Canticle* and the *Living Flame of Love* the full flower and perfection of ideas essentially present in St Bernard, but not developed in all the fulness of their psychological and experimental implications. They will soon find out for themselves that the writings of St John of the Cross are capable of throwing a dazzling light on the cistercian school of the twelfth century, while St Bernard in turn provides a strong foundation of tradition for the thoughts developed by the mystics of Carmel.

Yet this study has far more importance than this. It is not aimed merely at satisfying the curiosity of the erudite. Transforming union is not and can never be only a matter of curiosity and idle speculation for contemplative monks. On the contrary, it is the very end to which we must tend, not as contemplatives but as Christians, for it is the end for which we were created in the image of God.[4]

St Bernard tells us that the divine image was implanted in our natures by God as an ineradicable reminder of our destiny to perfect union with him. *Et utique ad hoc auctor ipse Deus divinae insigne generositatis perpetuo voluit in anima conservari, ut semper haec in sese ex Verbo habeat, quo admoneatur semper, aut stare cum Verbo, aut redire si mota fuerit.*[5] And the full import of these words will be realized only when we consider the opening words of the Sermon in which they occur. These words are a challenge to Cistercians who may not yet have realized the possibilities of their vocation. St Bernard categorically sets forth his doctrine. *Docuimus* omnem animam, *licet oneratam peccatis, vitiis irretitam, captam illecebris... distentam negotiis, contractam timoribus... in sese posse advertere non modo unde respirare in spem veniae, in spem misericordiae queat,* sed etiam unde aspirare ad nuptias Verbi, cum Deo inire foedus societatis non trepidet, suave amoris jugum cum Rege ducere angelorum non vereatur.[6]

This magnificent passage sums up St Bernard's providential message to his world and to our own: the call to mystical union which did so much to fill Clairvaux with 'miraculous catches' of men.[7]

When St Bernard told his monks *qui perfecte diligit nupsit*[8] he was telling them to seek perfection in the mystical marriage: and St John of the Cross instructed the daughters of St Teresa that it was only when their souls were completely possessed by God who himself would 'keep in recollection all the energies, faculties and desires... both of spirit and sense so that all this harmony may employ all its energies in this love' that they would 'attain to a true fulfilment of the first commandment'.[9]

The reason for this is that the perfection of charity, as we shall see, is an absolutely pure love of God, and such a pure love, excluding every other affection and every shadow of fear or sorrow, inevitably brings with it fruition of the divine good. In fact, that fruition is of the very essence of a love that is totally pure. Such love is a participation in the divine life, and therefore a participation in beatitude.[10] St Bernard assures us that the moment we enter into possession of a love of God that is really pure we are snatched up in rapture to the 'third heaven' of union with the heavenly Father. *Ad tertium [gradum]* puritas rapit *qua ad invisibilia sublevamur.*[11] William of St Thierry clearly enunciates this principle of cistercian mystical theology. *Pro mensura profectus seu similitudinis sit mensura fruitionis quia nec similitudo potest esse nisi in fruitione eam afficiente nec fruitio nisi in similitudine eam afficiente.*[12]

In this remarkable statement William delivers up to us the secret of mystical marriage for the Cistercians: the perfection of the divine likeness, effected in the soul by a pure love of God. This, too, is clearly taught by St John of the Cross.[13]

1. The Subject of Transforming Union

HUMAN NATURE

Those who have only a superficial acquaintance with St Bernard and St John of the Cross might imagine that there was an irreconcilable difference in their view of human nature itself. And if the two saints hold radically different ideas about the nature of the subject to be transformed, how can we say that their doctrine on the transformation is the same?

It would seem at first sight that this difference was almost transparently evident. We have just alluded in passing to the fundamental doctrine of St Bernard: that there exists in human nature itself an ineradicable potentiality for divine union, which is the very image of God. St Bernard's stress on this makes the cistercian emphasis on the dignity of human nature *celsa creatura in capacitate majestatis*[14] something altogether unique in mystical and ascetical theology. Gilson calls it the 'bed-rock of all cistercian mysticism'.[15]

Because of this it is 'natural' for man to love God the author of nature above all things; *excellit in naturae donis affectio haec amoris, praesertim cum ad suum recurrit principium quod est Deus.*[16] What St Bernard means by saying that it is natural for us to love God is that our free will is destined, by its very nature, to reach out spontaneously for the only good which can be loved for its own sake: God. In other words, pure love, disinterested love, is part of our very nature itself in its integrity.

Man was created unselfish by nature. He was made to love God with a pure and perfect love. But it must be made clear that the perfection of this love of God could only be actualized in the soul by grace: what is natural, then, is the potentiality for receiving this love in us by our consent, our free

165

union with God's will. *Consentire enim salvari est.*[17] It is, indeed, above all in our freedom that we are made in the image of God, and it is this innate, indestructible freedom that is to be as it were the point of contact, the point of union of the soul with God.[18] Perhaps one could work out an analysis of St Bernard's psychology of mystical union in which this freedom would occupy the place given to the *apex mentis* by other mystics.

Unfortunately original sin has covered over this inborn capacity for divine union. It has twisted and perverted our freedom, bending it back upon itself so that God's grace cannot get into it, cannot establish contact with it. *Istiusmodi ergo curvae animae non possunt diligere Sponsum quoniam non sunt amicae Sponsi cum sint mundi.*[19] Cupidity robs us of our natural *rectitudo,* the uprightness that keeps our free will lifted heavenward with desire of God, and bends us to the earth. In this position we are free and yet our liberty is captive, the prisoner of its own lust for pleasure and honor.[20] We have lost our *libertas a peccato.* We cannot avoid sin: *non possumus non peccare.*[21] We have lost all taste for the things of God and our will is possessed by that wisdom of the flesh, *sapientia carnis* which is death.[22] *Quaerere et sapere quae sunt super terram curvitas animae est; et e regione, meditari ac desiderare quae sursum sunt, rectitudo.*[23]

Therefore the indispensable condition for Divine Union is the recovery of what is natural to us, our inborn freedom, our spontaneity, our *rectitudo.* And that is why the central problem of cistercian mysticism, paradoxical as it may seem, is the re-establishment of the *integrity of human nature.* The reason is now quite clear: for as soon as we are once more in a position to receive God's love in our souls there is no doubt that he, whose grace has already done the work of bringing us to our primitive condition of capacity for his friendship, will not delay in completing the good work which he has begun in us.[24]

Hence it is that St Bernard considers that the principal work of the cistercian ascesis, of the Rule of St Benedict, is to restore the proper balance and essential perfection of human nature first of all, in order that we may become fit subjects for the gifts of God's love that will eventually raise us to transforming union with him. *Jugo disciplinae insolentia morum domanda est quousque... bonum in se naturae quod superbiendo amiserat, obediendo recipiat.*[25]

This indicates what should be the attitude of the cistercian monk who gives himself wholeheartedly to the *labor obedientiae*[26] prescribed by St Benedict: he is not crushing his nature or destroying it but on the contrary he is perfecting it and raising it up from the mire of concupiscence that it may become a fit subject for the supernatural work that God has desired, from all eternity, to perform in our free souls. And that is why the yoke of obedience truly makes us free. So St Bernard concludes the tremendous opening paragraph of the eighty-third sermon on the Canticle, from which we have already quoted at length the invitation to the mystical marriage, with these words which sum up the entire program of the monk who aspires to transforming union. Let him remove the obstacles to God's action by purifying his nature of all that has corrupted it — that is to say, by keeping the Rule. *Tantum est ut curet naturae ingenuitatem vitae honestate servare, imo caeleste decus, quod sibi inest, dignis quibusdam studeat morum affectuumque venustare et decorare coloribus.*[27]

What a contrast to all this is the categorical statement of St John of the Cross: 'It is needful that in a certain manner the soul itself should be annihilated and destroyed... *by nature the soul is so weak and impure that it cannot receive all this* [namely all the blessings of mystical union with God].'[28] In fact, the cornerstone of the doctrine of this great Carmelite is precisely that since the infused love and knowledge which prepare the soul for divine union are infinitely above nature and cannot be apprehended by human nature, all natural operations must cease, must 'die' and be 'annihilated' before the mystical action of God can really take hold of us and gain complete possession of our souls. 'If, as I say, and as in truth is the case,' St John tells us, 'the soul receives this loving knowledge passively and after the super-natural manner of God and not after the manner of the natural soul it follows that in order to receive them this soul must be *quite annihilated in its natural operations.*'[29] In the same passage we read: 'It is clear that at this time [that is, when the soul is entering the mystical life] if the soul were not to abandon its natural procedure of active meditation it would not receive this blessing in other than a natural way. It would not in fact receive it, but would retain its natural act alone, *for the supernatural cannot be received in a natural way, nor can it have aught to do with it.*'

One could multiply such passages without end, but there is no need to do so. Anyone who has ever opened one of the works of the carmelite saint recognizes that this is a doctrine in which 'nature' has to be entirely consumed by grace and vanish from the scene, leaving nothing but the love of God.

And for this reason some are tempted to think that the teaching of St John of the Cross flatly contradicts the sort of thing that is taught by St Bernard. Yet surely, this is a strange confusion. A mere glance should tell us that if these two saints are really using the word 'nature' in the same sense and are really in such categorical opposition to one another it would be hard to deny that one or the other of them must be preaching a grave error. How could they both be orthodox, and differ so widely on a point so fundamental?

And if a glance could tell us this much, the same glance should also tell us that St John does not literally mean that our souls must be annihilated before they can receive the fulness of the divine love, for if they no longer have any ex-istence in any sense whatever, the subject of transforming union has ceased to be, and there is nothing left to transform. In any case we must observe that whenever St John of the Cross speaks of the 'annihilation' of the soul he is always careful to qualify it as a metaphor and even to give a full explanation of it. Finally, however, the easiest way to loose this particular knot is to cut it with one stroke, by reminding the reader that St Bernard himself uses the very same language as St John of the Cross, with the same qualifications, when he comes to speak of the higher states of union: *Te enim* quodammodo perdere... *a teipso exinaniri et* paene annullari *coelestis est conversationis et non humanae affectionis.*[30]

Nevertheless, there is still the difficulty of an apparent contradiction in two categorically opposed statements of the two saints. Saint Bernard sees man as *celsa creatura in capacitate majestatis* and St John of the Cross asserts '*by nature* the soul is so weak and impure that it cannot receive [mystical graces]'. In other words St Bernard says we have a natural capacity for divine union and St John says we have a natural incapacity for it. One says our nature fits us to love God and the other that it makes us radically incapable of his love, and stands in opposition to it.

The answer of course is simple. St Bernard is talking about nature in its essential definition, in itself. St John is talking about nature as it finds itself, *per accidens,* in its present, actual, fallen condition.

Yet this confusion is possible and even great minds have fallen into it, to some extent. After all, is it not the same problem which Fr Rousselot thought he had discovered in St Bernard himself?[31] He accused the Abbot of Clairvaux of making 'pure love' grow out of cupidity, and all of one piece with it. We refer the reader to Professor Gilson's brilliant analysis of the question which need not detain us here, except to recall to our minds the truth that transforming union cannot consist in the sublimation of an essentially dcordinate

and vicious love. It is our natural obediential potency to love
God that is raised to these supernatural heights by the action
of the Word, but that natural love must not be confused
with 'cupidity' or with the self-love that has become 'natural'
to us in a purely relative sense since the fall. The perfection
of charity can never be achieved by a mere intensification of
an essentially selfish love because charity and self-love, in St
Bernard's sense, are opposed by their very nature. They
point in different directions. They have essentially contradictory objects. *Huic* [*sc. cupiditati, voluntati propriae*]
contraria est recte fronte charitas quae Deus est.[32]

On the other hand, if there is in human nature no capacity, in any sense, for union with God, how can St John of the
Cross raise it to union with him? How can he explain the fact
that a human soul can undergo a transforming for which it
has absolutely no potentiality whatever? The answer is that
he does not believe such a thing, and on the contrary he
teaches the radical potentiality of the human soul for divine
union, its essential need for mystical marriage to God with
an even more powerful emphasis than St Bernard himself.
Read, for example, the passage of the *Living Flame* in
which the carmelite doctor describes the 'yearnings of the
caverns of the soul' that is of the *natural faculties,* intellect,
memory and will, for divine union.

'These caverns are the faculties of the soul... of which the
depth is proportionate *to their capacity for great blessings
for they can be filled with nothing less than the infinite.* By
considering what they suffer when they are empty we can
realize in some measure the greatness of their joy and their
delight when they are filled with God.... When they are
empty and clean the hunger and thirst and yearning of their
spiritual sense become intolerable; for as the capacities of
these caverns are deep, their pain is deep likewise, as is also
the *food which they lack, which, as I say, is God.* [33] And in
this very passage where he has given us such a striking

testimonial of the capacity of human nature for divine love, the saint also goes on to give us one of those characteristic sentences in which we clearly see his manner of using the word 'nature'. 'For', he says, 'when the spiritual appetite is empty and purged from every creature and from every creature affection, and *its natural temper is lost*[34] and it has become attempered to the Divine and its emptiness is disposed to be filled... then the suffering caused by this emptiness is worse than death.'

For St John of the Cross, 'natural activity' since the fall, dominated and guided by the senses is nothing else but St Bernard's *curvatura,* the twisting and bending of our true nature upon itself. Therefore for both the saints, the only way to dispose ourselves for the perfect love of God is to 'draw the soul away and free it from the yoke and slavery of the weak operation of its own capacity, which is the captivity, of Egypt, where all is little more than gathering straw to make bricks... [let the soul go forth] from the limits and the slavery of the operation of the senses [which is to say from its scant understanding, its lowly perception, and its miserable loving and liking] so that God may give it the sweet manna....'[35]

The difference between the way this is expressed in the works of the cistercian and carmelite doctors is simply the difference in their points of view. St John tends to emphasize the cognitive aspect of the union with God by love and his ascesis directs its attention first of all to rectifying the radical incapacity of our faculties for God as long as they come under that domination of sense activity that is 'natural' to us.

St Bernard, on the other hand, sees the problem from the angle of the unworthy object which has captivated the will and dragged it down to its own level. It follows from this variation in points of view that carmelite mysticism will seek first of all to liberate the soul from attachment to 'natural' modes of knowing and loving which are incapable of arriv-

ing at God, and the Cistercians seek to detach the intellect
and will from baser things which keep them from rising to
God. St Bernard looks at the object to be rejected, St John
considers the preoccupation of the faculties. St Bernard re-
moves the object and thus liberates the faculties: St John
'blacks out' the faculties and thus frees them both from the
object and from the danger of becoming interested in a
seemingly worthy object. And his position never permits us
to forget that 'the clearer and more manifest are divine
things in themselves, the darker and more hidden are they to
the soul naturally; just as, the clearer is the light the more it
blinds and darkens the pupil of the owl.... In the same way
when this divine light of contemplation assails the soul
which is not yet wholly enlightened it causes spiritual
darkness in it....'[36] It is for this reason that St John insists
that the soul must reject even the most spiritual visions or
apprehensions even of God himself under some created form
for 'these [intellectual] visions, inasmuch as they are of
creatures with whom God has no proportion or essential
conformity, *cannot serve the understanding as a proximate
means of union with God.* And thus the soul must conduct
itself in a purely negative way concerning them... in order
that it may progress by the proximate means, namely by
faith'.[37]

This, incidentally, is one of the many points on which St
Bernard and St John of the Cross agree perfectly. The Abbot
of Clairvaux sounded the same note at the beginning of his
commentary on the Canticle of Canticles: *Merito proinde vi-
siones et somnia non recipio, figuras et aenigmata nolo; ip-
sas quoque angelicas fastidio species. Quippe et ipsos longe
superat Jesus meus specie sua et pulchritudine sua.*'[38] And
for those who ignore the profound and solid christological
foundations of the mysticism of St John of the Cross, we can
ring the echo of that cry from the rocks of Mount Carmel.
'He that would now inquire [directly] of God or seek any vi-

sion or revelation,' says St John of the Cross, 'would not only be acting foolishly but would be committing an offence against God *by not setting his eyes altogether upon Christ and seeking no new thing or aught beside....* For in giving us, as he did, his Son, who is his Word... he spake to us all together, once and for all, in this single Word, and he has no occasion to speak further.'[39]

2. The Ontology of the Transformation

St Bernard's ontology of transforming union is simply an elaboration of a symbol from St Paul—a symbol which has also become fundamental to the monastic life: the change of garments, the putting off of the old man and the putting on of the new *qui secundum Deum creatus est in justitia et sanctitate veritatis.*[40]

The Abbot of Clairvaux is very careful to explain that the human nature, the substance which underlies the two 'garments' does not itself change. The mystical *excessus* does not rob the soul of its substance, and there is no confusion of substances between the soul and God. In a passage of considerable metaphysical subtlety St Bernard defines the difference between the union of the Father and the Son and the union of the soul with God, between the *consubstantiale* and the *consentibile*, between the *unum* and the *unus*. And he sums it up in a sentence that definitely excludes every possibility of pantheism: *Quid tam distans a se quam unitas plurium et unius?*[41] What a difference between the union of persons in one Nature and a union of natures in a consent of wills. In fact, this is a point on which St Bernard is so cautious that St John of the Cross will go somewhat beyond the limits the great Cistercian imposed upon his language, as we shall see below.

Therefore the change that takes place is accidental and not substantial. Instead of the substance of the soul being destroyed to give place to the substance of God, transforming union means the acquisition of an accidental form. But although this new form is only an accident, it endows the soul with a participation in the substantial life of God, a

174

participation so close that the soul takes to itself the very perfections of God himself and lives by his life. 'Impossible to unite more closely two subjects that must needs remain substantially distinct', says Gilson. And without passing on to any further discussion that would involve us in unnecessary subtleties, we need only sum up the soul's new situation in the concise words of this same author:

> It [the soul] subsists, but now it is to be considered as a substance which, although irreducibly distinct from that of God, had no other function than to be the bearer of the Divine likeness. This likeness is its 'form'; the more it is enveloped by this form, as it is here below by charity and is destined to be the more so in glory, so much the more does it become indistinguishable from God. And so much the more is it itself. Of man, then, it may be said that he tends in effect, by way of love, to make himself invisible; for this image of God will never be fully itself till nothing is any longer to be seen in it save only God: *et tunc erit omnia in omnibus Deus*.[42]

Underlying these innocent words is something that amounts to a problem of the first magnitude which we will name without discussing it. If man is created for the supernatural end of union with God, natural perfection will never be perfect enough to fulfil his true destiny. It will never suffice for him to be nothing more than a man. As long as he is only a man, he is not yet what he was made to be. Therefore in some sense he is not yet a man. He can only truly become what God intends him to become, by being united to God, by becoming God. He is not really a man, then, until he is lost in God, or (as St John of the Cross would say) until his humanity has been 'annihilated'. His real identity will never be found merely in human nature. You can call him a rational animal until you get blue in the face and you will never have said the one important thing about him that will tell you who he really is.... As long as he is nothing but a rational animal he will end up in hell, that is in the complete frustration of his whole human nature in all its capacities.

That is why a mystic like St Bernard or St John of the Cross will be practically forced to look for man's true identity in this accidental form which is charity, the divine likeness, the supernatural perfection which integrates our nature and reveals its meaning and fulfils its ultimate supernatural destiny, and which alone really makes us what God intends us to be.

And this evidently accounts for the quotation marks with which M. Gilson surrounded the word 'form' in the passage we have just cited.

But what is even more interesting is that St Bernard shows that human nature cannot just exist all alone in a moral vacuum. If it does not reach its supernatural perfection under the action of charity, it will take on another identity which will be stamped upon it by another accidental form. It will work out its destiny, if not in the garments of charity, then in those of corruption. No created substance, in fact, reaches perfection all by itself: it must be perfected and completed by its accidents, and if man's nature does not invest itself in the character woven for it by virtuous operations, it will necessarily rot in the deformity imposed on it by corrupt ones. This is the significance of the psychological principles which St Bernard enunciates in *De gratia et libero arbitrio*.[43] And they are of cardinal importance. They show clearly that although nature cannot be said without contradiction to demand grace as its due, nevertheless it requires grace to reach the end for which it was created. There could be no more cogent expression of our almost infinite poverty. We have been created essentially beggars, and beggars in a sense which does not apply to the whole range of creation below us!

We briefly recall the theme of the *De gratia et libero arbitrio*. St Bernard distinguishes between three kinds of liberty: *liberum arbitrium* or the radical indetermination of the will, proper to our nature and inseparable from it. This is freedom from necessity, from compulsion; it is a tremendous dignity, no doubt, but it does not comport anything more than this negative character. It does not endow us with the ability to make choices that are invariably good, it only gives us the power to make choices, on our own initiative. In order to make consistently right choices we must have a higher freedom, freedom from sin, and this *liberum consilium* belongs not to nature but to grace. But this liberty does not guarantee that the choice of good over evil will always be easy and pleasant to us: on the contrary it may cost us bitter suffering to do what we know to be right, until we have a third liberty, *libertas a miseria* which is proper to heaven and to glory and is only found on earth in the transforming union or in the mystical *excessus*. *Fatendum est eos qui per excessum contemplationis rapti quandoque in spiritu, quantulumcunque de supernae felicitatis dulcedine degustare sufficiunt, toties esse liberos a miseria quoties sic excedunt.*[44] Such ones will find the highest joy in all things even in suffering.[45]

Hence it is evident that our natural liberty alone is practically helpless without the liberty of grace. We make choices, yes: but what choices! *Velle siquidem inest nobis ex libero arbitrio, non enim posse quod volumus. Non dico velle bonum aut velle malum, sed tantum velle.*[46]

St Bernard therefore considers our free will as a neutral factor, a potentiality waiting to be qualified as either good or evil by the union with good or evil from outside itself.

Velle etenim bonum profectus est, velle malum defectus. Velle vero simpliciter ipsum est quod vel proficit vel deficit. Porro ipsum ut esset creans gratia fecit (the saint would have us remember that creation itself is a free gift of God and a grace in the broad sense) *ut proficiat, salvans gratia facit; ut deficiat, ipsum se dejecit.*[47]

Then, in order to drive home the point that by ourselves

we are helpless and that our own nature alone cannot achieve its supernatural destiny St Bernard tells us in one of the strongest passages he ever wrote:

Creati quippe quodammodo nostri in liberam volun-tatem, quasi Dei efficimur per bonam voluntatem. Porro bonam facit qui liberam fecit; et ad hoc bonam ut simus in-itium aliquod creaturae ejus: quoniam expedit profecto nobis omnino non fuisse quam nostros permanere. *Nam qui voluerunt sui esse, utique sicut dii... facti sunt* non tantum jam sui sed et diaboli.[48]

Human nature then is an essential nakedness waiting to be clothed with a form that will fulfil its eternal destiny. It has in its hands the capacity to choose between glory and shame — and since the fall that capacity is in the hands of the blind! More than that, we are born clothed in a disfigure-ment that makes the choice of our eternal good impossible.

We have considered this form of disfigurement already as the soul's *curvatura*. It is now time to discuss it in a little more detail, for the purpose of showing precisely what this form is, and what part it plays in the doctrines of St Bernard and St John of the Cross.

This form, this false nature is what St Bernard calls the *proprium* and what St John of the Cross simply refers to as our nature. He can afford to do so, because in our actual condition the operations of our natural faculties are govern-ed and determined by the disfigurement imposed on our will by selfishness, cupidity. And we are all forced to realize this even when we are in the state of sanctifying grace and our soul has been clothed in the power of a freedom that is higher than nature; even then our faculties are still subject to the tyranny of habits that are left over from the condition of sin, and it is a lifetime of labor to get rid of all the shreds of the old man's garments clinging to our skin.

Ask St Bernard what this *proprium* is, and ask St John of the Cross what he means by 'nature' and you will get the same answer. *Voluntatem dico propriam,* says St Bernard, *quae non est communis cum Deo et hominibus, sed nostra tantum: quando quod volumus, non ad honorem Dei, non ad utilitatem fratrum, sed propter nosmetipsos facimus, non intendentes placere Deo et prodesse fratribus* sed satisfacere propriis motibus animorum.[49] And the great carmelite theologian tells us, in the same words, that St Paul's *animalis homo*[50] means 'the man that *still lives according to natural desires and pleasures'.*[51] The life of the 'old man' is described for us by the saint in another passage.[52] It is nothing but the familiar use which tradition has given to this term ever since the apostles. This life is 'the employment of the faculties—memory, understanding and will—and the use and occupation of them in the things of the world, and the occupation of the desires in the pleasure afforded by created things'. So far from being common to the soul and God, this 'natural desire' must be killed, destroyed, before the soul can arrive at perfect union with God in charity. The only thing lacking in St John of the Cross is St Bernard's *term* 'common will' and the explicit reference to the good of one's neighbor proper to a cenobitic ascesis.

The conclusion is clear: this false 'form', 'clothing' the soul, obscures its 'naked' natural dignity and freedom which therefore cannot take on the supernatural form of divine likeness for which it is destined by God. The two saints both use the same language on this point also. St John of the Cross says 'the affections which the soul has for creature are pure darkness in the eyes of God and when the soul is *clothed* in these affections it has no capacity for being enlightened and possessed by the pure and simple light of God'.[53] This at once recalls the famous passage in the eighty second sermon on the Canticle of Canticles, in which St Bernard applies the words of the Psalmist, *sicut diploide confusione sua,*[54] to the fall of man. *Quia ergo naturae ingenuitatem morum probitate defensare neglexit, justo auctoris judicio factum est,*

*non quidem ut libertate propria nudaretur, sed tamen
superindueretur* [necessitate] sicut diploide confusione sua.[55]
This double cloak is nothing else than the subjection of the
free will to creatures which are inferior to it. Indeed, the
false form which Eve took on by her sin was a likeness to
creatures as well as an unlikeness to God. *Non est tua, o
mulier, ista suavitas, ista delectatio... Quid tu animae tuae
aliam formam, imo deformitatem imprimis? Enimvero quod
delectat habere id etiam perdere timet:* et timor color est. Is
libertatem dum tingit, tegit, et eam nihilominus sibi reddit
dissimilem?[56]

The special cast of the psychological considerations about
timor, fear, is proper to the cistercian context but the
underlying truth is pure John of the Cross. And the
carmelite saint tells us exactly the same thing: 'The affection
and attachment which the soul has for creatures renders it
like to these creatures.... And thus he that loves a creature
becomes as low as is that creature and in some ways lower;
for love not only makes the lover equal to the object of his
love but even subjects him to it. Wherefore in the same way
it comes to pass that the soul that loves anything else
becomes incapable of pure union with God and transformation in him. For the low estate of the creature is much less
capable of union with the high estate of the Creator than is
darkness with light.'[57]

Both saints agree that the love of creatures for the sake of
the pleasure they give to ourselves covers the soul with a
form or rather a deformity, an unlikeness to God. And when
such a soul comes into contact with the light of God's truth,
and sees this horrible deformity which is in us all, both saints
agree again that the only result can be tremendous interior
suffering.[58] This is St John of the Cross' Dark Night — all the
elements of which are present in St Bernard, though in an
undeveloped state.

It would consume too much paper to go into all the details

of the similarity in thought and language between the two mystics all along the line. Let us pass over all that in order to pause on one very revealing fact. It is this.

The resemblance between St John of the Cross and St Bernard of Clairvaux, in spite of their somewhat different personal points of view, is so close and so fundamental that the psychological apparatus devised by the Abbot of Clairvaux in the *De gratia et libero arbitrio* gives us the surest vindication of St John's doctrine of 'emptiness' and 'annihilation' and 'night' and, indeed, makes it thoroughly understandable.

If our present condition is as St Bernard describes it—a 'naked' freedom covered over by the deformity of a false nature which is servitude to creatures, self-love, and if that 'naked' soul was created to be clothed with another form, a supernatural life which is the likeness to God, then it follows that the only way to prepare it for the reception of the new form is to strip it of the old and reduce it to its primitive natural indetermination and 'nakedness' in order to start again to clothe it with an altogether new life. And since, as both agree, this 'false nature'—Gilson calls it 'the illusory personality of self-will'[59]—is woven about us by the activity of our faculties reaching out in concupiscence towards the created world, then the process of stripping it off must mean nothing else but the 'darkening' and 'starving' of these faculties with respect to all these created satisfactions which raise an obstacle to the light of God. In fact, the operations of the faculties with respect to natural goods will be so reduced that at a given moment the soul will be seemingly left with nothing but its 'naked' indeterminate freedom, hanging as it were in a void between heaven and earth. This is the term of the painful process by which the old, false nature is literally consumed in the flames of infused love.[60]

> Everything becomes insufficient for this soul; it finds no pleasure either in heaven or on earth; it is filled with griefs even unto darkness.... What the soul here endures

is affliction and suffering without the consolation of a certain hope of any light and spiritual good.... [Then all the energies and faculties of the soul are wounded with burning love] yet without the possession and satisfaction thereof, in darkness and in doubt. They will then doubtless be suffering hunger like the dogs of which David speaks as running about the city; finding no satisfaction in this love they keep howling and groaning. [And yet] in the midst of these dark and loving afflictions the soul feels within itself a certain companionship and strength which bears it company and strengthens it.[61]

St Bernard tells us the same thing at least in principle, although one would not dare say he was definitely describing the same state, when he writes: *Trahitur in desperationem pro tanto malo sed revocatur in spem a tanto bono. Inde est ut quo sibi plus displicet in malo quod in se videt, eo se ardentius ad bonum, quod aeque in se conspicit, trahat.*[62]

The reader will no doubt have observed that so far all that has been said applies to the ontology of sanctifying grace itself. That is true, and it must be so because transforming union develops logically and harmoniously from the life of grace of which it is the perfection and the fulfilment. We have been describing a process which begins not with some extraordinary illumination but with the grace of baptism. Nevertheless, there are certain special features about the mystical marriage which is the end of this supernatural growth of the soul.

The new 'form' of divine life has begun to live in the soul as soon as it is in sanctifying grace. But all traces of the old form are not yet expelled by any means. On the contrary, below transforming union the christian soul will always be a battleground between those two contrary forms. If we are in the state of grace, the old form is indeed gone, but our faculties, guided by sense appetites, will always be acting as spies and allies of the enemy, and will always be working within us to break down the resistance of grace and open the way for the old deformity's return. And so the Christian who follows his 'nature' in St John of the Cross' sense, even though he may be in a state of grace, is living in fact according to the 'old man', the *animalis homo* and his operations are not in harmony with his new supernatural life but with the old. That is why St John of the Cross tends to speak of anyone who retains any attachment to creatures, whether mortally sinful or not, as being still possessed by the old form. Practically speaking, that is just the case. And that is why the carmelite saint usually does not speak of a soul as being possessed by the new divine life *until the life of grace has reached its final peak of perfection on earth by transforming union.* For St John of the Cross that means impeccability[63] as well as everything that is implied by St Bernard's *libertas a miseria.*

The particular feature that makes transforming union different from every lower state in the spiritual life is that in it the soul has not only given itself entirely to God, but God has given himself to the soul as completely as the Infinite can give himself to a finite being outside the beatific vision. This sets the final seal upon the 'total transformation of the soul in the Beloved'.[64] 'On either side there is made surrender by total possession of one to the other in consummate union of love... wherein the soul is made Divine and becomes God by participation in so far as may be in this life.'[65] St Bernard agrees: *Sic affici deificari est.*[66]

It may be quite correct for any man in the state of grace to say 'I live, now not I but Christ liveth in me'.[67] But that statement will never achieve its full significance short of a permanent and total transformation in which it becomes literally true to say that the soul has no other life than the life of Christ. St Bernard saw this, and that was why his youthful treatment of the mystical marriage was troubled with an uncertainty. It was evident to him that the marriage had to be something permanent and that it had to involve such a total surrender of the lover to the Beloved that the soul would vanish into God and live by his life only. Could such a union be achieved on earth?

With the same uncompromising accents as St John of the Cross, St Bernard described the transforming union in these terms:

> Quomodo stilla aquae modica, multo infuso vino deficere a se tota videtur, dum et saporem vini induit et colorem; et quomodo ferrum ignitum et candens igni simillimum fit, pristina propriaque forma exutum; et quomodo solis luce perfusus aer in eamdem luminis claritatem, adeo ut non tam illuminatus quam ipsum lumen esse videatur: *sic omnem tunc in sanctis humanam affectionem quodam ineffabili modo necesse erit a semetipsa liquescere atque in Dei penitus transfundi voluntatem.*[68]

No need to stop and comment on the well-known traditional symbols, or on the metaphysical language which has already been sufficiently discussed. No need either to point out how the saint is here using St John of the Cross' own language: 'every *human affection* must melt away....'[69]

What is important is the saint's concern about the fact that as far as he was aware, at the time, this transformation did not take place permanently in this life. Indeed it lasts only a short time *modicum, hora videlicet quasi dimidia, silentio facto in coelo,*[70] and then the cares of this life reclaim possession of the soul. *Heu, redire in se, recidere in sua compellitur.*[71] It did not seem to St Bernard in those days that the soul could arrive at permanent *libertas a miseria* before entering into glory. The reason he gave was that as long as the soul was united to a body that was not completely subjected to it by being spiritualized, it would be subject to the necessities of the body and therefore it would be compelled in spite of itself to take some thought for itself and to look after its own interests. And thus its love could not yet rest completely in God in that pure union in which the soul would live entirely for and by him alone.[72]

To the question when this transforming union would be perfect, he answers: *Ego puto non sane ante perfectum iri: Diliges Dominum Deum tuum ex toto corde tuo et ex tota anima tua, et ex tota virtute tua, quousque ipsum cor cogitare jam non cogatur de corpore, et anima eidem in hoc statu vivificando et sensificando intendere desinat, et virtus ejusdem, relevata molestiis,* in Dei potentia roboretur.[73]

Among the many interesting points in this passage we select the last four words which are those that most concern us here. They prove how much St Bernard demanded of the mystical marriage. It is not enough that the soul should possess a supernatural life as a habit from which proceed from time to time certain more or less supernatural acts, mingled with many purely natural acts whose overwhelming majority stamps our everyday life with their own imperfect character. It was not even enough that grace should gain such mastery over us that every rebellious movement of nature be conquered and our rebellious natural affections be kept under constant control: that is still only *libertas consilii, libertas a peccato.* But in transforming union the soul must literally live by God. And that would have to mean among other things that all its operations should take their rise not in human nature aided by ordinary grace, but in the nature of God, and starting from him they should also terminate in him. *Alioquin quomodo omnia in omnibus erit Deus, si de homine in homine quidquam supererit?*[74]

So far the image of the change of garments has served our turn. Now it can hardly do so any longer. It is too indefinite because it is too static. What we are describing is a marriage of two wills in which the human will, by a perfect purity of love for God is transformed into the divine will, and as a result all the other faculties of the soul undergo the same transformation and become divinized.

According to St Bernard this must follow immediately upon the elimination of all self-will from the human soul. As soon as our love is absolutely pure, as soon as we have renounced all other affections, all human affections, the marriage with the divine will is complete because he is charity—that is, he is infinitely pure love and what is more *prior dilexit nos*,[75] he has first loved us and it is his love that has brought us to this purity in order to unite us to himself.

> Talis conformitas maritat animam Verbo, cum cui videlicet similis est per naturam [the image] similem nihilominus ipsi se exhibet per voluntatem, diligens sicut dilecta est. Ergo si perfecte diligit, nupsit.... Merito cunctis renuntians affectionibus aliis soli et tota incumbit amori, quae ipsi respondere amore habet in redhibendo amore.... Proptera ut dixi, sic amare nupsisse est: *quoniam non potest sic diligere et parum dilecta esse,* ut in consensu duorum integrum stet perfectumque connubium. Nisi quis dubitet, animam a Verbo et prius amari et plus.[76]

Now from the moment that the likeness between the soul and the Word is reestablished everything that belongs to the Word belongs to the soul. This too follows from the absolute purity of their love: for there is no trace left of that *proprium* which was the root of exclusiveness and division, *quippe quibus omnia communia sunt, nil proprium, nil a se divisum habentes.*[77] St John of the Cross uses the same words, at the same time showing us how and why it is that the pure love of God desires us to be as perfect as he is perfect, in order that we may share all his infinite perfections: 'God,' he says, 'is pleased with naught save love.... He desires nothing for Himself, since He has no need of anything; and thus, if anything pleases Him it is that the soul may be exalted; and since there is no way wherein He can exalt it so much as by making it equal with Himself, for that reason alone He is pleased when the soul loves Him. For the property of love is to make the lover equal with the object of his love.[78] Wherefore since this love is now perfect the soul is called Bride of the Son of God, *which signifies equality with Him; in the which equality of friendship all the things of both are common to both.'*[79]

What happens therefore is that the divine nature becomes ours; the divine perfections become ours; the life of God becomes our life. His truth, his goodness, his love, his might not only entirely possess the substance of our souls but overflow into our faculties so that it is God himself that moves them and not we ourselves. So great then are the joy and power and perfection of the soul that it feels itself to be almost in the light of glory from which, indeed, it is only divided by 'a slender web'.[80]

St John of the Cross describes this magnificent language at the beginning of the *Living Flame of Love.*

> This flame of love is the Spirit of its Spouse — that is, the Holy Spirit.... The soul that is in the state of transformation of love may be said to be, in its ordinary habit, [i.e., habitually, constantly, uninterruptedly] like to the log of wood which is continually assailed by fire; and the acts of this soul are the flame that arises from the fire of love: the more intense is the fire of union, the more vehemently does the flame issue forth. In this flame the acts of the will are united and rise upwards, being carried away and absorbed in the flame of the Holy Spirit even as the angel rose upward to God in the flame of the sacrifice of Manue.[81] In this state therefore *the soul can perform no acts but it is the Holy Spirit that performs them; wherefore all its acts are divine, since it is impelled and moved to them by God.* Hence it seems to the soul that whensoever this flame breaks forth, causing it to love with a divine temper and sweetness, it is granting it eternal life, since *it is raising it to the operation of God in God.* [82]

Under the complete domination of the Holy Ghost the soul no longer knows objects merely in the natural way, through the knowledge afforded by the senses, although it goes through its ordinary life doing all things not only well but with a consummate perfection. Far from being trance-like and strange, all the outward actions of such souls are carried out with such effectiveness and so smoothly as to be absolutely free from any deordination or lack of balance.[83] All the soul sees or understands, it sees and understands in God by the light of his own truth, for 'the natural light of the soul is united to the supernatural light of God and *the supernatural light alone shines*'[84] It is the same with the will which 'being united with divine love no longer loves with its natural strength after a lowly manner, but with strength and purity from the Holy Spirit'.[85]

All these statements of the carmelite doctor are echoes of St Bernard's *in potentia Dei roboretur*,[86] *osculum... est infusio gaudiorum, revelatio secretorum,* mira quaedam et quodammodo indiscreta commixtio superni luminis et illuminatae mentis,[87] for this kiss is the Holy Spirit himself, *in quo sibi [sponsae] et Filius reveletur et Pater... qui Patris Filiique imperturbabilis pax est, gluten firmum, indivisibilis unitas.*[88] What meaning these saints have found in the Apostle's *Qui adhaeret Domino unus Spiritus est.*[89]

3. Spiritual Betrothal and Marriage

Characteristic of the mystical doctrine of St John of the Cross is the emphatic distinction he makes between the spiritual betrothal and spiritual marriage, introducing as it were two degrees into transforming union. And it is only in the second of these that the transformation has really taken place. Perhaps there is no other mystical writer who has ever set such high standards in the spiritual life as St John of the Cross. Nevertheless, as Fr Garrigou Lagrange points out, his restriction of the unitive life to the ways of mystical contemplation is so truly traditional that the Carmelite 'agrees perfectly with St Augustine, Dionysius, St Thomas Aquinas and also with St Bernard, St Bonaventure and the true disciples of these masters'.[90] What is peculiar to St John of the Cross is that he also says that the unitive life really begins with the spiritual betrothal, which is an inferior degree of transforming union or more properly the immediate prelude to true transforming union.[91] In that case for him the unitive life means not only mystical union but a high degree of mystical union, and according to the plan of the *Spiritual Canticle* the terrible trials of the dark night of the soul, which very few have to go through,[92] are absolutely necessary before one can enter spiritual betrothal with God. And so spiritual betrothal must be carefully distinguished from the period of spiritual consolation which marks the state of progressives or proficients who are mystics and have passed through the night of the senses in which infused contemplation begins.[93]

When St John tells us that these proficients, because of their 'weakness' and 'imperfection' cannot prevent themselves from falling into raptures and ecstasies,[94]and

189

when on the other hand the night of the senses is described as a grace given to 'beginners'[95] we begin to realize that St John of the Cross' degrees of prayer are lofty indeed. However, we must remember that they are exclusively degrees of *prayer*. It does not necessarily follow from the absence of the unitive way of prayer that a soul is not in the unitive way in a broad sense.[96] The carmelite school today interprets St John of the Cross and St Teresa in the sense that mystical union is absolutely necessary if a soul is to be perfect in all the integral wholeness of perfection: but it is not essential to the bare substance of perfection.[97]

But the mystical marriage is something so sublime and so completely above every human mode in the spiritual life that it is in a sense beyond all degrees. Indeed, the soul has been transformed into God in whom all degrees have disappeared. So:

> this marriage is without comparison far greater than the spiritual betrothal, because it is a total transformation in the Beloved wherein on either side there is made surrender by total possession of the one to the other... the soul is made divine and becomes God by participation... this estate is never attained without confirmation in grace... this is the loftiest estate which in this life is attainable... there are two natures in one spirit and love... even as when the light of a candle is united with that of the sun so that that which shines is not the candle itself, but the sun which has absorbed the other lights in itself... [the soul] has gone out from all that is temporal and all that is natural and from all spiritual manners and modes and affections, and having left behind and forgotten all temptations, disturbances, griefs, anxiety and cares is transformed in this lofty embrace.[98]

Nevertheless, at first sight it is hard to see the precise difference between marriage and betrothal, since betrothal is described by St John of the Cross in such exalted terms that it reminds us of the usual descriptions of mystical marriage. Here are the terms which he applies to betrothal:

> When the soul has attained to such purity in itself and in its faculties that the will is well purged of other strange tastes and desires according to its lower and higher parts[99] and when it has given its consent to God with respect to all this, and the *will of the soul and the will of God are as one in a free consent of their own*, then it has attained to the possession of God through grace of will, in so far as can be by means of will and grace.[100]

The sense of these expressions 'grace of will', 'by will and grace' is that betrothal is the highest state attainable by the will aided by grace by the will still living and working outside of God. When transforming union has taken place the situation is quite different: for then our will not only works *with* God's will in perfect harmony and concord, but the union has transformed one into the other and the two are identical. When the saint says betrothal is the highest union attained 'by the will and grace' he means in effect it is the highest union conceivable to those who have not passed beyond. Mystical marriage transcends language entirely. Betrothal can still be fitted in some measure into human words. Continuing the same passage we read of betrothal that:

> this [union] signifies that God has given it, through its own consent, His true and entire consent which comes through His grace.[101] And this is the lofty state of spiritual betrothal of the soul with the Word, wherein the Spouse grants the soul great favors, and visits it most lovingly and frequently, wherein the soul receives great favors and delights.[102]

Elsewhere this union of spiritual betrothal is described as 'the inner cellar of love' in which the soul and God 'are united through the communication of Himself to her...and

the communication of herself to Him when she surrendered
herself to Him indeed and wholly, without reserving aught
for herself or for another and declaring herself His forever...
and God communicated to her His love and His secrets....
God communicates to the soul this science [mystical
theology] and knowledge in the love wherewith He communicates Himself to her... the soul is immersed in God and
surrenders itself most willingly and with great sweetness to
Him.'[103] All these statements are very confusing since they
seem to be a description of mystical marriage even in St
John's own terms, and the distinction between the two states
seems to vanish altogether when he goes on to declare:

> God grants it in the said union [betrothal] the purity and
> perfection that are necessary for this [immersion in God]
> for inasmuch as He *transforms the soul into Himself*, He
> makes it to be wholly His and empties it of all it possessed
> and that was alien from God. Wherefore the soul is in-
> deed completely given up to God, reserving naught, not
> only according to its will, but also according to its works
> *even as God has given Himself freely to the soul.*[104]

The trouble with this passage of St John of the Cross is
that it occurs in a part of the *Spiritual Canticle* which is really concerned with mystical *marriage*.[105] This particular stanza (xxvii) harks back to betrothal, which was the subject of
stanzas fourteen to twenty two. But the saint seems to have
become so well warmed to his new subject of the perfect
transforming union that he attributes its characteristics to
betrothal. Nevertheless, he uses the word betrothal
(desposorio) and not marriage *(matrimonio)* so that we cannot mistake his intention to discuss the former rather than
transforming union. Whatever the solution of this particular
difficulty may be, and even if we allow that St John of the
Cross intended the remark about actual transformation to
be taken in a relative or incomplete sense, the description of

spiritual betrothal is clearly in his text, and we single out its main elements.

In the first place the soul has now been perfectly purified. It has passed through the dark night of the soul, it is *pura y purgada;* no question of any creature attachments or of the slightest imperfection. Its love for God is unmixed with the slightest shadow of selfishness. It is absolutely pure in the traditional christian sense of St Bernard and the Fathers, that it desires to possess God alone; or rather, by its very purity, it already does possess God alone having left all else for him. There can be no question here of the 'pure love' of the Quietists which rejects even the desire to possess God as selfish and therefore 'impure'. In actual fact such a conception of pure love is itself pitiably low in comparison with the ardent love of a St John of the Cross or a St Bernard. We need only remind the Quietists, with Gilson,[106] that the very fact that they had time to spend in airy speculations, trying to work out an abstract formula of the purest possible love, and composing statements about wanting to love God even without ever possessing him, showed that they were not in fact possessed by that Love which is God himself and the possession of whom drives every other thought, and *a fortiori* all idle, abstract considerations, out of the mind.

As a consequence of its purity, then, the soul that has reached spiritual betrothal has also reached the perfection of union with God's will. It has nothing left to give him, and by that very fact nothing to refuse. It has given all, and without return.

God, in his turn, frequently visits the soul with exquisite favors and intimate contacts with his own divine substance inflaming the mind and will with a knowledge and love that belong to heaven rather than earth and far transcend in purity the visions and raptures which represent 'mysticism' to the popular mind and which the saint holds in such low esteem.

So no matter what ambiguities there may be in the use of the term 'transformation', St John has at least told us this much quite clearly: *betrothal is a perfectly pure love for God, a perfect union of wills with God, and yet something less than mystical marriage.*

He also gives us the reason for the existence of such a state. This reason is a subtle but very important detail. The mere purity of the soul is not enough, by itself alone, to bring it into the mystical marriage. St Bernard had said *Si perfecte diligit,* nupsit.[107] St John of the Cross would have said: *Si perfecte diligit,* desponsata est.

Besides the negative purification in which all natural imperfections and attachments are burned out of the soul by infused love, the soul needs other, positive preparations for the immediate union with the divine substance which is mystical marriage. St John of the Cross characteristically speaks of this as the anointing of the soul symbolized by the preparations of the brides of King Assuerus.[108] Under the image of these anointings he describes the work of exalted mystical graces in the soul preparing it and strengthening it for that marriage which is to be, after all, an immediate union with him whom no man shall see and live![109] It is to be an 'essential communication of his Divinity without any kind of intermediary in the soul through a certain contact thereof with the Divinity... in a touch of pure substances, that is of the soul and the Divinity.'[110]

It is not enough that the soul have a natural capacity to love God purely, or that disinterested love should enter into its very essence: all its capacities must still be enlarged by the final work of grace. This final preparation for the perfect union of the soul with God consists above all in intense desires produced in the soul by the gifts and visits of the Betrothed, 'whereby He purifies the soul ever more completely and beautifies and refines it so that it may be more fitly prepared for such lofty union.... During the time, then,

of this betrothal and expectation of marriage in the unction
of the Holy Spirit, when there are choicest unctions preparing the soul for union with God, the yearnings of the caverns
of the soul are wont to be extreme and delicate. For, as those
ointments are a most proximate preparation for union with
God, because they are nearest to God and for this cause
make the soul more desirous of Him and inspire it with a
more delicate affection for Him, the desire is more delicate
and deeper; for the desire for God is a preparation for union
with God.'[111]

Another clue to the reason for these positive preparations
leads us to the chief distinction between betrothal and marriage. In betrothal, although the soul is pure of every imperfection as far as the will is concerned, nevertheless there
can still occur rebellious movements of the imagination or of
the sense appetites, and consequently the peace of the soul is
not altogether guaranteed from surface storms. On the contrary, it may happen that the evil spirits, in a last despairing
attempt to ruin the wonderful work that God has done, ex-
cite wild and sudden tempests in the imagination and the
senses, in order to trouble the soul's peace if they can. 'And
what is worst of all,' says St John of the Cross, 'they do battle
against the soul with horrors and fears amounting at times
to a terrible torment...' but nevertheless these things cannot
seriously disturb the soul which often, as soon as they arise,
'will very quickly become recollected in the deep hiding
place of its inmost being, and then those terrors which it suffers are so far away and so greatly removed that not only do
they cause it no fear, but they make it to be glad and
rejoice.'[112]

Evidently the unctions of the soul not only strengthen it in
view of union with God but also against these incursions of
imagination, the emotions and the devil.

Nevertheless, in the mystical marriage, the soul is buried
in God himself by its identification with him and has conse-

quently passed entirely out of the reach of all such things.
For then the devil not only cannot disturb her but he does
not 'even dare to approach her, but flees very far from her in
great terror and dares not even appear...' and at the same
time 'the sensual part of the soul with all its powers, faculties
and desires is conformed with the spirit and its rebellions are
quelled and are all over'.[113] The soul in this condition, says
St John of the Cross, has recovered the primitive innocence
of Adam and knows no evil 'for it is so innocent that it
understands not evil nor judges aught as evil; and it will hear
things that are very evil and will see them with its eyes and
will be unable to understand that they are so because it has
no habit of evil whereby to judge it, God having rooted out
its imperfect habits and ignorance with the perfect habit of
true wisdom'.[114]

In short, the soul 'is changed in God, as to all its desires
and operations into a new manner of life and it is destroyed
and annihilated concerning those old things which it used
aforetime'.[115] There is no question of relapsing into the old
life for this transformation is permanent and habitual. That
is what the new form amounts to: the life of God informs the
soul as a habit or permanent quality. 'The soul is *forever in
this high estate of mystical marriage after God has placed it
therein.*'[116]

In the light of this detailed treatment of mystical marriage and betrothal by St John of the Cross there immediately arises a question about the famous descriptions of the
transforming union in St Bernard's earlier works. Does the
tenth chapter of the *De diligendo Deo* describe St John of
the Cross' mystical marriage or mystical betrothal?

Here a distinction must be made. That chapter evidently
contains a description of mystical marriage, that is, of a
perfect and permanent transformation into God. The
language indicates this beyond question:

Quoniam   tamen   Scriptura   loquitur   Deum   omnia

fecisse propter semetipsum; erit profecto ut factura sese quandoque *conformet et concordet* auctori.... Oportet proinde in eumdem nos affectum *quandocunque transire....* O pura et defaecata intentio voluntatis! Eo certe defaecatior et purior quo in ea *de proprio nil admistum relinquitur:* eo suavior et dulcior quo *totum divinum* est quod sentitur. *Sic affici deificari est.*[117]

Then follow the classical comparisons: the drop of water in wine *deficere a se tota videtur,* the iron in the fire igni simillimum fit pristina *propriaque forma exutum,* and the air full of sunlight *non tam illuminatus quam ipsum lumen esse videtur.*[118] And he concludes: *sic omnem tunc in sanctis humanam affectionem quodam ineffabili modo necesse erit a semetipsa liquescere, atque in Dei penitus transfundi voluntatem.* Alioquin quomodo omnia in omnibus erit Deus, *si in homine de homine quidquam supererit?*[119]

Here we have the uncompromising term of St John of the Cross,[120] *omnem* humanam affectionem *penitus transfundi,* and the rest. But the trouble is that St Bernard felt, at the time of writing, that this perfect union was only for the next life![121]

At the same time, it is easy to find in the same tenth chapter of *De diligendo Deo* what is clearly a description of the spiritual betrothal. Or rather to be precise it is a description of the *excessus* or the momentary contact with the Beloved in an ecstasy, of pure love which would correspond to the 'visits' and 'touches' of the Beloved in the passages quoted from the writings of the great Carmelite.[122] Then St Bernad goes on to lament the necessary relapse from momentary ecstasy into the habitual state of *languor* or purifying desire. In other words it is a description of that *vicissitudo* which, in its highest form, corresponds to the alternations of union and desire for union which characterise St John of the Cross' spiritual betrothal.

Passing rapidly over some details of the passage from *De*

diligendo Deo we find that they fit in perfectly with parallel texts on betrothal in the *Spiritual Canticle* or the *Living Flame*. St Bernard's *excessus* takes the soul out of itself in the inebriation of love: *divino debriatus amore, oblitus sui.*[123] St John of the Cross tells us that the inebriation of love belongs to the *desposorio,* or betrothal.[124] This self-forgetfulness is also characteristic, in different degrees, both of the *excessus* and of the whole state of betrothal in the sense that the soul's love is habitually pure and perfect, but not in the sense that involuntary movements of the emotions cannot disturb us, as we have seen.

Beatum dixerim et sanctum,[125] exclaims St Bernard of one who has tasted this *excessus* of pure love in this life, even were it only rarely, or only once! That seems strange no doubt to those who know well that sanctity does not consist in extraordinary experiences; but they forget that for St Bernard perfection of charity and mystical experience coincide. His ecstasy is nothing but a movement of absolutely pure love for God, and for that reason it must be an integral element of sanctity.

At the same time St John of the Cross agrees that the state of spiritual betrothal can properly be called a state of perfection.[126]

Te enim quodammodo perdere... omnino non sentire teipsum et a teipso exinaniri et paene annullari:[127] all this is very strong, and it is stronger still with the qualification that it belongs to heaven rather than earth, *caelestis est conversationis non humanae affectionis.*[128] But it fits in perfectly with the rapture described by St John of the Cross which takes souls out of themselves even before they have reached the state of spiritual betrothal. So we read, for instance, that 'in that visitation of the Divine Spirit the spirit of the soul is enraptured with great force to commune with the Spirit and abandons the body and ceases to experience feelings and to have its actions in the body, since it has them in God...'[129]

and he adds: 'Very willingly was the soul leaving the body upon that spiritual flight thinking that its life was coming to an end and that it would be able to have fruition of its Spouse forever and remain with Him unhindered by a veil.'[130]

But in this state both St Bernard and St John of the Cross tell us that the soul has still far to go before it arrives at a stable and permanent union of the faculties with God. In St Bernard's language, the inevitable necessities of physical life and the duties of one's state conspire with less worthy agents, the world and the flesh, to rouse the soul from this sweet rest in God. *Subito invidet saeculum nequam, perturbat diei malitia, corpus mortis aggravat, sollicitat carnis necessitas, defectus corruptionis non sustinet, quodque hi violentius est fraterna revocat charitas.*[131] Gilson gives us a technical commentary on these terms[132] and we learn, among other things, that *diei malitia* is sometimes used by St Bernard to refer to the abbot's duty of receiving and entertaining important guests.[133] But at any rate, the result of the conspiracy is to draw the soul out again from the sanctuary of pure love into the open forum of the active life. It is therefore very curious to observe that St Bernard speaks of this as *recidere in sua*.[134] Surely there is nothing selfish about the exercise of these relatively unpleasant duties. The term cannot go altogether without comment. It applies differently to all the agents the saint has just listed. The world is *sua* because it is the soul's own level as a fallen creature, and no doubt that also applies to *diei malitia! Corpus mortis* means the involuntary movements of sense appetite and this is *sua* in the strict sense, because it is a trace of the old *proprium* that has not yet been entirely eliminated from the outer fortifications of the soul's castle, even though the inner citadel may be at peace in a pure and uncompromising love of God. The soul does not fall back from *excessus* into self-love. God forbid! But though the resistance to these movements is an act of love of God, the soul tastes something of its own misery, is reminded of its potentiality to reassume the old deformity.... *Carnis necessitas* is *sua* for even though the legitimate care of the body, being willed for us by God, belongs to the 'common will' nevertheless it distracts us from the pure love of him alone. But in what sense is fraternal charity *sua?* Only relatively can it be called so, in so far as it brings us down to the human level. St Bernard was surely as familiar as any of the great mystics with the necessity of 'leaving God for God'[135] and he did not attempt to deny that it sometimes cost a considerable sacrifice. So much so that it would be selfish to prefer the consolations of prayer to the spiritual profit of those whom God has given us to direct.[136]

However, all this goes to prove that the saintly abbot of Clairvaux was only telling us, in the tenth chapter of *De diligendo Deo* that he thought the perfect union with God described by St John of the Cross as mystical marriage was only to be attained in the next life.

Turning back the pages to the *De gradibus humilitatis*, we also find that the celebrated description of mystical union in the seventh chapter does not necessarily represent a higher state than the one we have just discussed. The soul is described as perfect, *propter humilitatem sine macula, propter charitatem sine ruga; cum nec voluntas rationi repugnet nec ratio veritatem sine ruga; cum nec voluntas rationi repugnet nec ratio veritatem dissimulat*[137] but we have seen that this perfection belongs to St John of the Cross' spiritual betrothal. True, St Bernard calls the soul a *spouse.* Gloriosam *sibi sponsam Pater conglutinat.*[138] But we shall soon see what a broad meaning *sponsa* could have for St Bernard. Besides, the expression *conglutinat* is an extremely weak one to use for transforming union. Strictly, the notion of transformation is not to be found in it. It does, however, have the merit of at least suggesting a more or less permanent state, and one might add that the temporary character of the *raptus*[139] is described in terms that need not necessarily indicate the *vicissitudo* of betrothal. After all even in mystical marriage the union of the *faculties* in God is not continual,[140] for this is something which St John of the Cross agrees must be left until we get to heaven.[141]

Nevertheless it cannot be said that this passage of St Bernard's *De gradibus humilitatis* clearly portrays the state of mystical marriage as we find it in St John of the Cross.

The question then arises: where does St Bernard give us a complete description of the mystical marriage *in this life?* Or did he continue to the end of his life to believe that it could only be achieved in heaven? This at once suggests the final sermons on the Canticle of Canticles, and if the solution is to be found at all we must look for it there.

4. Mystical Marriage in St Bernard

We have now reached the point where it has become evident that the central problem, in discussing the treatment of transforming union by St Bernard and St John of the Cross, is to find out whether St Bernard believes that the soul can reach what St John calls 'mystical marriage' in this life, or whether St Bernard's 'mystical marriage' is St John's 'spiritual betrothal' and nothing more. It is by no means an easy problem to solve, because St John's distinctions are not as clear as they appear to be at first sight, and St Bernard never entered into the subject systematically, so that his terminology seems to vary widely in different occasions, situations and contexts.

To begin with, St Bernard uses the word *sponsa*, spouse, to describe the soul in every degree of the spiritual life from plain sanctifying grace up to the mystical marriage. After all, since the Church is the mystical bride of Christ, all her members are individually in some sense brides of the Word. *Quae est sponsa et quis est Sponsus? Hic Deus noster est: et illa, si audeo dicere, nos sumus, cum reliqua multitudine captivorum, quos ipse novit.*[142]

However this is not the usual sense in which the word is used in the Sermons on the Canticles. Indeed, St Bernard could hardly help defining the term before beginning his commentary on this *carmen nuptiale*.[143] In the first Sermon of the long and beautiful series the abbot told his monks in clear and definite language that he thought they were contemplatives already or at least destined to become so,[144] and therefore there was not much use in his teaching them merely the ways of the purgative and illuminative life, urging them to avoid sin and practice vitue: what they needed was no longer the milk of children but the bread of the strong. The very first words of the first sermon are, then: *Vobis, fratres, alia quam aliis de saeculo, aut certe aliter dicenda sunt.*[145] And what better subject for contemplatives than to discuss the ways of infused prayer and infused love which are the normal fruit of the zealous practice of the virtues: *caeterorum omnium est fructus?*[146]

The spouse of the canticles is then the contemplative soul, the mystic, who has entered upon the ways of infused prayer, who is leading a life that may be called a state of perfection and is passing through the proximate preparation for mystical marriage, *facta nuptiis caelestis Sponsi idonea.*[147]

It is well enough known that St Bernard did not find the mystical life set forth in a well-ordered sequence of ascending steps in the Canticle of Canticles, and therefore we must not look for parallel structure in his series of sermons and in St John's *Spiritual Canticle.* But nevertheless it is in the final sermons, which represent at once the climax of St Bernard's teaching and of his own interior life, that we find the highest expression of the mystical life in his works. Before that point is reached, however, we find the *sponsa* in many different stages and attitudes of the ascent.

In the seventh sermon he keeps the promise he made in the first[148] and explains in greater detail what he means by the spouse, the contemplative soul who is disposed for the mystical marriage. She is one who has reached a point where she loves God for himself alone. She is in the 'third degree of love' according to the plan of the *De diligendo Deo* where there is at least a hint that this degree brings with it more than a taste of contemplation. *Ita fit ut ad diligendum pure Deum* plus jam ipsius gustata alliciat suavitas *quam urgeat nostra necessitas.*[149] And it must be noted that this *gustata suavitas* is by no means a mere sensible consolation. After all that would come under the heading of *necessitas* since sensi ble pleasure is not something which our sense appetite is free to refuse: and the proof that this 'taste' of divine love is really pure is to be found in the tangible evidence of unselfishness: fraternal charity, good works, obedience.[150]

The spouse then is essentially one who loves, and loves not for the sake of any reward or consolation, but merely for the sake of love itself. And what is more, she not only loves, but she thirsts for the perfect possession of God who is infinite Love. The spouse then is defined as *anima sitiens Deum.*[151] How is this thirst expressed? By the desire of union. *Amat autem quae osculum petit. Non petit liberatem, non mercedem, non haereditatem, non denique vel doctrinam, sed osculum.*[152] This love, with its three principal qualities of disinterested purity, spirituality, and a burning ardor which excludes every other affection[153] is already in a sense a union between the soul and God because it establishes her in true likeness to him. Therefore division between them, self-will, has already disappeared and consequently the obstacle that prevented God's communicating himself to the soul is out of the way. It can already be said that they share all things in common — *quippe quibus omnia communia sunt nil proprium, nil a se divisum habentes.*[154]

From this it can be seen that the spouse in these sermons of St Bernard is more than a contemplative soul. This passage gives us all the elements of St John of the Cross' spiritual betrothal, and since it is offered us by St Bernard as a general statement of what *sponsa* is to mean throughout his commentary, we can safely say that his words *nuptiis idonea* can be interpreted strictly, and that therefore the sermons on the Canticle deal principally with the state of spiritual betrothal.

This becomes very clear when we consider a passage like the following, in which the word *sponsa* is again defined: *Et nunc da mihi animam quam frequenter Verbum Sponsus invisere soleat, cui familiaritas ausum, cui gustus famem,*

*cui contemptus omnium otium dederit: et ego huic incunc-
tanter assigno vocem pariter et nomen sponsae.*[155] We are
immediately told, however, that the visits of the Bridegroom
are brief and fleeting, and that he quickly departs again *quo
avidius revocaretur, teneretur fortius.*[156] The spouse then
knows something of the delight of his presence, but has not
yet tasted the joy of the full communication of his love and
perfections: *meruit praesentiam etsi non copiam.*[157]

All this at once recalls the 'frequent and loving visits' of
the Word to the soul that is betrothed to him, in St John of
the Cross' *Living Flame,* together with the 'anointings' we
have already sufficiently discussed.[158] Such thoughts are
characteristic of the *Sermones in Cantica.*

Let us now turn our attention to the most important of
these sermons, where St Bernard tells us explicitly that he is
treating of the mystical marriage. From the eightieth sermon to the eighty-fifth, the holy Abbot of Clairvaux has
given us what amounts to a summary of his whole mystical
doctrine, as if he were taking stock of it once more before
laying down the pen. And yet these pages, perhaps the most
brilliant he ever wrote, do not give one the feeling that they
were written in a nostalgic and retrospective mood, by any
means! On the contrary, if they are a summary, they have
also many of the elements of a new beginning. It is as if the
saint not only wanted to sum up his doctrine but to start it
all over again, and that is why the reflections on the
character of the divine image in the soul have something of
an experimental quality about them.

We do not need to go into these details which have
already been sufficiently discussed. We take up the thread
of the argument where the soul has been stripped of the
'double-cloak' of cupidity overlying and disfiguring the
divine image, and once more takes on the lost likeness to
God by charity. Indeed charity itself is this likeness, because
it is also the vision of God. *Charitas illa visio, illa similitudo*

est.[159] The more perfect is our charity, the more perfectly do we see God, and the more lovingly does he look upon us and, in consequence, the greater is the likeness that grows up between us. The full perfection of this vision and likeness will be a complete identification of the soul with God, when we love God as he loves us *diligens sicut dilecta est.*[160]

The eighty-third sermon opens with the magnificent declaration that the mystical marriage, *nuptias Verbi,* is something to which all may aspire. All we need to do is to return to the Word by charity, and this work will be performed in our souls by the Word himself. *Animae reditus conversio ejus ad Verbum, reformandae per ipsum, conformandae ipsi.*[161] If St Bernard likes the words 'reformation' and 'conformation' better than 'transformation' it is because of his emphasis on the fact that we are 'made in God's image and likeness'.[162]

This 'conformity', when it amounts to a perfect likeness, will by that very fact constitute the mystical marriage of the soul and the Word. *Talis conformitas maritat animam Verbo, cum cui videlicet similis est per naturam, similem nihilominus ipsi se exhibet per voluntatem, diligens sicut dilecta est. Ergo, si perfecte diligit, nupsit.*[163]

No ambiguity about the fact that St Bernard is telling us what mystical marriage means to him. It is a perfect union of wills, a perfect union of love with God, perfect likeness to God. All this, we know, will take place in heaven: but now the saint is talking about the relative perfection which can constitute perfect likeness and therefore mystical marriage even on earth. For the language of the eighty-third sermon leaves no doubt that the saint is now talking not about heaven but about this present life.[164]

Before we go any further we must meet the objection that is bound to arise at this very point. St Bernard has described the mystical marriage as a conformity of wills with God. If he said nothing more than this, his definition would be so vague that it would be unacceptable. After all, every degree of the spiritual life implies conformity of will with God. But very few souls ever reach the mystical marriage on earth. So Fr Poulain rightly marks this down as a 'confusion to be avoided' and he says: 'We must not suppose that the mystical marriage consists in a perfect conformity to the will of God. That would be to confuse a state of prayer, a special mode of divine communication, that is to say, with a virtue, which is something very different.' However, he goes on to add at once that this virtue is *one of the consequences* of the transformation.[165]

Perhaps Fr Poulain's distinction is not quite as clear as he thinks. After all, when God purifies our will by infused love and brings it into perfect conformity with his own, the love and the conformity, which are the same thing, constitute a mystical state and a special divine communication. At least this is the way both St Bernard and St John of the Cross would look at it.[166]

However, we shall see that the context of this passage in St Bernard definitely proves that he is talking about the communication of divine love to the soul. Whether or not he considers it a 'state of prayer' is another matter. After all, St Bernard was concerned with degrees of love and not states of prayer, but that did not make his final degrees of love any the less mystical for all that, nor did it exclude an essential cognitive element.

The real difficulty to this conception would be one that is raised not by Fr Poulain but by a passage in St John of the Cross. It is the famous definition of spiritual betrothal which has already claimed our attention.[167] We remember that the betrothal is described as the highest state that can be attained 'by grace of will'. Now this is clarified by the saint's statement that betrothal consists in an agreement, a consent between the two parties, and this consent gives us possession of God 'by mutual love' *(bien quererse)*. The Spanish expression which Professor Peers translates as 'consent by agreement and a unity of will'· is *un igualado si y una sola voluntad.* This would seem to be saying nothing but 'a perfect conformity to the will of God' which Fr Poulain will not admit as a description of a 'state of prayer'.

Actually, this could not be mere 'conformity to the will of God' in the sense of psychological conformity, the ordering of the will by a series of virtuous acts corresponding to a series of divine commands, which is what Fr Poulain is talking about, and which certainly does not constitute a state of prayer. Yet it certainly is an approach to complete identification, *in the concrete,* between a created faculty and the Love which is the very substance of God: and this implies a mystical state.

However, what concerns us particularly is this: if St Bernard's language, *talis conformitas maritat... similis per voluntatem... diligens sicut dilecta est* is to be translated into St John's *igualado si y una sola voluntad,* then we have once more failed to prove that St Bernard's mystical marriage goes beyond what the carmelite saint would call 'betrothal' and we would have to admit that for St Bernard a true transforming union was not possible in this life.

That would mean that the 'Mellifluous Doctor' who has been considered for many centuries as one of the greatest of mystical writers in the Church was preaching a relatively impoverished and limited doctrine.

The problem can now be attacked directly and it will not be too hard to solve.

What St John of the Cross demands here is naturally that mystical marriage be something more than an *agreement.* It must be a real possession of the soul by God and of God by the soul, not through grace alone but by union. In other words, the soul must be no longer merely 'like' God, but so much like him as to be identified with him. And the saint makes the obvious comparison to human betrothal and marriage. Two persons may agree perfectly on everything, and enjoy one another's company in frequent visits, and give one another presents: but that does mean that they are married, united as two in 'one flesh'.

So mystical marriage demands more than a consent, an agreement: it means that the soul and God must share not ideas, not affection, not mere mutual love but their very being and substance. It means the most exalted, unimaginably sublime transformation of the soul in God, something that we can hardly discuss intelligibly let alone comprehend, something that must always remain a mystery, but one of the most dazzlingly fruitful mysteries that the Church offers us for our contemplation!

St Bernard does not leave us long in doubt on this score. In repeating (in the same sermon) that the union he is talking about is a true marriage, he lets slip the word *contractus* and corrects himself in a way that can leave little doubt he was of the same mind as St John of the Cross on this point. *Parum dixi contractus:* Complexus est. *Complexus plane, ubi idem velle, et nolle idem,* unum facit spiritum de duobus.[168] And then he goes on at once to explain how it is that this union of wills is as it were the channel which opens up the intercommunication between the divine essence and the substance and faculties of the soul. When the two wills are inseparably joined there necessarily follows the free and uninterrupted participation in that Love which is also the Holy Spirit, the bond between the Father and the Son.[169] The thoughts developed in the rest of the sermon leave no doubt that *complexus* here means transforming union, because it fills the soul with a pure love which is not merely a virtue, not merely a grace, but the very life and substance of God himself: *Adde quod iste Sponsus non modo amans, sed Amor est.*[170] Once this is understood, once we see that the Spouse is Love itself, infinite and uncreated Love, a perfect conformity of wills must obviously be not only the result of union with him but the necessary condition for union with him. Also, since he is pure love, he cannot communicate himself perfectly to a soul in which love is mixed with any other affections. To prove it, St Bernard mentions some of the other affections which cannot immediately unite us to the divine substance: fear, for instance, or reverence; honoring God will not make me one spirit with him because he is not honor, he is Love. *Solus est amor ex omnibus animae motibus, sensibus et affectibus, in quo potest creatura, etsi non ex aequo, respondere Auctori* vel de simili mutuam rependere vicem.[171] Note the last phrase, which again tells us that we are dealing with a perfect sharing, intercommunication, interchange; in other words, with transforming union. And the language which proves this most clearly of all is in the saint's admirable metaphor comparing God to a fountain of love that flows out into the soul and fills it and flows back again into himself.

Magna res est amor si tamen ad suum recurrat principium, si suae origini redditus, si refusus suo fonti semper ex eo sumat unde jugiter fluat.[172] To appreciate fully the strength and depth of this sentence we must compare it with a similar passage from St John of the Cross, and we will see that here, as on so many occasions, the Carmelite of the sixteenth century develops and amplifies ideas implicitly contained in the writings of the great Cistercian of the twelfth.

St Bernard is talking of a fountain of water: St John of the Cross tells of the same thing, calling it a fountain of fire, although he does not hesitate to make it also 'flow' and 'bathe' the soul with its glory, for it is, he tells us, the river of living water promised to us by Christ.[173] In other words both the fountain and the fire are the same Holy Spirit of Love.

These are the words of St John of the Cross:

> The soul feels itself at last to be wholly enkindled in Divine Union, and its palate to be wholly bathed in glory and in love, and from the inmost part of its substance to

be flowing rivers of glory, *(hasta lo íntimo de su sustancia
está revertiendo no menos que rios de gloria)* abounding
in delights, for it perceives that from its belly are flowing
the rivers of living water which the Son of God said would
flow from such souls.... That delicate flame of love that
burns within it is, as it were, glorifying it with a glory
both gentle and powerful whenever it assails it.... This
flame of love is the spirit of its Spouse, that is the Holy
Spirit. And this flame the soul feels within it not only as a
fire that has consumed and transformed it in sweet love,
but also as a fire that *burns within it and sends out flame*
and that flame, each time that it breaks into flame,
bathes the soul in glory and refereshes it with the temper
of divine life.[174]

When St John goes on to explain that the substance of the
soul is enveloped by this fire (that is, by the habitual possession of divine Love) and the faculties from time to time flame
out with intense acts of this love, 'which are the enkindling of
love, wherein the will of the soul is united, and it loves most
deeply being made one with that flame of love', we hear the
echo of St Bernard's *si perfecte diligit, nupsit... similem per
voluntatem... semper ex suo fonti sumit unde jugiter fluat.*[175]

Of course, we were under no obligation of proving that St
Bernard conceived perfect transforming union in the same
terms as St John of the Cross: that was already clear from the
tenth chapter of *De diligendo Deo*. Yet there is a great advance to be noted in the passage we have just quoted. For all
its intensity, the description of transforming union in *De
diligendo Deo* was the description of a state which the saint
did not yet know from experience—for obviously if he had
already reached it, he would not have wasted his time
wondering whether it could be possessed this side of heaven.
But now he not only describes the mystical marriage in a sermon that places it definitely in the present life, but does so in
the language of personal experience.

5. The State of Pure Love

One big difficulty remains. It is the biggest of all. We know that St Bernard has tasted the highest *excessus* of pure love, but has he reached permanent union with God? Has he risen above the *vicissitudo* which called forth his lamentations in all his earlier writings, and even most of the way through the *Sermones in Cantica?* If he has not, then it is still not the mystical marriage. Marriage is a permanent state. The 'flame', it is true, may not always be blazing forth through the faculties, but the soul remains conscious of its identification with God and its faculties cannot even act at all except in him and by him.[176]

The true test of St Bernard's mystical marriage remains this: does it endure? Is it a state? For if there is any question of falling out of the union, *recidere in sua,* it is not the mystical marriage; there has been no transformation, but only a 'visit' of the Beloved. Nor does this hinge on the famous questions in impeccability. That has nothing to do with it. Whether or not one might be capable of sin in this union, it must be a permanent state: both sides in the controversy agree on that much. It must, in other words, endure at least in the same way that sanctifying grace endures, as a habit.

Since St Bernard believes that mystical marriage is nothing else but pure love, the question boils down to this: is pure love a state?

Here we have no less an authority against us than M. Gilson. He admits that 'pure love as conceived by St Bernard *is essentially a mystical experience'*, which is useful to us as an added argument that for the Abbot of Clairvaux perfect conformity to the will of God belonged to the mystical order.

But Gilson continues. 'What we have to do with here is neither an idea, *nor an habitual disposition,* but the brief and perpetually interrupted *excessus* of the soul of the mystic, when God unites it with Himself by exceptional graces.' And he concludes that for St Bernard, pure love is '*in no way a state*'.[177]

These remarks are much easier to understand in their context — they occur in a comparison between St Bernard and Fénelon, and they represent Gilson's effort to clear the Abbot of Clairvaux of every taint of quietism. He means, then, that St Bernard's pure love is by no means the 'state' of pure love described by someone like Mme Guyon. But in proving it, he says too much, and thereby does St Bernard less of a service than he thinks.

Obviously there can be no connection between the pure love we have been discussing and the pure love of quietism. The latter is a state in which the soul is conceived as being indifferent even to the possession or the loss of God, and therefore unconcerned about hell and judgement or any of God's gifts, including grace and glory. It has simply made up its own mind to love him through thick and thin, regardless of what he may have to say about it. And so the soul that has come to this pass is conceived as remaining there permanently, and as being therefore in a state. Nothing, not even hell, can change its 'pure love' of God. Of course, everyone admits, even the Quietists themselves, that there must be generous elements of fantasy in such a conception. But what is important for us is that it is poles apart from St Bernard, for whom pure love is precisely a love so ardent that it excludes all other desires but the desire of God and which by its intensity proximately disposes the soul for perfect union with him in mystical marriage. *Talis conformitas maritat animam Verbo.*[178]

It is difficult to see what usefulness Gilson found in proving that St Bernard's 'pure love was by no means a state'.

Evidently the early texts we have discussed at such length were so obvious and so inviting that the distinguished writer could not resist making use of them. But the result is that his portrait of St Bernard's interior life in its final and most complete development is the following:

> A continual pining desire interrupted by the fleeting and always unforeseeable joys of divine union — there we have the picture of his life.... St Bernard's confidence is a charity which, not by any means for a whole lifetime, but for short instants, succeeds in transcending the normal state in which the question of punishment still arises.[179]

This is clearly not the picture of a soul in the state of mystical marriage as it is described by the majority of mystical theologians and above all by St John of the Cross. Needless to say Fr Poulain makes permanency the first of his principal elements of the transforming union. It is a 'mystic state'.... 'A union that is almost permanent, persisting even amidst exterior occupations, and this in such a manner that the two diferent operations do not interfere with one another'.[180]

St John of the Cross, in a typical description of the mystical marriage, calls it a state over and over again, so much so you can count the word a dozen times in a couple of paragraphs. There is a passage in the Spiritual Canticle which fairly echoes with the word *estado*. Here are a few characteristic sentences.

> The Spouse Himself invites the soul, now made His bride, to this estate saying: *Veni in hortum meum*.... He has now gathered His fragrant myrrh and aromatic spices, which are the fruits of the flowers now ripe and made ready for the soul, the which fruits are the delights and grandeurs which He Himself communicates to her in this estate.... For the whole desire and aim of the soul and that of God in all the works of the soul is the consumma-

tion and perfection of this estate; wherefore the soul
never rests until it reaches Him; for in this estate she finds
much greater abundance and fullness of God, and a
peace more sure and stable, and a sweetness more perfect
without compare than in the spiritual betrothal, since she
is now placed in the arms of such a Spouse, Whose close
embrace the soul *habitually feels,* — a true embrace
[remember St Bernard's *complexus*] by means whereof
the soul lives the life of God.[181]

Over and over again St John of the Cross insists that in
mystical marriage the soul rests in a union of practically
uninterrupted fruition of God in a way that seems to be only
a little short of beatitude itself.

Nothing in the world, high or low, can cause her unrest,
disturb her or even move her; for being now free from all
the disturbance of the natural passions, and withdrawn
and detached from the torture and diversity of temporal
cares, the soul has fruition, in security and tranquillity, of
the participation of God.[182]

It remains only to show that St Bernard himself no longer
has any hesitation in calling this union of love a permanent
and habitual state. The language of the eighty-third sermon
on the Canticle leaves us little doubt on that score. Not only
is there nowhere a trace of the old lamentation, at the brevi-
ty and rarity of the fleeting moments of union with the
Spouse, but now we read the following serene sentences:

Quid hac conformitate jucundius? Quid optabilius
caritate qua fit ut humano magisterio non contenta, per
temet, o anima, fiducialiter accedas ad Verbum, *Verbo
constanter inhaereas,* Verbum familiariter percuncteris,
consultesque de omni re, quantum intellectu capax, tantum audax disiderio?[183]

Even if the clear, unequivocal *constanter inhaereas* were not
there to prove our thesis, we could still find it proved in

such expressions as *quid optabilius*. In the tenth chapter of
De diligendo Deo the saintly Abbot of Clairvaux left us no
doubts about his opinion that there was definitely something
more desirable than a life in which, after a brief and transient visit of the Spouse, the soul was left to fall back into
itself and struggle alone in the cares and trials of a workaday
world. As for the word *fiducialiter,* surely it seems to say exactly the opposite to what Gilson would have us believe
about St Bernard's confidence at this stage of his mystical
life; for it seems plainly to tell us that this soul is confident of
finding the Word close by, indeed in her very self, whenever
she needs to consult him in any special way. And how could
she consult him *de omni re* if, for most of her life, he were
far away?

We could go through the whole sermon and subject line
after line to the same scrutiny with the same felicitous
results. *Hic nexus vincit etiam quod natura arctius vinxit,
vinculum parentum ad filios.*[184] But the love of parents and
children is not something that endures only for five or ten
minutes at a time. And, of course, St Bernard immediately
quotes; *Propter hoc relinquet patrem suum et matrem suam
et* adhaerebit *sponsae.*[185]

What a change, too, from the *vicissitudo,* the 'continual
pining desire interrupted by the fleeing joys of divine
union'[186] characteristic of spiritual betrothal is the love that
now fills the soul. It is a love of fruition. *Is per se sufficit*—he
does not say it suffices for a brief moment—*is per se placet,
et propter se. Ipse meritum, ipse praemium est sibi. Amor
praeter se non requirit causam, non fructum. Fructus ejus,
usus ejus. Amo quia amo; amo ut amem. Magna res amor,
si tamen ad suum recurrat principium, si suae origini redditus, si refusus suo fonti semper ex eo sumat unde jugiter
fluat.*[187] Nothing could be more clear than that for St Bernard mystical marriage is a state in which pure love is a continuous loving union with the divine source of all love and

joy, by whose life the soul now lives in perfect likeness, transformed into him by virtue of the very purity which it has received from him.

It remains now only to trim off all the rough edges of this notion and follow St Bernard as he completes his summary description of the mystical marriage in the eighty-fifth sermon on the Song of Songs. And here we find not only the fullest confirmation of what we have just read, but also the one remaining distinction that remains to be made. This distinction is the important one, that in mystical marriage the union of the *faculties* in fruition of the divine substance is not continual although the substance of the soul remains not only in an uninterrupted union, but in *an uninterrupted joy*.

Here indeed we touch upon a subject which has inspired the finest pages of mystical theology—pages which the contemplative soul never tires of savoring, and which all of us in the cloister, no matter what may be our level in the spiritual life, ought to keep constantly before our eyes because they represent the ideal for which we were created, in so far as it is attainable on earth.

But first, St Bernard repeats and emphasizes what he has said about the permanency of pure love in the mystical marriage. Once again he quotes the scriptural text *adhaerebit uxori suae,* and supports it with another from David: *Mihi autem adhaerere Deo bonum est*[188] and goes on:

> Ergo quam videris animam relictis omnibus *Verbo votis omnibus adhaerere, Verbo vivere, Verbo se regere, de Verbo concipere quod pariat Verbo* quae possit dicere: 'Mihi vivere Christus est et mori lucrum' puta conjugem, Verboque maritatam. Confidit in ea cor viri sui, sciens fidelem, quae prae se omnia spreverit, omnia arbitretur ut stercora, ut sibi ipsum lucrifacere.[189]

The saint then goes on to the interesting and important distinction betwen the two aspects of mystical marriage. The two aspects are the result of the twofold precept of charity and of St Bernard's own principle: *nec cuiquam sibi sed omnibus esse vivendum.*[190] It is the old question of action and contemplation in which St Bernard follows St Gregory and St Augustine in the traditional view that contemplation is more perfect but it must be supplemented by the fruitful, but less delectable labor of fraternal charity.[191]

Indeed, the mystical marriage must not be sterile: it must bring forth children to the Spouse, that is, souls to the mystical life. But since the faculties cannot give themselves to the work of preaching and the care of souls when they are completely absorbed in the fruition of the highest graces of union, there must remain even in the mystical marriage some alternation between the pure love of God in himself and the love of God through our fellow men.

Notice that on this point St Bernard represents a definite development over the western Fathers — he is a step on the way to St John of the Cross and, for that matter, to Pius XI's *Umbratilem.* St Augustine does not allow that Rachel, the contemplative life, is anything but sterile. *Rachel clara aspectu mente excedit Deo et vidit in principio Verbum Deum apud Deum, et vult parere et non potest quia generationem ejus quis enarrabit?...* vacare vult ab omni negotio et ideo sterilis.[192]

St John of the Cross on the contrary will tell us that: 'A very little of this pure love is more precious in the sight of God and the soul, *and of greater profit to the Church, even though the soul appear to be doing nothing than are all these works together.*[193]

St Bernard, half-way in between, considers that the ecstasy of the faculties in mystical marriage is certainly not sterile in a purely mystical order: *intelligentias pariunt spirituales.*[194] But it needs to be supplemented by a spiritual fertility in the apostolic field as well. And so he describes the *duo genera pariendi.* There is nothing

especially new in the language in which he talks of the
faculties in ecstatic fruition of the Word.

> Interdum exceditur et seceditur etiam a corporeis sen-
> sibus, ut sese non sentiat quae Verbum sentit. Hoc fit
> cum mens ineffabilis Verbi illecta dulcedine, quodam-
> modo se sibi furatur, imo rapitur atque elabitur a seipsa
> ut Verbo fruatur.[195]

And immediately he passes on to the distinction: Aliter
sane afficitur mens fructificans Verbo, aliter fruens Verbo.
*Illic sollicitat necessitas proximi, hic invitat suavitas
Verbi.*[196] And yet it is evident that here the situation is quite
different from that *vicissitudo* which made him exclaim:
Heu redire in se, recidere in sua compellitur![197] True, he admits even here that the perfect experience of rapture is transitory. *Dulce commercium, sed breve momentum et ex-
perimentum rarum.*[198] But he accepts this quite peacefully,
and without special comment. What need was there of comment, after all? For the union with the Spouse is by no
means interrupted. The joy of that union is less intense,
perhaps, but it is still the same joy: Laeta in prole mater; sed
in amplexibus sponsa laetior. *Chara pignora filiorum, sed
oscula plus delectant. Bonum est salvare multos; excedere
autem et cum Verbo osse multo jucundius.*[199]

However, in order to appreciate fully what this means we
must recall to mind that this is far more than a voluntary
submission to the dictates of the Beloved's divine will. It is
something that far transcends a mere self-surrender, abandonment, even the most complete and uncompromising.
And the reason for this transcendence is that such abandonment is a gift of one's self, by the aid of grace, while the
mystical marriage is a transformation, a receiving of God's
gift of his own self, 'beyond all grace'.

Therefore, when the soul and God have bcome 'one spirit'
the fruition of the soul is God's fruition of himself, and the
working of the soul for other souls is God's love reaching out

to them. It is thus God who rests in the soul and God who works in the soul. How then can there be any cause for lamentation where there has been no loss and none but a superficial change?

Much light is thrown on this mystery when we reflect, with another great mystic, Blessed John Ruysbroeck, that the divine life, which is now the life of the soul is at the same time eternal activity and eternal rest.

The divine persons in the fecundity of their nature are one God eternally in action, and in the simplicity of their essence, they are Godhead, perpetual rest; *and so with respect to his persons God is an eternal operation, but with respect to his essence eternal rest....*

And in the soul united to God:

> between action and rest live love and fruition. Love would ever be at work, since it is an everlasting interaction with God, but fruition must ever be at rest, above all will or desire, the embracing of the Well-beloved in the Well-beloved, in a love pure and without images. Therein the Father together with His Son clasps His beloved in the restful unity of His Spirit above the fecundity of His nature; ...so great is the mutual joy and delight between God and His beloved spirits that they are rapt out of themselves and melt and flow to become one spirit with God in fruition, being drawn eternally into the abyssal blessedness of His essence.[200]

St John of the Cross, with his usual psychological finesse explains this uninterrupted joy:

> Since the soul lives a life so happy and blessed as this life of God, let each one consider, if he can, what a life of the soul this will be, wherein neither can God perceive aught that is displeasing to Him, nor can the soul perceive it, but the soul enjoys and *perceives the delight and glory of God in its very substance* which is now transformed in Him.[201]

And besides that, in everything that the soul does, its faculties are directly moved by God alone.

> Not only does He guide her in her solitude, but it is He Himself alone who works in her; using no other intermediary.[202]

Therefore it is small wonder that:

> Even as the bee extracts from all plants the honey that is in them and has no use for them for aught save for that purpose, even so the soul with great facility extracts the sweetness of love that is in all the things that pass through it; it loves God in each of them whether pleasant or unpleasant; and being as it is informed and protected by love it has neither feeling nor taste nor knowledge of it [i.e. the pleasantness or unpleasantness of the thing itself] for, as we have said, *the soul knows naught but love and its pleasure in all things and occupations is ever, as we have said, the delight of the love of God.*[203]

This language of St John of the Cross takes us back immediately to St Bernard's earlier writings, to the 'fourth degree of charity' and to *libertas a miseria*. And so it should, for now at last the saint of Clairvaux has found both of these fulfilled in his own experience to the extent that they can be fulfilled in this life — and he has found that that extent is far greater than he imagined in his younger days.

Now indeed he knows what it is to experience such union with God that:

> quomodo Deus omnia esse voluit propter semetipsum, *sic nos quoque nec nosipsos nec aliud aliquid fuisse vel esse velimus nisi aeque propter ipsum, ob solam videlicet ipsius voluntatem, non nostram voluptatem.*[204]

Now the will, perfectly emancipated from cupidity, from self-seeking, is able fully and effortlessly to fulfil the whole program which St John of the Cross was to set forth in such terse axioms: '*In order to arrive at having pleasure in everything, desire to have pleasure in nothing... In order to arrive at possessing everything, desire to possess nothing.*'[205] To have pleasure in everything? That is precisely St Bernard's *libertas a miseria,* the end and culmination of the spiritual life! It is *libertas complaciti* which belongs to those who *ab omni proinde quod displicere potest, hoc est ab omni miseria, se liberos sentiunt... omnia quae tamquam recta et commoda consulte observant* etiam ut beneplacita libenter amplectuntur.[206] That phrase *omne quod displicere potest* is echoed by St John's 'aught that can be displeasing': there is nothing left in such a soul that can displease God, and finally, inevitably, since the soul is now married to him and finds its supreme delight in all that pleases him, therefore it finds nothing displeasing in itself, nothing displeasing in anything that happens in the world around it.

> So the Beloved (says St John of the Cross) likewise conjures all the four passions of the soul (joy, hope, fear and grief) making them to cease and be at rest... so that not only can these things not reign in her but they cannot even cause her the least degree of displeasure. For the grandeur and stability of the soul in this estate are so complete that if formerly there reached the soul the waters of any grief whatsoever, even those of its own sins (remember the soul is now impeccable!) or the sins of some other person, which is what spiritual persons habitually feel the most, now, although it still realizes their importance, they cause it neither pain nor sorrow... for in this transformation of love the soul is made like the angels, who apprehend perfectly things that are grievous without feeling grief... And thus naught can either reach it or molest it, since it has entered, as we have said, into the pleasant garden of its desire, where it enjoys all peace, tastes all sweetness and delights itself in all delight... since it sees and feels itself to be full of the riches of God and thus in life and in death it is conformed and reconciled to God's will.[207]

St Bernard in his turn shows us such a soul as being completely 're-formed', that is, transformed by wisdom. And for St Bernard wisdom is nothing else but another aspect of the same notion he expresses in his *libertas complaciti:* it is an intensity and purity of love so great that it finds delight in all things, irrespective of what they may be in themselves; for in everything that exists the goodness of God may be found and sapientia, *sapor boni,* is the pure love that tastes his goodness and sees that it is sweet even in what the natural man would find most bitter. But the 'natural man' has ceased to exist in such a soul that lives entirely by love, that is, 'informed' by love as by a new life and a new nature and a new soul. *Qui autem transierunt in affectum cordis sapientes sunt et ipso delectantur sapore boni.... Beata mens quam sibi* totum vindicavit sapor boni *et odium mali. Hoc reformari ad sapientiam est, hoc sapientiae victoriam feliciter experiri.*[208] That phrase *totam vindicavit sapor boni* is paralleled by one of the strongest expressions of John Ruysbroeck, who says that the souls in rapture, lost in the divine essence, become fruition, they *'are fruition'.*[209]

Continuing in the same passage, St Bernard asks us: *Nam in quo evidentius sapientia vincere malum comprobatur, quam* cum excluso sapore mali, *qui non aliud quam ipsa malitia est,* boni quidam intimus sapor mentis intima occupare tota suavitate sentitur?[210] What a picture this is of a soul so penetrated with goodness that it has, in a sense, become itself goodness and joy! It has lost all sense of evil, it can no longer understand or apprehend evil, as St John of the Cross has already told us[211] and it can, indeed, no longer know anything except by the power of this affinity for God's own goodness which belongs to it in virtue of God's purity and love into which it has been transformed: and so it finds the whole universe saturated with his goodness, is lost in his love, and no longer knows anything but his immense delight! St Bernard concludes that such a soul has risen far above the level of mere virtues, the level of good habits and good acts or what St John of the Cross would call the level of 'will and grace'.[212] *Itaque*, St Bernard continues, *ad virtutem spectat tribulationes fortiter sustinere: ad sapientiam gaudere in tribulationibus. Confortare cor tuum et sustinere Dominum virtutis est; gustare et videre quoniam suavis est Dominus, sapientiae est.*[213] By now it should be clear that this rejoicing in tribulation, proper to the highest wisdom, is far above the concept of an interior joy that persists in the depths of the soul *in spite of* tribulation. This is a flame of love which consumes every other affection. *Amor sibi abundat, amor ubi venerit, caeteros in se omnes traducit et captivat affectus. Propterea quae amat, amat et aliud novit nihil.*[214] This love elevates the soul beyond virtues, beyond any heroism of sanctity that can be seen or understood by men, and places it in an entirely different world, or rather in heaven. Such a soul will pass through the midst of the world not catching the attention of others, but, as it were, invisible, neutral and indifferent to them because it belongs to an entirely different order of things.[215] It will be clothed in the kind of sanctity that belonged to Our Lady, whose life seemed ordinary to men because it was so exalted that it was beyond their comprehension and could not be measured by the standard of virtues, even the most sublime supernatural virtues operating *humano modo*.

Only one thing remains to be settled before we conclude. If the mystical marriage brings a soul into such perfect conformity and possession of God that it is transformed entirely into him and no longer lives on the human level at all, having passed beyond even the level of the most heroic human sanctity, one may ask what there is left for the soul to expect? Its heaven has already begun: what more can the light of glory give such a soul?

Strange to say, St John of the Cross can still find an immense distance for the soul to travel! It rests already in perfect peace, and yet the end of the *Spiritual Canticle* shows us how the soul is consumed with an ever greater and greater desire for this still more perfect union of heaven and the theme of the *Living Flame* is the pleading of the soul that God may brush aside the 'thin veil' which still obscures the perfection of face to face vision of his essence.

> It is not to be understood [he says] that because this which the soul understands [in the mystical marriage] is naked substance [of God] that it is perfect and clear fruition as in heaven. For although it is free from accidents it is not for that reason clear, but rather it is dark, for it is contemplation which as St Dionysius says, is in this life a ray of darkness; wherefore we can say it is a ray and *image of fruition.*[216]

And so the saint has to set about explaining the marvelous paradox of this desire which persists in the midst of satisfaction and this longing which is enkindled in the heart saturated with peace. For although the soul is now perfect, as perfect as it can be on this earth, there is still something—and something essential—lacking to its perfection: obscurity must give place to light, and fruition must come out of darkness and secrecy into the full light of glory. God has now communicated himself entirely to the soul, it is true, but as long as the soul remains in a mortal body it cannot bear the full weight of his perfections in their own essential clarity and magnificence. And so the desire of the soul and the desire of God cannot be fully consummated as long as the soul remains in this life, and it is because of the desire of God to pour out the torrents of his glory into the soul that the soul also desires this with all its being. St John of the Cross adds a very particular reason for this desire: it is only in heaven that the soul can enter, together with Christ, into the full profundity and meaning of his mysteries.[217] What is even more important, it is only in heaven that Christ will be fully glorified in that soul by the soul's perfect participation by adoption in his divine sonship.[218] Ultimately, the full glory of Christ and his complete triumph will only be when all the elect have reached the state of glory predestined for them, and so this too is a powerful element in the soul's desire for heaven. In a word, the culmination of St John of the Cross' doctrine on the mystical marriage is a hymn of praise and glory not only to the Holy Trinity, not only to the Divine Word who is the Bridegroom of the soul but in a very special way to the Man-God, Jesus Christ, Christ the King.

One final sentence from St Bernard will complete the picture. The whole process, the whole spiritual life is the work of her through whom God willed us to receive all gifts and graces.[219] St Bernard does not hesitate to give us another of his summaries of his spiritual doctrine in which the mystical marriage, our transformation by wisdom into God is assigned to the Mother of God as her mission *par excellence* among the children of men. Through one woman we were born to the living death of cupidity; from our mother Eve we received the disfiguring form of the *proprium:* but God allowed this only in order that his wisdom might triumph through another woman and that our natural integrity might be clothed in the freedom of his divine glory and exult forever in the gladness of his infinitely pure love.

> Ita insipientia mulieris saporem boni exclusit, quia serpentis malitia mulieris insipientiam circumvenit. Sed unde malitia visa est vicisse ad tempus, inde se victam dolet in aeternum. Nam ecce denuo sapientia mulieris cor et corpus implevit, *ut qui per feminam deformati in insipientiam sumus, per feminam reformemur ad sapientiam.*[220]

Notes

1. We have not attempted to discuss the question of direct influence that may have been exercised by St Bernard on St John of the Cross. The probability of such influence is very slight, although St John himself seems to claim that it existed in heading one of the chapters of the *Dark Night* 'Begins to explain the ten steps of the mystic ladder of Divine love according to S. Bernard and S. Thomas' (Book 2.19; Peers translation 1:463). The reference is to St Thomas' *De dilectione Dei et proximi* (*Opusculum* LIV; Vives edition, chapter 27). Here St Thomas gives ten degrees of love *secundum Bernardum*. St John of the Cross follows this closely in this particular chapter, but whether or not the degrees have much to do with St Bernard is another matter altogether. Even if they have, they would only constitute an indirect influence upon the carmelite theologian, who was not a voluminous reader. The question falls entirely outside the field of the present article which is doctrinal rather than bibliographical or historical.

2. Fr Augustin Poulain was a French jesuit mystical theologian and writer who published in 1901 his enormously successful *The Graces of Interior Prayer*, which considerably revived interest in mystical theology — editor.

3. For instance, *Sermons on the Song of Songs* (SC) 31.6, 75.5-6, 23.16. Cf. Dom Anselme le Bail OCR 'Bernard, saint,' in *D Sp* 1.

4. St John of the Cross, *Spiritual Canticle* b. 22.5 (Peers 2:309): 'For the whole desire and aim of the soul and that of God in all the works of the soul is the consummation and perfection of this estate, wherefore the soul never rests until she reaches Him....' Cf. William of St Thierry, *Expositio in Cantica* (PL 180:473 C): *Domine Deus noster qui ad imaginem et similitudinem tuam creasti nos, scilicet ad te contemplandum, teque fruendum.* [O Lord our God, who has created us in your image and likeness that we might contemplate you and enjoy you in fulfilment.] Cf. St Bonaventure, *Coll. ii in Hexaemeron*, 32; ed. Delorme (Quaracchi, 1934) p 32: *Haec sapienta reddit hominem divinum et Christus venit hanc docere.* [This wisdom renders man divine and Christ came to teach it.]

5. SC 83.2 [And this is why God, its very author, wanted this mark of divine excellence to be preserved forever in the soul; that it might always have within itself something by which it can always be admonished either to remain with the Word or, if it has changed, to return.]

6. SC 83.1 [We have taught that *every soul,* even one laden

227

with sin, ensnared by vice, trapped by enticements... overwrought by business, constricted by fear... has within itself the ability of turning back, not only to where it can breathe in the hope of pardon, in the hope of mercy, *but even to where it can aspire to the nuptials of the Word, where it, a base creature, shall not be afraid to enter into fellowship with God, nor be hesitant to bear, with the King of angels, the yoke of love.*] Those who have any further doubt that transforming union is the end to which all Cistercians may and even should tend, may consult SC 9.2, and study the context of the following words: *ut holocaustum meum pinguefiat osculetur me quaeso osculo oris sui.* [Let him kiss me with the kiss of his lips, I pray, that he may make my whole-offering acceptable = Ps 19:4].

7. See David Knowles, *The Monastic Order in England* (Cambridge, 1941) 223.

8. SC 83.3 [whoever loves perfectly has been wedded].

9. *Dark Night* II, x, 3 (Peers 1:434). Cf. Bernard, Dil 10.29.

10. Etienne Gilson, *The Mystical Theology of St Bernard* (New York, 1940) 142.

11. Hum 6.19 [purity snatches (us) to the third (degree); by it we are lifted up to things invisible].

12. *Expos. in Cantica* 1; PL 180:505B. [The measure of advancement or likeness should be the measure of fruition, because there can be no likeness except in the fruition bringing it about, and no fruition except in the likeness bringing it about].

13. An important text, *Spiritual Canticle* a, xi, 6 (Peers 2:67)l: 'The image of the Beloved is outlined in the soul and so completely and vividly pictured when there is union of love that it is true to say that the Beloved lives in the lover and the lover in the Beloved.'

14. SC 80.2 [a lofty creature in its capacity for greatness].

15. *Mystical Theology,* 54.

16. SC 7.2 [Among the natural gifts this affection of love stands first, especially when it is directed back to its own source, which is God].

17. Gra 1.2 [For to consent is to be saved]. Ibid.; *Tolle liberum arbitrium, non erit quod salvetur; tolle gratiam, non erit unde salvetur.* [Take away free choice and there will be nothing to be saved; take away grace and there will be nothing by which to be saved].

18. SC 82 and 83.

19. SC 24.7 [Souls warped like this are not able to love the Bridegroom, for they are not friends of the Groom while they are friends of this world]. See Gilson, *Mystical Theology,* 53 ff. In two interesting notes (p 226, nn. 52,53), he likens St Bernard on this point with the franciscan tradition. The link is in the common parentage of St Anselm, from whom St Bernard stems on the one hand, while the collateral line culminates in St Bonaventure and Duns Scotus. The Subtle Doctor's treatment of the *affectio commodi* and *affectio justitiae* (natural capacity for disinterested love) throws great light on St Bernard's doctrine of freedom. See *II Oxoniense d.* vi, *q.* 2, especially *n.* 8 (Wadding 12:353).

20. Gra 4.10; *Cum autem non valemus quod volumus, sentimus quidem ipsam quodammodo libertatem peccato esse captivam, vel miseram, non tamen amissam.* [But when we do not manage to do what we will, we perceive that that liberty has somehow been ensnared by sin, or has been made wretched, but has not, however, been lost].

21. Ibid. 7.21: *[Adam] corruit de posse non peccare in non posse non peccare, amissa ex toto consilii libertate.* [Adam tumbled from being able not to sin to not-being-able-not-to-sin and liberty was lost from full counsel].

22. Rom 8:7-8. *Sapientia carnis inimica est Deo, legi enim Dei non est subjecta* nec enim potest. (Cf. St Bernard above: *non possunt diligere Sponsum.) Qui autem in carne sunt Deo placere non possunt.* [The wisdom of flesh is at enmity from God, for it is not and cannot be subject to God's law.... But who is in the flesh cannot please God].

23. SC 24.7 [It is the soul's warp to seek and to savour what is upon earth; and its uprightness, on the contrary, to meditate on and to yearn for what is above it].

24. Phil 1:6.

25. SC 23.6. Note the play on the language of the Rule. [By the yoke of discipline the insolence of our manners must be harnessed until... the good of nature which was lost in us by pride may be restored by obedience].

26. Prologue, RB.

27. SC 83.1 [All he needs to do to heal his natural free-state is to serve straightly, or better, to endeavor to beautify and adorn with the natural hues of affections and manners the heavenly splendor which is within himself]. Then follows a discussion of the *grande donum naturae* which is *industria,* a term which sums up our work of cooperation with grace.

28. *Dark Night of the Soul* II, vi, 5 (Peers 1:411) and II, ix, 4 (425).

29. *Living Flame* b, III, 34 (Peers 3:179).

30. Dil 10.27 [For somehow to lose yourself... to be emptied of yourself and almost to be annihilated pertains to heavenly conversation, not to human affections].

31. p 86. [Incomplete reference, most likely to *Pour l'histoire du problème de l'amour au Moyen âge.* Paris, 1933. — ed.]

32. *Sermo iii in tempore resurrectionis,* 3 [To this (selfishness, wilfulness) that love which is God is clean contrary].

33. III, 18 (Peers 3:171).

34. We apologize for Professor Peers' unintentional pun, although it is psychologically rather apt when we consider the earlier stages of purification. The Spanish is *el Templo natural.*

35. *Living Flame* III, 38 (Peers 3:181).

36. *Dark Night* II, v, 3 (Peers 1:406).

37. *Ascent of Mount Carmel* II, xxiv, 8 (Peers 1:191).

38. SC 2.2 [With good reason then do I not accept visions and dreams, I do not want figures and riddles. I shrink even from angelic appearances. For my Jesus surpasses them all in his appearance and his beauty].

39. *Ascent* II, xxii (413).

40. Eph 4:22-24 [which is created after God in justice and the holiness of truth].

41. SC 75.7-11.

42. *Mystical Theology*, p 129.

43. English translation: *On Grace and Free Choice* in *Bernard of Clairvaux: Treatises II*, Cistercian Fathers Series, Number 19, pp 51-111.

44. Gra 5.15 [We must acknowledge that those who are snatched up at times in a contemplative rapture—however little they may reach a taste of the sweetness of heavenly joy—are free from misery to the degree that they are thus enraptured].

45. Cf. SC 85.8.

46. Gra 6.16 [Even though willing is innate in us by free choice, to be able (to do) what we will is not. I am not saying 'to will good' or 'to will evil', but simply 'to will'].

47. Ibid. [For to will good is a step forward, to will evil a sliding back. But simply to will indicates the thing which goes either forwards or backwards. Yet saving grace lets it go forward just as creating grace lets it be. What backslides hurls itself down].

48. Gra 6.18 [Created somehow as our own with free choice, we are made God's, as it were, by good choice. Yet He makes the choice good who made it free. And he makes it good to this end, that we may be the beginning of his creatures. For it would actually be better for us never to have been at all than to remain forever our own. Those who have chosen to be their own, like gods indeed... become not merely their own, but the devil's].

49. *Sermo 3 in tempore resurrectionis*, 3. [I call our very own will the one which is not mutual between God and men; when we will a thing not for God's glory, not for the brothers' advantage, but we do it for our own sakes, not intending to please God or to advance the brothers, but to satisfy our very own stirrings of mind].

50. 1 Cor 2:14. Douay has 'sensual man'.

51. *Living Flame*, b, III, 74 (Peers 3:202).

52. Ibid. a, II, 29 (Peers 3:56).

53. *Ascent*, I, iv, 1 (Peers 1:24).

54. Ps 108 (Heb. 109):29 [with their own confusion, as with a double cloak].

55. SC 82.5 [Because therefore it has neglected to defend the ingenuousness of its own nature by uprightness of behaviour, it has been made—by the just judgement of its Author—not stripped of its own freedom, but covered over (necessarily) by its own confusion as by a double cloak].

56. SC 82.4 [That sweetness, that pleasingness is not your own, o woman.... *Why do you impress upon your soul another form—indeed a deformity?* But what it delights to have, it still fears to lose; *and fear is a color. It discolors freedom, covers it over, and renders it dissimilar to itself at the same time*].

57. 57. *Ascent,* I, iv, 3 (Peers 1:24-5).

58. Compare, for instance, St Bernard, SC 82.6-7, with St John of the Cross, *Dark Night,* II, ix, 11 (Peers 1:428): 'In contemplation and the Divine inflowing there is naught that of itself can cause affliction but they rather cause sweetness and delight. The cause is rather the weakness and imperfection from which the soul then suffers and the dispositions which it has in itself and which make it unfit for the reception of them....' Also, *Dark Night,* II, x, 3 (Peers 1:420).

59. *Mystical Theology,* p 128.

60. Note the parallel in St Bernard: self-will is the fuel for all the flames of suffering: *Sermo iii in tempore resurrectione,* 3: *Cesset voluntas propria et infernus non erit.* [Let self-will cease, and there will be no hell].

61. *Dark Night,* II, xi, 5-6, 7 (Peers 1:435, 436).

62. SC 82.7 [It is drawn toward desperation by so great an evil (that is, its deformity) but recalled to hope by such great goodness (the image of God perceived beneath the deformity). Hence it is that the more it is displeased by the evil it sees within itself, the more ardently is it drawn to the good, which it likewise spies in itself. (Parenthetical explanations are Father Merton's — ed.)].

63. *Spiritual Canticle,* a, xxvii, 2 (Peers 2:140): 'I think that this state is never without confirmation in grace.'

64. *Spiritual Canticle,* a, xxvii, 2 (Peers 2:140).

65. Ibid.

66. Dil 10.28 [to be affected like this is to be made like God].

67. Gal 2:20.

68. Dil 10.28 [As a drop of water seems to disappear completely when a great deal of wine is poured into it, while at the same time taking on the taste and color of the wine, and as molten, fiery iron becomes very much like fire, divested of its own original form, and as air shot through with sunlight seems to be not so much enlightened as to become light in the brightness of that light, so it will somehow be necessary that all human affection in the saints be melted in some inexpressible way from itself and flow utterly into the will of God].

69. An interesting point of comparison between the two saints is St Bernard's declaration of the insufficiency of the human affection and love of Jesus *(amor carnalis Christi)* if it is not completed by something deeper and more spiritual. SC 20.5; *Non sapienter diligis humanum sequens affectum* [Following this human affection, you do not love wisely]. Cf. St John of the Cross on the inadequacy of 'methods' of meditation, etc., *Living Flame,* III, 30 ff.

70. Hum 8.21 [for a moment, perhaps an hour, half an hour, (there is) silence in heaven].

71. Dil 10.27 [Alas, one is compelled to return to himself, to be cut down to his own being].

72. Cf. St John of the Cross, *Dark Night,* II, x, 3.

73. Dil 10.29, citing Mt 22:31 [I myself think it cannot be perfect before you love the Lord your God with all your heart, and all your soul, and all your strength, until the heart is no longer compelled to think about the body, and the soul may give up endowing it with life and senses in its present state, and virtue, relieved of these burdens, may be *made strong in God's power.*

74. Dil 10.28 [Otherwise how will God be all in all, if something of man survives in man?]

75. 1 Jn 4:19 [loved us first].

76. SC 83.3, 6 [Such conformity marries the soul to the Word, when she who is like him by nature (the image) shows herself like him too by will, loving as she is loved. If she loves perfectly therefore, she has been married.... Deservedly renouncing all other affections, she lies down completely in this love alone.... Therefore, as I have said, to love like this is to have been married, *in that she cannot love like this and not equally be loved,* so that a complete and perfect marriage arises in the consent of the two. No one may doubt that the soul is loved first and more by the Word].

77. SC 7.2 [for all things are common to them. They have nothing of their own, nothing divides them].

78. St John has already made the same remark about the love of creatures. See note 57 above.

79. *Spiritual Canticle*, b, xxviii, 1 (Peers 2:341).

80. *Living Flame*, a, I, 1 (Peers 3:19).

81. Jdg 13:20.

82. *Living Flame*, I, 3-4 (Peers 3:20).

83. *Ascent*, III, 1 (Peers 1:225).

84. *Living Flame*, b, III, 71 (Peers 3:20).

85. *Dark Night*, II, iv, 2 (Peers 1:405).

86. Dil 10.29 [strengthened in God's power].

87. SC 2.2 [the kiss... in an inpouring of joys, a revealing of secrets, *a kind of wonderful and somehow undistinguishable commingling of heavenly light and the enlightened mind*].

88. SC 7.2-3 [in whom is revealed to her (the bride) both the Son and the Father... who is the imperturbable peace of Father and Son, the fast glue, the indivisible unity].

89. 1 Cor 6:17 [He who cleaves to the Lord is one Spirit].

90. *Christian Perfection and Contemplation* (1945) 175.

91. *Spiritual Canticle*, II, xxii, 3 (Peers 2:307); mystics below this degree are in the *vida contemplativa.*

92. *Dark Night*, I, viii, 1 (Peers 1:371).

93. Ibid. I, 1-2 (Peers 349).

94. Ibid. II, ii (Peers 400 ff).

95. Ibid. I, 1-2 (Peers 349).

96. St Teresa, *The Interior Castle*, V, iii, 11: 'If you possess fraternal charity I assure you you will certainly obtain the union I have described.'

97. Gabriel de Saint-Marie-Madeleine OCD, 'Carmes-dechausses,' in *D Sp* 2;198-199.

98. *Spiritual Canticle*, b, xxii, 3 (Peers 2:307).

99. See *Ascent*, I, 1, 2-3 (Peers 1:18).

100. *Living Flame*, III, 23 (Peers 3:12): *ha llegado a tener a Dios por gracia de voluntad, todo lo que puede por via de voluntad y gracia.*

101. The Spanish is somewhat clearer: *esto es haberle Dios dado en el sí de ella su verdadero sí entero de su gracia.* The translation cannot get the effect of the 'yes' of God and the 'yes' of the soul united in the soul's 'yes' which is at the same time the fulness of God's grace. Thus mystical marriage is indicated as something in some sense more than a fulness of grace since it is transformation into God himself. The saint's true meaning is hard to grasp here.

102. *Living Flame*, III, 24-5 (Peers 3:103).

103. *Spiritual Canticle*, b, xxvii, 3 ff (Peers 2:338).

104. Ibid., xxii, 3 (301).

105. Ibid.

106. *Mystical Theology*, 140-147. These pages of 'pure love' in St Bernard are among the most brilliant of a brilliant book.

107. SC 83.3 [If you love perfectly, you have been married. Cf. John: If you love perfectly, you have been betrothed].

108. Est 2:12.

109. Ex 33:20.

110. *Spiritual Canticle*, xix, 4 (Peers 2:292).

111. *Living Flame*, III, 25-26 (Peers 3:174). The following passages (27 ff) indicate that this anointing by desire belongs to the whole mystical ascent and is indeed one of the essentials of the mystical life. But in the state of spiritual betrothal it takes on a particularly intense and refined form.

112. *Spiritual Canticle*, b, xvi, 6 (Peers 2:277).

113. Ibid., b, xl, 1 (403).

114. Ibid., xxvi, 14 (334).

115. Ibid. 17 (335).

116. Ibid., xvii, 9 (104).

117. Dil 10.28 [In that Scripture says that God made everything for his own purpose, however, it shall someday come about that all things made shall conform themselves to and agree with their Author.... In like manner it behooves us someday to pass over into that same state of affection.... O pure and cleansed intention of the will! All the more cleansed and purer in that nothing of its own is left mixed up with it; all the sweeter and more gentle in that what it senses is wholly divine. To be affected like this is to be made like God].

118. [See above, note 68].

119. Dil 10.28. [so then it will somehow be necessary that all human affection in the saints be melted away in some inexpressible way and be poured out utterly into the will of God. Otherwise how will God be all in all, if something of man remains in man. See above, notes 66, 68, 74].

120. See the texts quoted above, as well as *Spiritual Canticle*, a, xi, xvii, xxvii, xxviii, xxix, etc.

121. Dil 10.29.

122. The language of St Bernard's *excessus* with its 'forgetfulness of all external things' is not to be interpreted as anything physiological. The graces described in these higher states by St John of the Cross and St Bernard alike are not concerned with bodily effects.

123. [drunk with divine love, forgetful of self].

124. *Spiritual Canticle*, a, xvi, 6-7 (Peers 2:98).

125. [Blessed, I say, and holy].

126. *Spiritual Canticle*, xiii, 21 (Peers 2:86): 'the state of illumination and perfection'.

127. [for to lose you somehow... not to sense your very self at all and to be emptied of you and to be almost annihilated...].

128. [pertains to heavenly converse, not to human affections. Dil 10.27: see above, note 30].

129. *Spiritual Canticle*, a, xii (Peers 2:71).

130. Ibid., 7 (72). This section of the *Spiritual Canticle* is one that can be applied to 'progressives' who have not yet entered the unitive way (spiritual betrothal) and in it St John of the Cross takes advantage of an opportunity to indicate the imperfection and weakness implied by raptures that cause a violent physical reaction and bodily unconsciousness as distinct from the *spiritual* exinanition of pure love belonging to higher states in which 'all these raptures cease' (Peers 2:72). St Bernard only considers the spiritual *excessus*.

131. Dil 10.27 [Suddenly the wretched world lodges a grudge, the spites of the day disturb him, the body of death weighs down on him, the needs of the flesh demand attention, the flaw of corruption gives no support, and, even more violently, brotherly love calls him back].

132. *Mystical Theology*, 130 ff.

133. SC 3.6.

134. [Above, note 71.]

135. SC 9.9 [greater the fruit at the breasts than in the embraces]. Cf. SC 52.7.

136. SC 41.6: *Docemur ex hoc sane, intermittenda plerumque dulcia oscula propter lactantia ubera; nec cuiquam sibi sed omnibus esse vivendum.* [We learn from this that sweet kisses must often be interrupted for the sake of milky breasts, that one must live not for himself but for others].

137. Hum 7.21 [for the sake of humility without stain, for the sake of

charity without wrinkle, since the will does not blench from reason nor reason disguise the truth].

138. Ibid. [The Father cements the glorious bride to himself].

139. Ibid.: *Ibi modicum, hora videlicet quasi dimidia, silentio facto in coelo, inter desideratos amplexus suaviter quiescens ipsa quidem dormit sed cor ejus vigilat, uo utique interim veritatis arvana rimatur: quorum postmodum memoria statim ad se reditura pascatur.* [There for a moment, for half an hour, as it were, in the silence caused in heaven, she sleeps gently, quietly, in the longed-for embrace, but her heart keeps watch, while there it explores the hidden recesses of truth by which, as soon as she has returned to herself, her memory may be fed].

140. *Spiritual Canticle*, a, xvii, 9 (Peers 2:104). 'The soul is not forever in union according to the faculties although it is so according to the substance of the soul.'

141. Ibid. (105).

142. SC 68.1 [Who is the bride and who the Groom? He is our God and, if I dare say it, we are she, along with the whole throng of captives whom he acknowledges].

143. SC 1.11.

144. Ibid. *Experti recognoscant, inexperti inadrescant desiderio, non tam cognocendi quam experiendi.* [Let the experienced recognize it; let the inexperienced burn with desire, not to recognize it, but to experience it].

145. SC 1.1 [To you, brothers, must we say different things than we would to those in the world, or at least, say them differently].

146. SC 1.11 [it is fruit for all the others].

147. SC 1.12 [made fit for the wedding with the heavenly Bridegroom].

148. SC 1.12.

149. Dil 9.26 [It comes about that, once tasted, his sweetness binds us more to loving God purely than our own needs drive us to it].

150. Ibid. *Amat caste, et casto non gravatus obedire mandato, castificans magis cor suum ut scriptum est in obedientia caritatis (1 P 1:22).... Amor iste merito gratus quia gratuitus. Castus est quia non impenditur verbo neque lingua sed opere et veritate....* See the whole passage, which is very important. [Chaste love, one not weighed down at obeying a chaste command, makes one's heart yet chaster, as it is written, in the obedience of love.... This love is gratifying because it is gratuitous. It is chaste because it depends neither on word nor on tongue, but on deed and on truth...].

151. SC 7.2 [a soul athirst for God].

152. Ibid. [She loves who seeks a kiss. She seeks not freedom, not reward, not inheritance, not even doctrine, but a kiss.].

153. SC 7.3. *Amat profecto caste quae ipsum quem amat quaerit. Amat sancte quia non in concupiscentia carnis sed in puritate spiritus. Amat ardenter quae ita proprio debriatur amore, ut majestatem non cogitet.*

Cf. Gilson, *Mystical theology,* p 131, notes, and p 141. [Clearly she loves chastely who seeks the person she loves.... she loves spiritually because she loves not in the lust of flesh but in purity of spirit. She loves ardently who is so intoxicated by that very love that she does not pause to think of his majesty].

154. SC 7.2 [for to them all things are common, they have nothing of their own, nothing separating them].

155. SC 74.3 [And now give me a soul whom the Bridegroom, the Word, is accustomed often to visit, whom familiarity has given boldness, taste hunger, contempt of things leisure; and I will immediately assign it the voice and equally the name of the Bride].

156. Ibid. [that the more eagerly she calls him back, the more tightly she may cling to him].

157. Ibid. [she has deserved his presence, if not his abundance].

158. *Living Flame,* III, 25-26 (Peers 3:174).

159. SC 82.7 [Charity is that vision, that likeness].

160. SC 83.5 [loving as she is loved].

161. SC 83.2 [the return of the soul is her conversion to the Word, to be reformed by him and conformed to him].

162. Gn 1:26.

163. SC 83.3 [Such conformity marries the soul to the Word, when she who is like him by nature shows that she is no less like him by will, loving as she is loved. Then, if she loves perfectly, she has been married].

164. The context stresses *industria,* cooperation with grace.

165. *The Graces of Interior Prayer* (London, 1912) p 291. Poulain is evidently not thinking of the language of great mystics, taken in a context which clearly shows that they are talking about a mystical state. He is justly reproving the loose talk which leads some pious authors to define the mystical marriage in terms which include no notion of such a state.

166. This should be evident from all the quotations we have considered, as well as from a particular passage like *Spiritual Canticle,* a, xi, 6 (Peers 2:67).

167. *Living Flame,* III, 24 (Peers 3:173).

168. SC 83.3 [I said agreement too slightingly. It is an encompassing. Clearly there is an encompassing where two become one spirit, willing alike and not willing alike].

169. SC 8.2.

170. SC 83.4 [Add to this that the Bridegroom is not only loving, but is Love].

171. Ibid. [Love is the only one of all the movements of the soul, all the senses and affections, by which the creature, although not from any equality, can respond to its Author and requite his mutual interchange in like manner].

172. Ibid. [Love is a great reality if it runs back into its source, if returned

to its origins, if it flows back always to the fount from which it springs and flows].

173. Jn 7:38.

174. *Living Flame*, I, 1 and 3 (Peers 3:118-119). Cf. *Spiritual Canticle*, a, xvii, 3-5 (Peers 2:102).

175. Above, note 76.

176. *Spiritual Canticle*, a, xxxiv, 5 (Peers 2:162).

177. *Mystical Theology*, p 143.

178. [Such conformity marries the soul to the Word]. See above, note 163.

179. *Mystical Theology*, 143-6. The remark about confidence is directed against Luther's 'faith in which the sinner feels himself a sinner and nevertheless feels that he is saved by Jesus Christ'. Nothing could be further from St Bernard's absolutely pure love, the way to which can only be prepared by the long and generous struggle against imperfections demanded by the cistercian ascesis! But once again, it is irrelevant to prove that, for St Bernard, *fiducia* to the point of self-forgetfulness was 'not a state'.

180. *Graces of Interior Prayer*, p 283. The word *almost* is inserted to indicate that the rule may admit of exceptions. Fr Poulain gives examples of mystics for whom this union was so continuous that it was felt even during sleep (p 286).

181. *Spiritual Canticle*, b, xxii, 5 (Peers 2:309).

182. Ibid., b, xxiv, 5 (317) *Ninguna cosa del mundo alta ni baja la puede inquietar ni molestar, ni aun mover, porque estando ya libre de toda molestia de las pasiones naturales, y ajena y desnuda de le tormenta y variedad de los cuidados temporales, como aqui lo esta, goza en seguridad y quietud de la participacion de Dios.*

183. SC 83.3 [What is happier than this conformity? What is more to be wished for than the charity by which it happens that you, not content with any human instruction, by yourself confidently approach the Word, cling steadfastly to the Word, investigate the Word intimately, consult him in every matter; in so far as you are capable in your understanding, you are daring in desire].

184. Ibid. [This bond is stronger even than the tighter bond nature ties between parents and children].

185. Ibid. [For the sake of this a man shall leave his father and his mother and shall cleave to his bride]. Cf. Mt 19:15.

186. Gilson, *Mystical Theology*, 143-6.

187. SC 83.4 [It is sufficient of itself. It gives pleasure of itself and for its own sake. It is its own merit. It is its own reward. Love needs no reason, no fruit, beyond itself. It is its own fruit, its own usefulness. I love because I love. I love that I may love. Love is a great thing, if it runs back to its source, if it returns to its origins, if it flows back always to the fount from which it springs and flows].

188. Ps 72 [Hebr. 73]:28 [But for me to cleave to God is good].

189. SC 85.12 [Therefore any soul you see clinging with all its might to the Word, having left everything else, living for the Word, disciplining itself for the Word, conceiving by the Word what by the Word she will bring to birth, someone who can say 'for me to live is Christ and to die is gain' (Ph 1:21), consider her a wife, married to the Word. The heart of her husband trusts in her, knowing she is faithful who has spurned everything for his sake, has counted everything as dung that she might win him for herself].

190. SC 41.6 [one is to live not for himself but for everyone].

191. *Rachel videns sed sterilis; Lia vero lippa sed fecunda* [Rachel, sighted but sterile; Leah, blear-eyed but fecund]. St Gregory the Great, *Homilia 2, Lib. ii in Ezech.; PL* 76:954. Ibid. *Sicut bonus ordo vivendi est ut ab activa in contemplativam tendatur, ita plerumque utiliter a contemplative animus ad activam reflectitur....* [It is a good ordering of life that one move from active to contemplative (life), and most often useful that the mind reflect from the contemplative on the active].

192. *Contra Faustum* 53; PL 42:434. [Rachel, clear of sight, goes out in her mind to God and sees the Word, God in the beginning with God, and she wants to give birth but she cannot, for who will tell of his begetting? (Is 53:8, Ac 8:33) ...*she wants to be at rest from all busyness and, in that way, sterile*]. Not exactly encouraging words for contemplatives. The saint also explains the sterility of Rachel by the fact that what she sees of God is incommunicable. *Sed et ipsa procreandi charitate inardescit.* The result is that she too takes to preaching, clothing her visions of the Word in poetic symbols. It must be noted that in this passage St Augustine does not consider the question whether the contemplative merits more *grace* for the Church.

193. *Spiritual Canticle*, b, xxix, 2 (Peers 2:346).

194. SC 85.13 [Spiritual persons give birth to understandings].

195. Ibid. [She goes out and leaves behind even her physical senses so she may not sense herself in sensing the Word. This happens when the mind, enraptured by the ineffable sweetness of the Word, somehow escapes itself, or better is snatched or transported away from self that she may enjoy the Word].

196. Ibid. [The mind fruitful in the Word is affected one way; that enjoying the Word in another. The first the needs of a neighbor beckon; the second the gentleness of the Word summons].

197. Dil 10.27 [Alas it is constrained to return to itself, to come back down into itself].

198. SC 85.13 [A sweet exchange, but a brief moment and a rare experience].

199. Ibid. [A mother is happy with her child, but a bride is happier in the embrace (of her Groom). The pledge of children is dear, but kisses are more pleasing. It is good to save many persons, but to go out and to be with the Word is much more pleasant].

200. John Ruysbroeck, *The Seven Steps of the Ladder of Love* (London, 1943) p 58.

201. *Spiritual Canticle,* a, xxviii, 4 (Peers 2:142).

202. Ibid., xxxiv, 5 (162).

203. Ibid., b, xxvii, 8 (340). This last quotation is taken from the problematical passage that describes spiritual betrothal in terms so close to those proper to mystical marriage. The problem does not affect the application of this text which applies *a fortiori* to perfect transforming union.

204. Dil 10.28 [Just as God willed that everything be for his sake, so we too should will that neither we nor anything else be or have been except for his sake, too. For his will alone, that is, not for our own will].

205. *Ascent of Mount Carmel,* I, xiii, 11 (Peers 1:62).

206. Gra 4.11 [feel themselves free from everything that can displease, that is, from all misery... they do not even freely embrace as pleasing everything which they observe reflectively to be right and suitable].

207. *Spiritual Canticle,* a, xxix, 7-8 (Peers 2:149-50).

208. SC 85.9 [But those who have passed over into affection of heart are wise and are delighted with that very taste of good.... Happy the mind which that taste of good and hatred of evil totally liberate. This is what it is to be re-formed to wisdom. This is cheerfully to experience wisdom's victory].

209. *The Seven Steps....,* 60.

210. SC 85.9 [Now in what is wisdom more evidently proven to conquer evil than when (once the taste for evil, which is nothing but malice is cut away) the inmost savor of the mind feels itself intimately and utterly occupied with sweetness?].

211. *Spiritual Canticle,* b, xxvi, 14 (Peers 2:334). Note how St John of the Cross insists like Saint Bernard: 'It has no habit of evil (cf. *sapor mali*) whereby to judge evil, God having rooted out its imperfect habits and ignorance... *with the perfect habit of true wisdom.*'

212. *Living Flame,* III, 23 (Peers 3:72).

213. SC 85.9 [It looks to virtue to sustain tribulations bravely, to wisdom to rejoice in tribulation. To strengthen your heart and wait upon the Lord pertains to virtue; to taste and see how gracious the Lord is, to wisdom].

214. SC 83.3 [Love overflows itself. Where love goes, it carries along and captivates to itself every other affection. What it loves, then, it loves and it knows nothing else]. Cf. St John of the Cross, *Spiritual Canticle,* b, xxvi, 14 (Peers 2:333): 'That deification and exaltation of the mind in God wherein the soul is as if enraptured, immersed in love and wholly one with God, allows it not to take notice of aught in the world soever; and it is withdrawn not only from all other things but even from itself, and is annihilated, as though it were transformed and dissolved in love, which transformation consists in passing from itself to the Beloved.'

215. *Dark Night,* II, xxi (Peers 1:470).

216. *Spiritual Canticle,* b, xiv, 16 (Peers 2:269).

217. Ibid., xxxvii (387).

218. Ibid., xxvi, 5 (381).

219. Nat BVM, 7.

220. SC 85.8 [So it was that silliness cut the woman off from the taste of good because the serpent's malice got around the woman's silliness. Yet the reason why malice seemed for a time to have won is why it endures being overcome in eternity. For, look! wisdom again fills the heart and body of a woman so that we who were deformed into silliness through one woman might through a woman be reformed to wisdom].

ABBREVIATIONS

PL   J.-P. Migne, *Patrologiae cursus completus, series latina.* Paris, 1844-64.

RB   *The Rule of St Benedict*

References to the works of St Bernard have been abbreviated in the notes in conformity with the standard adopted by the Association of Cistercian Scholars and Cistercian Publications.

Ann	Sermo in annuntiatione dominica
Asspt	Sermo in assumptione Beatae Virginis Mariae
Conv	Sermo de conversione ad clericos
Csi	De consideratione libri v
Dil	Liber de diligendo Deo
Div	Sermones de diversis
Epi	Sermo in epiphania domini
Gra	Liber de gratia et libero arbitrio
Hum	Liber de gradibus humilitatis et superbiae
Miss	Super Missus est in laudibus Virginis Matris
Nat	Sermo in nativitate domini
Nat BVM	Sermo in nativitate B.V.M.
O Asspt	Sermo dominica infra octavam assumptionis
Pent	Sermo in die sancto pentecostes
Pre	Liber de praecepto et dispensatione
SC	Sermones super Cantica canticorum

Translations not enclosed in brackets were made by Thomas Merton. Quotations from the works of St John of the Cross were made from *The Complete Works of Saint John of the Cross,* translated and edited by E. Allison Peers from the critical edition of P. Silverio de Santa Teresa OCD. Westminster, MD: The Newman Press, 1949 (reprinted from London: Burns Oates & Washbourne, Ltd., 1935).

The Works of St Bernard of Clairvaux appear in new translation in the Cistercian Fathers Series. All translations are made from the critical edition of Jean Leclercq and H. M. Rochais, *Sancti Bernardi Opera*, Rome 1957–.

CF 1   *Treatises I* (Apologia to Abbot William, On Precept and Dispensation)

CF 4   *Sermons on the Song of Songs I* (Sermons 1–20)

CF 7   *Sermons on the Song of Songs II* (Sermons 21–46)

CF 31   *Sermons on the Song of Songs III* (Sermons 47–66)

CF 40   *Sermons on the Song of Songs IV* (Sermons 67–86)

CF 13   *Treatises II* (The Steps of Humility and Pride, On Loving God)

CF 19   *Treatises III* (On Grace and Free Choice, In Praise of the New Knighthood)

CF 10   *The Life and Death of St Malachy the Irishman*

CF 18   *Magnificat: Homilies in Praise of the Blessed Virgin Mary* (Super Missus Est)

Other works to appear at regular intervals.

Cistercian Publications
WMU Station
Kalamazoo, Michigan 49008

CISTERCIAN PUBLICATIONS INC.

Titles Listing

THE CISTERCIAN FATHERS SERIES

THE WORKS OF BERNARD OF CLAIRVAUX

THE WORKS OF WILLIAM OF SAINT THIERRY

THE WORKS OF AELRED OF RIEVAULX

THE WORKS OF GILBERT OF HOYLAND

OTHER EARLY CISTERCIAN WRITERS

THE CISTERCIAN STUDIES SERIES

*   out of print